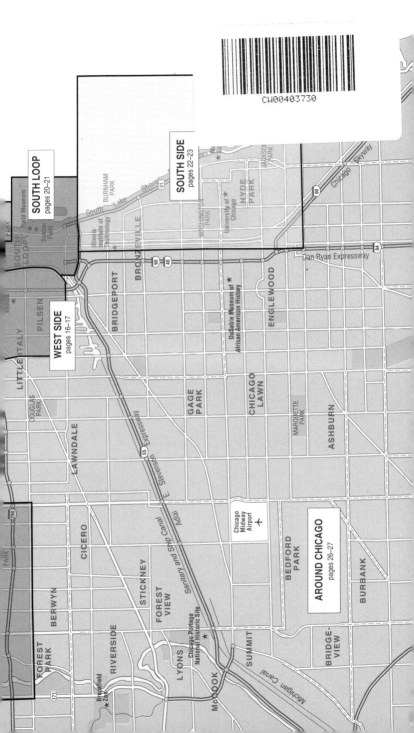

INSIGHT GUIDES

CHICAGO

smart guide

Discovery
CHANNEL

APA PUBLICATIONS
Part of the Langenscheidt Publishing Group

Areas

Contents

A–Z

Below: family-friendly Navy
Pier is a big attraction.

Left: 'The Bean' is a new Chicago landmark.

Below: the 'el' (elevated train) is a good way to get around.

Chicago

Asked what Chicago brings to mind, most people will mention skyscrapers, deep-dish pizza, and the blues. But as residents have long known, there is much more to the Windy City: miles of easily accessible shoreline, a cutting-edge restaurant scene, and world-class arts institutions. Even the cold winters are a source of pride, considered a trade-off for the luscious summers.

Chicago Facts and Figures

Population: **2.8 million**
Area: **237 sq miles (615 sq km)**
Miles of lakefront: **29 (46km)**
Number of hotel rooms in central Chicago: **30,000**
Number of cities in the world with more Poles: **1 (Warsaw)**
Percentage of residents who are foreign-born: **21.8**
Rank of Sears Tower in top ten tallest buildings list: **5**
Month of highest average snowfall: **January**
Coldest temperature on the official record: **-27°F (-33°C) on January 20, 1985**
Height above sea level: **576ft (175m)**
Number of locations on National Register of Historic Places: **306**

A Rough and Ready History

Chicago has a history of reinventing itself that goes back to the destruction caused by the Great Chicago Fire in 1871. This disaster made room for new growth that included experimentation in architecture and planning. Daniel Burnham's Reliance Building showed the possibilities of the high-rise, while in suburban Oak Park a young man named Frank Lloyd Wright started to imagine an architectural style inspired by the broad, flat plains of the Midwestern prairie. As immigrants flocked to what became known as the 'Second City' (in population after New York), they tended to stick together in pockets, creating ethnic enclaves that would come to define Chicago's demographic character for decades to come. The poet Carl Sandburg celebrated Chicago's stockyards, tough-minded inhabitants, and pride in its working-class character in his ode 'City of the Big Shoulders,' while another Chicago scribe, writer Nelson Algren, said of having a preference for Chicago: 'Like loving a woman with a broken nose, you may well find lovelier lovelies, but never a lovely so real.' A Midwestern-style straightforwardness and attitude are still part of the civic temperament, but today they are just one of many layers in a constantly evolving city.

21st-Century City

In recent years, the city has heightened its national and international profile with cutting-edge architecture, green initiatives, and landscape development. One of the greatest of these successes is Millennium Park, a new lakefront green space featuring an undulating bandshell designed by Frank Gehry and other works that add to the city's long tradition of public art. The city's Center for Green Technology researches and promotes environmentally friendly processes and technology for businesses, industry, and residents, including a lauded 'green roof' program. Other beautification plans are more literal: the city has put a lot of muscle into promoting its nascent fashion industry, with support

Below: catch classic Chicago blues at the Kingston Mines *(see p.87).*

4

for local designers. Dining is another area where the city distinguishes itself, with local chefs such as Charlie Trotter, Grant Achatz, and Rick Bayless attracting attention for their sophisticated, innovative, and tasty concoctions.

The Windy City

There's a well-known saying in Chicago: 'If you don't like the weather, wait five minutes.' In early spring you might be teased by a summer-like day that invites you to dig out your shorts, while the next day – or even that afternoon – you'll have to pull out that winter coat again to face blustery winds. The winters can be snowy, gray, and long, and while it's a citywide pastime to complain about them, they do create a sense of community. But the summer always beckons, the light at the end of a cold, dark tunnel, when residents take delight in being out and about outdoors. It can be hard to decide between all of the options on offer: taking a leisurely boat trip on the lake, planning a trip to a farmers' market, stopping at one of the many ethnic and music festivals taking place in parks and on city blocks, or simply dining alfresco and watching the crowds go by. Anyway, Chicagoans will gleefully tell you that if it weren't for the winters, too many people would want to live in their beloved city.

Highlights

▲ **Architecture** From early skyscrapers to todays record-breaking high-rises, the city's architecture has always been a big draw.
▶ **Lake Michigan** It's not called a Great Lake for nothing. Sail on it, swim in it, or just stroll along by it.

▲ **Art Institute** One of the world's premier art museums, it's a must-see on any itinerary.
▶ **Millennium Park** Chicago's newest lakefront green space boasts stunning public art and a Frank Gehry-designed bandshell.

▶ **Groundbreaking cuisine** There are few cities with so many chefs stretching the boundaries of cooking.

▲ **Wrigley Field** Spend a day at the atmospheric 'Friendly Confines' to understand why Chicagoans remain so loyal to the Cubs.

The Loop

As the oldest part of Chicago as well as its business and financial center, the Loop – named after the elevated CTA trains that circle downtown – is the city's living, breathing heart. Many of the city's most famous architectural treasures and museums are located here, including the Sears Tower and the Art Institute, while an increasing residential population in recent years and students from the design and art colleges located here have helped spawn a lively nightlife, exciting new cultural events, and a reinvigorated retail scene. With a little bit of all the elements that make Chicago so special, it's a microcosm of the city at large.

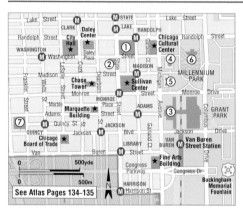

There's a lot of public art in the Loop if you know where to look. Two of the most notable pieces are an untitled Picasso sculpture in Daley Plaza, which has had people scratching their heads over what it's supposed to be since 1967, and the four-sided mosaic *The Four Seasons*, by Marc Chagall, in the plaza of the Chase Tower. *See also Public Art, p.100–101.*

State Street

It's 'that great street,' as Frank Sinatra sang, and while its fortunes have gone up and down through the years, its status as the city's main drag still seems indisputable. For many Chicagoans, State Street immediately brings to mind the seminal department store **Macy's** ①, formerly the local retail institution, Marshall Field's, since the middle of the 19th century. Locals were dismayed when the store was transformed into a Macy's following a buyout in 2005, although the grand 13-story interior remains largely unchanged. Just down the street is another once popular retail destination, the now closed Carson Pirie Scott & Company department store, dating from 1899. At the time of writing the **Sullivan Center**, as the building is officially known, is under construction for redevelopment, but you can still admire the elaborate ironwork over the main entrance and the first couple of floors, featuring swirling organic motifs.

Yet another architectural masterpiece is on view here, the 1894 Reliance Building, now the **Hotel Burnham** ②, named after one of its architects, Daniel Burnham. After a massive renovation in the late 90s, the building has been restored to its former glory. The ground floor features an intricate mosaic floor that was discovered during restoration work, while the elevator bay is covered with ornate iron filigree. Al Capone's doctor had his office here, in room 804, where he used to treat the gangster and his girlfriends. SEE ALSO ARCHITECTURE, P.33; HOTELS, P.64; SHOPPING, P.113

Michigan Avenue

The city's other celebrated roadway is sometimes referred to as the 'Boul Mich,' a name that refers both back to its beginnings as Michigan Boulevard and its stunning cliff-like streetscape of contiguous structures on its east side. One of them is the **Chicago Cultural Center**, a grand neoclassical structure that once was the location of the main public library. It's worth a look

Left: the Sears Tower rises above the city.

During warm weather, concerts take place in the Frank Gehry-designed **Jay Pritzker Pavilion** ⑥, notable for its undulating waves of stainless steel on the bandshell.

Just to the south, the more traditionally landscaped Grant Park is the site of many summer festivals as well as the majestic **Buckingham Memorial Fountain**, modeled after one at the Palace of Versailles in France.

SEE ALSO CHILDREN, P.41; PARKS AND BEACHES, P.96; PUBLIC ART, P.100; WALKS, TOURS, AND VIEWS, P.127

Financial District

The Art Deco **Chicago Board of Trade** looms over a canyon-like stretch of LaSalle Street, topped by a statue of Ceres, the goddess of grain. Visitors are welcome to observe daily trading, which has grown a little less frenetic with the introduction of electronic trading. To the west is the 110-story **Sears Tower** ⑦, the tallest building in the world until 1996. On a clear day it is said you can see into the neighboring states of Indiana, Wisconsin, and Michigan from its skydeck.

SEE ALSO ARCHITECTURE, P.32, 33; WALKS, TOURS, AND VIEWS, P.129

inside, or taking the free hour-long tour to admire the Carrera marble staircase, inlaid with green marble and mother-of-pearl designs, as well as the sumptuous third-floor Preston Bradley Hall, topped by a stunning Tiffany dome, the world's largest.

On the opposite side of Michigan Avenue lies the **Art Institute of Chicago** ③, one of the world's foremost art museums, with over 30,000 works from ancient times to the present day. As of the time of writing, a new Modern Wing, designed by Renzo Piano, is under construction, scheduled to open in 2009.

SEE ALSO MUSEUMS AND GALLERIES, P.76

Millennium and Grant Parks

The lakefront here is the site of two of the city's loveliest green spaces, known as 'Chicago's front yard': **Millennium Park** and **Grant Park**. Opened in 2004, Millennium Park draws strollers admiring Anish Kapoor's curving, reflective steel sculpture **Cloud Gate** ④, known colloquially as 'The Bean.' Nearby, the **Crown Fountain** ⑤, two facing towers outfitted with video screens, on which appear the faces of Chicagoans, spew streams of water every few minutes into the granite basin below. It is thronged with splashing children in summer.

Below: trading in action at the Chicago Board of Trade.

North Side

Packed with shopping, cultural venues, and some prime tourist sights, the North Side is one of the most visited areas of the city. Old mansions and plaques whisper of the city's early history, and students of modern and contemporary architecture from all over the world come here to view some of the most groundbreaking buildings in the discipline. It is easy to spend a lot of time here and particularly tempting to concentrate on Michigan Avenue, which heaves with the city's flagship stores. However, detours both west and east offer plenty of worthwhile diversions, from the intellectual to the kid-friendly.

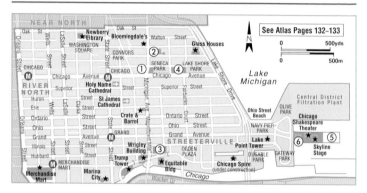

Michigan Avenue

Known as the 'Magnificent Mile' (it's actually not quite a mile), this is truly the city's Main Street, where office workers rush past goggle-eyed visitors admiring the buildings and the chic store-fronts. The city's answer to the Champs-Elysées, shopping is a big draw here: the street is an amalgam of big-name department stores, chains, and high-end boutiques. Here you'll find the flagship location of **Crate & Barrel**, a home furnishing company that started in Chicago in 1962.

Near the north end of the strip are two highly recogniz-able landmarks. On the west side of the street is a little square that houses the historic **Water Tower** ①, one of the few structures in the area that survived the Great Chicago Fire. You can visit the visitor

Left: the twin 'corncobs' of Marina City.

center and a City Gallery inside, which hosts a rotating exhibit of photographs with a local bent, or hire one of the horse-drawn carriages that wait around its periphery for a genteel tour. On the other side of the street is the **John Han-cock Center** ②, the third-tallest building in the city, which gradually narrows over the course of 100 stories. The observatory offers grand views of the lake and cityscape in clear weather, which many claim is superior to the one from the taller Sears Tower. You can also skip the lines and have an expensive drink in the elegant **Signature Lounge** on the 96th floor.

As you head south on Michigan, the shops thin out in favor of office buildings.

Left: having a mid-shopping bite on Michigan Avenue.

until it started silting up. These days it's one of the most densely packed residential areas of the city, known mostly for a few hotels and restaurants. One must-see is the **Museum of Contemporary Art** ④, whose permanent collection includes work by such 20th-century names as Francis Bacon and Andy Warhol. The wide front plaza hosts a weekly farmers' market from May to October.

Just off Lake Shore Drive are Ludwig Mies van der Rohe's seminal **Glass Houses**, two steel-and-glass apartment towers dating from 1951 that set the standard for skyscrapers for decades to come. Heading further south you arrive at **Navy Pier** ⑤, a one-time municipal site that, after many different roles over the years and an intensive restoration, is now a hugely popular family destination, thanks to such attractions as a Ferris wheel, a miniature golf course, and the **Chicago Children's Museum** ⑥. Bike rental is available, and the weekly fireworks display over the lake in summer is fun, especially when viewed from one of the boat tours leaving every few hours from the pier.

SEE ALSO ARCHITECTURE, P.31; CHILDREN, P.40; MUSEUMS AND GALLERIES, P.76, 77

The Gothic **Tribune Tower** ③ is one of the city's most recognizable landmarks. It houses the offices of the *Chicago Tribune* as well as the studios of WGN Radio. Inside the building the lower-level walls are embedded with fragments from historical buildings across the globe, among them the Taj Mahal and the Colosseum, brought home by *Tribune* correspondents through the years. A little further down, there's a plaque set in the pavement commemorating the site of the home of the official founder of the city, Jean Baptiste Pointe DuSable, who ran a trading post here.

As you cross the Chicago River, heading into the Loop, take a detour down West Wacker Drive and have a look at the highly distinctive 'corncobs' of **Marina City**.
SEE ALSO ARCHITECTURE, P.30, 32; BARS, P.34; SHOPPING, P.114; WALKS, TOURS, AND VIEWS, P.129

West of Michigan

Although new construction has obliterated some of the vintage charm from this area, there is still enough remaining to make a walk worthwhile. The rose-toned **Newberry Library** holds a fine collection of rare books, local histories and other printed paraphernalia, which are exhibited to the public on a rotating basis. **Washington Square Park** out front has its own literary history. Known as 'Bughouse Square,' during the first half of the 20th century this was where a motley assemblage of thinkers, poets, and assorted oddballs perched on soapboxes to declaim on subjects dear to their hearts. The tradition is repeated over one weekend every summer.
SEE ALSO FESTIVALS AND EVENTS, P.54

Streeterville

The area east of Michigan was once part of Lake Michigan

Streeterville is named after 'Cap' George Streeterville, a wily character who claimed ownership of the area after his boat ran aground in the shallow waters here in 1886. In 2007 construction crews working on a new parking garage unearthed an anchor – perhaps the very one from Streeter's ship.

Gold Coast

Ever since the successful dry-goods retailer Potter Palmer set up house here in the 1880s, the Gold Coast has been one of the city's most desirable addresses. This heavily residential area nearest the lake has for the most part been spared from major development in recent years, allowing strollers a glimpse of its grandest era. It's a must-see for architecture buffs, who can visit a few of the more significant homes. Lacking any significant tourist attractions other than its architectural heritage, the area is known mainly for its expensive shops and restaurants, as well as the sunbathing and people-watching opportunities at the beach.

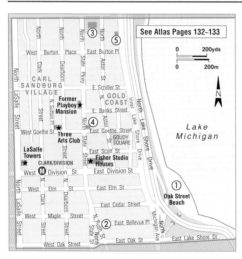

See Atlas Pages 132–133

Oak Street and the Beach

The block-long stretch of Oak Street between Michigan and Rush is the city's most glittering shopping destination, with designer boutiques and independent high-end retailers tucked into elegant town homes, including the three-story Prada store.

Tucked into the curve made by Lake Shore Drive as it turns east here is **Oak Street Beach** ①, where the heady combination of sun, sky, sand, and skyscrapers makes this a rather glamorous summer destination. On weekends, traffic on the combination bike, jogging, and walking path can be extremely heavy, and it can seem like the entire metropolitan area has descended on the place. There are usually a couple of hot-dog and ice-cream stands

More recently the nightlife scene in the blocks around Rush Street has earned it the nickname the 'Viagra Triangle' for the shape of the streets forming the area's boundary and the graying would-be Casanovas who frequent its clubs and bars.

around, and the **Oak Street Beachstro** offers sit-down dining as well as alcohol.
SEE ALSO BARS, P.34; FASHION, P.52; PARKS AND BEACHES, P.97

Rush Street and Division Street

Back in the 1970s, '**Rush Street**' ② was shorthand for singles bars and a thriving meat-market pick-up scene. These days, it's much easier to find an expensive dinner than a drink special on Rush itself, although it's hardly less crowded than in its heyday. Popular stops among the moneyed, well-dressed crowds include **Gibson's** for steaks and Martinis and **Le Passage** for dancing. Meanwhile the drink-'til-you-drop action has moved a few blocks north to Division Street, where there are still plenty of saloons offering fast ways to get effectively inebriated or meet up with the opposite sex, such as **The Original Mother's**, where Demi Moore and Rob Lowe met in the movie *About Last Night*.
SEE ALSO BARS, P.35; NIGHTLIFE, P.92; RESTAURANTS, P.107

Astor Street District and Environs

While many of the opulent mansions dating from the

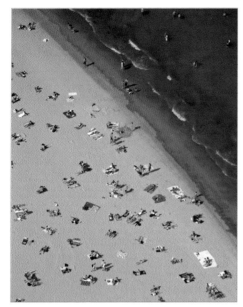

Left: sun-worshipping on the Oak Street Beach.

Don't forget to check out the back wall of the LaSalle Towers, which the mural artist Richard Haas adorned with a *trompe l'œil* masterpiece mimicking the terracotta cladding, bay windows, and other signature features of the Chicago School of architecture.

neighborhood's 19th-century beginnings no longer exist, one excellent surviving example is the **Archbishop's Residence** ③, the home of the leader of the city's Catholic diocese. A brick structure studded with towers, turrets, and chimneys, it is set apart from its neighbors by a wide lawn. In back is one of the few remaining alleys lined with cedar blocks treated with creosote – used instead of brick because it was cheaper and safer for horses.

Just a few blocks away is a building in which no doubt many activities occurred that the Catholic Church would frown on: the **Playboy Mansion**, where magazine publisher Hugh Hefner lived and worked until he left for Los Angeles in the 80s. Today the 'Bunny Hutch,' which has been divided into condominiums, hosts a much more sedate lifestyle.

Other notable buildings include the **Three Arts Club**, a grand building with mosaics celebrating the arts and bas-relief figures built to house young women studying the arts (it was sold by the club in 2007), and the **Fisher Studio Houses**, an unusually modern structure with rounded edges and glass block windows. After your tour you can stop for a drink at the **Pump Room** in the **Ambassador East Hotel** ④, which is lined with images of visiting celebrities. It's past its prime as a fashionable dinner spot, but the elegance of an earlier age lingers.

Not well known even among residents, the **International Museum of Surgical Science** ⑤ is of interest both for its collection of oddities and for the building itself, a creamy-gray structure designed by noted architect Howard Van Doren Shaw in the style of the Petit Trianon, Marie Antoinette's hideaway at Versailles.

SEE ALSO HOTELS, P.69; MUSEUMS AND GALLERIES, P.77; RESTAURANTS, P.107

Below: the Pump Room at the Ambassador East Hotel.

Lincoln Park and Old Town

Originally settled by German immigrants in the 19th century, a surge of redevelopment in the 1970s transformed Lincoln Park and Old Town into the upscale neighborhoods they are today. Rising real-estate prices mean that this affluent area is home to mainly white professionals, although the presence of DePaul University in Lincoln Park injects a bit of youthful energy to the area. The presence of the city's zoo and beautiful landscaping in the park makes it a magnet for families. Old Town, though just as pricey, retains a few vestiges of its recent past as a bohemian enclave, and, further back, one of Chicago's earliest residential neighborhoods.

Lincoln Park

It's hard to believe that this vast park was once the city's cemetery. After the bodies were moved to other locations in the 19th century, the city brought in landfill and dug canals to create the lagoons, ponds, and paths you see today. The free **Lincoln Park Zoo** ①, one of the oldest such institutions in the country, is almost seamlessly integrated into the park and remains a popular draw for its sophisticated exhibits and animal enclosures. The paddleboat rental at the South Pond attracts families and romantic-minded couples.

Other attractions in the park include the child-oriented **Peggy Notebaert Nature Museum**, with interactive exhibits on everything from plant biology to recycling, as well as a live butterfly haven. The **Lincoln Park Conservatory**, a complex of four iron-and-glass greenhouses from the Belle Epoque era, can be a warm shelter on a chilly day.
SEE ALSO CHILDREN, P.41; MUSEUMS AND GALLERIES, P.80; PARKS AND BEACHES, P.97, 98

Intersection of Fullerton, Lincoln, and Halsted

If there's a center to this neighborhood, this is probably it. Although the affluent residents have largely driven out most of the music clubs, there are a few decent blues bars remaining, including long-time businesses **b.l.u.e.s.** and the respected **Kingston Mines**. Rock-lovers can head a few blocks northwest on Lincoln to **Delilah's**, where the DJs might just be moonlighting from their 'day job' in a band.

There's nothing on the facade to commemorate it, but the **Biograph Theatre** ② marks the spot where Public Enemy Number 1 John Dillinger, a notorious bank robber and gangster, was shot by federal agents in 1934 as he exited the theatre. The theatre itself is still in business after many reinventions over the years; it's now the home to the Tony-Award winning **Victory Gardens Theater**.

A couple of blocks southeast is **Oz Park** ③, a much smaller green space than Lincoln Park, but a favorite

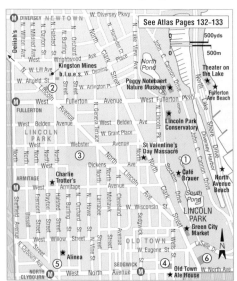

See Atlas Pages 132–133

500yds

500m

Left: the statue of Abraham Lincoln in his namesake park.

performers as John Belushi, Tina Fey, and Alan Arkin. Cast members hit the stage nearly every night, while classes in performance and comedy writing are also held here. Students and performer alike often head across the street to the comfortably worn **Old Town Ale House**, whose history is pretty much concurrent with Second City's. Look for the famous faces among the portraits of the regulars along the walls.

Fans of more dramatic performance should find their way to the **Steppenwolf Theatre Company** ⑤, where actors from the ensemble – including John Malkovich, Gary Sinise, and Joan Allen – can often be seen in both revivals and original dramatic plays.

The recently renovated **Chicago History Museum** ⑥ is often called the city's attic and displays a wide range of exhibits that trace the growth of the city from the days of a small frontier town to the metropolitan center it is today. SEE ALSO BARS, P.36; COMEDY, P.44–5; MUSEUMS AND GALLERIES, P.80; THEATER AND DANCE, P.122

among children for its sculptures of the Tin Man, the Cowardly Lion, the Scarecrow, and Dorothy and Toto – the main characters from the classic book and movie *The Wizard of Oz*. The book's author, L. Frank Baum, lived in Chicago and was said to have entertained neighborhood kids with his stories about a strange land. SEE ALSO BARS, P.35; MUSIC, P.86, 87; THEATER AND DANCE, P.122

Armitage Avenue

One of the city's most popular clusters of boutiques, sweet shops, and restaurants, the strip caters to an upmarket lifestyle. While chains have made inroads here in recent years, several local shops remain, offering everything from shoes to exotic chocolates. This is also where you'll find the internationally known restaurant **Charlie Trotter's**, discreetly tucked away in a townhome. This stretch of

Armitage enjoys landmark status for its 19th-century streetscape, with delightful touches like ornate turrets and decorative masonry. SEE ALSO RESTAURANTS, P.108

Old Town

Just as gentrified as Lincoln Park, Old Town has nevertheless hung on to some institutions from its days as a bohemian quarter. Here are the headquarters of **Second City** ④, the comedy improv troupe known for catapulting the careers of such acclaimed

Hungry? The **Green City Market** is one of the city's most popular outdoor farmers' markets (from May to October), featuring products and vendors grown locally and produced in an ecologically responsible manner. Chefs from some of the city's best eateries are regulars. *See also Food and Drink, p.57.*

Below: fresh goods at Green City Market.

Lakeview to Andersonville

It's hard to make generalizations about the communities north of Lincoln Park, as their characters are so distinct. Lakeview is perhaps known best for Wrigley Field, the gracious home of the luckless Cubs baseball team, while others know it for its thriving gay community in Boys Town. Andersonville, once home to a large Swedish community, hosts a smaller, quieter gay scene, Uptown still shows remnants of its glamorous past amid the occasionally seedy present, and Argyle Street hosts restaurants and businesses catering to relatively new Vietnamese arrivals. In other words, each area provides a peek into the lives of Chicagoans of all stripes.

Cubs fans blame some of team's dismal history on the Curse of the Billy Goat. In 1945 Billy Sianis, the owner of the famous Billy Goat Tavern, tried to bring his pet goat to the ballpark for a World Series game but was denied entrance. He decreed that the team would never win another pennant. Attempts over the years by Sianis's relatives to break the curse have not yet met with success.

Boys Town

Southeast of the ballpark the nightlife scene changes from beer-swilling sports fans to loud, pumping dance music and same-sex couples, a sign that you have arrived in the heart of the city's main gay neighborhood. The preponderance of rainbows on storefronts and sidewalk pylons are another clue. At night crowds throng to down-and-dirty dance clubs, but for a more sedate atmosphere, head to **Roscoe's**, where the dance floor is complemented by a beer garden and pool tables.
SEE ALSO GAY AND LESBIAN, P.60

Southport Corridor

The anchor of this West Lakeview business district is the **Music Box Theatre** ②, a gorgeous temple to film built in

Wrigleyville

Yes, it's named after **Wrigley Field** ①. The park, which was built in 1914, surprises many visitors by being right in the middle of a busy neighborhood – making it best to arrive here via public transportation on game days. Although the team hasn't won the World Series since 1908, hope springs eternal, and there are plenty of sports bars situated throughout the neighborhood in which fans can celebrate the occasional victories as well as drown their sorrows.
SEE ALSO SPORT, P.116

Left: Cubs fans pack out Wrigley Field.

Swedish American Museum Center ③ chronicles their culture and history with art, concerts, and other events and festivals. While you probably won't hear the language spoken on the street, there are still several storefront delis and restaurants specializing in Scandinavian fare. One of the most popular – although it's not quite as Swedish as it used to be – is **Ann Sather**, a friendly place to indulge in Swedish meatballs, lacy pancakes with lingonberry sauce, and legendary cinnamon rolls. Meanwhile, **Simon's Tavern** is a friendly local bar that salutes the neighborhood's history with spicy glogg around the holidays and Abba on the jukebox (much to the bartenders' annoyance).

1929. The main theater inside resembles a Mediterranean street scene at night, with the ceiling painted to resemble a star-filled sky, complete with twinkling lights. There are lots of restaurants here at which to grab a bite before or after a movie, or stop at the **Southport Grocery and Café** for a quick snack.
SEE ALSO MOVIES, P.75

Uptown

In the early years of the 20th century, Uptown was one of the city's most glamorous neighborhoods, due in no small part to the presence of **Essanay Studios**, where silent-movie stars Gloria Swanson and Charlie Chaplin churned out the hits during the silent era. The studio went out of business long ago, but its building is now the home of St Augustine College.

People crowded Uptown's swanky speakeasies and gracious dance halls, especially the **Green Mill**, which was co-owned by an associate of Al Capone during Prohibition. These days it's known as one of the best places to hear jazz.
SEE ALSO MUSIC, P.87

Argyle Street

The informal family-run Asian restaurants around here – mainly Vietnamese – are low on atmosphere but big on taste, as crowds who flock here every weekend prove. Favorite dishes include *pho*, a fragrant beef noodle soup, and *banh mi*, baguette sandwiches that show Vietnam's French colonial history.

Andersonville

As one might guess from the name, this area was once home to a sizable community of Swedish immigrants, once the largest in the country. The

Members of the neighborhood gay community – more lady-based than Boys Town further south – meet up at **Star Gaze**, which features a beer garden, a pool table, and occasional free salsa lessons. **Women and Children First**, a neighborhood institution, is one of the dwindling number of independent bookstores in the city, stocking books and magazines with a feminist and GLBT bent as well as plenty of general interest titles.
SEE ALSO BARS, P.36; GAY AND LESBIAN, P.60; LITERATURE, P.73; MUSEUMS AND GALLERIES, P.80

Right: a jazz show at the Green Mill.

15

West Side

In the 19th century the West Side was an address with serious cachet, as the pockets of faded grandeur that dot the area testify. After many years of poverty and decline, an influx of new residents is driving the area's rebirth. Restaurants and boutiques are springing up in the formerly desolate West Loop, while home-buyers are enticed by the large, relatively inexpensive houses. Not everyone is happy with this gentrification; some suggest that it is erasing local history and culture, although many enclaves are stubbornly retaining their immigrant characters. While more populated areas are generally safe, visitors should exercise caution when on foot, especially at night.

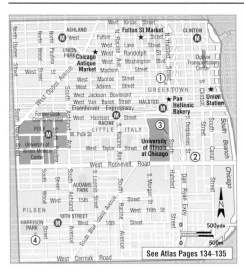

See Atlas Pages 134–135

The neighborhood is home to Harpo Studios, the TV home of the spectacularly popular daytime talk-show host Oprah Winfrey. Tickets are reserved far in advance, but for latecomers there's always the Oprah Store at 37 North Carpenter, which carries Oprah's 'favorite things' and even a selection of her gently used clothing.

Fulton Street Market

The most obvious manifestation of the changing nature of the West Side is perhaps in the blocks surrounding this stretch. You'll still dodge forklifts and trucks from the many meatpacking companies in the area, which now compete for space with sleek shops, art galleries, and clubs.

Randolph Street

Known locally as Restaurant Row, this is a blocks-long stretch lined with chic eateries. A favorite is **Sushi Wabi**,

which specializes in superfresh seafood. A few of the restaurants have stalls in the nearby **Chicago Antique Market**, held the last weekend of the month from May to October. Modeled after the giant flea markets of Paris, Rome, and London, it offers everything from vintage clothes to mantelpieces.
SEE ALSO RESTAURANTS, P.109; SHOPPING P.113

Greektown

Clustered around Halsted Street between Monroe and

Van Buren are the Greek pastry shops, restaurants, and cafés that are the remnants of a once large Greek community here. While most of the original residents were displaced by the construction of the nearby highway and the expansion of the University of Illinois at Chicago in the 1960s, plenty of them still make the trek back to the old neighborhood for supplies and conversation. For a taste of authenticity, try the almond and apricot cookies with a traditional Greek-style coffee at the family-owned **Pan Hellenic Bakery**. For background on the area, the **Hellenic Museum and Cultural Center** ① offers displays on the Greek immigrant experience filtered through art, food, and dance. The area also hosts several summer festivals that bring back the sights, sounds,

Left: authentic Mexican dishes at a Pilsen eatery.

resources. The museum is made up of the original mansion and dining hall, which house original furnishings (including the inside of Addams's office) and displays of letters, photos, and other items from the museum's archives.
SEE ALSO MUSEUMS AND GALLERIES, P.81

Pilsen

The happy exception to the rapidly gentrifying West Side, Pilsen is proudly and undeniably Mexican. The main drag, 18th Street, is bustling with record stores blaring the latest south-of-the-border hits, taco stands, and cafés, while walls and sometimes even buildings are gilded with colorful murals. The western edge of the neighborhood houses the **National Museum of Mexican Art** ④, with a collection ranging from folk art to work by Diego Rivera and José Clemente Orozco. The museum also hosts an annual Dia de los Muertos (Day of the Dead) exhibit, featuring the holiday as interpreted in various media by contemporary artists.
SEE ALSO MUSEUMS AND GALLERIES, P.81

and tastes of the neighborhood's heyday, including the **Greek Independence Day Parade** and the **Taste of Greece** street fair.
SEE ALSO CAFÉS, P.39; MUSEUMS AND GALLERIES, P.80

Around the University of Illinois at Chicago

Throughout the years the university has found itself mired in controversy about its development and displacement of communities and landmarks. One of the most bitter fights revolved around the fate of the **Maxwell Street Market** ②, which for more than a century occupied several blocks around Maxwell and Halsted Streets every Sunday. That area is now a shopping and housing center, while the market was moved to Canal Street and Roosevelt Road. It's definitely not the same, although you can still find all sort of odds and ends, from socks to

CDs. Reportedly the market will be moved yet again, although a definitive date has not been set.

On the campus itself, the **Jane Addams Hull-House Museum** ③ is devoted to chronicling the life and work of the famous social activist, who opened the settlement in this West Side neighborhood to help poverty-stricken residents and recent immigrants find their footing with educational programs and other

Below: street artists work on a new mural in Pilsen.

Wicker Park

Since the 1990s, when musicians and bands like Liz Phair, the Smashing Pumpkins, and Urge Overkill catapulted Wicker Park to national prominence, the neighborhood's image has been that of a hipster utopia. While you still see artfully dressed young people wandering the streets, they probably live in cheaper neighborhoods, and big-name designer boutiques and chain cafés are slowly replacing the quirky independent businesses. Still, for now many of the more raffish elements of the area coexist with the glamorous newcomers, ensuring that Wicker Park remains a popular place to live, play, and visit.

cheaply, stop at secondhand bookstore **Myopic Books**, with its maze of shelves. The **Flat Iron Arts Building** ① still leases space to artists and holds an open studio evening the first Friday of every month.

SEE ALSO RESTAURANTS, P.110

North Avenue

A walk down North also shows vestiges of Wicker Park's past. One restaurant, Spring, is even housed in a former communal bathhouse. Head east of the intersection to check out the collection of comics, zines, erotica, and art books – everything anyone with an 'alternative lifestyle' could want – at **Quimby's Bookstore**. Clotheshorses should check out several storefronts on these blocks that make up the **Akira** empire, variously offering super-trendy men's and women's clothing, shoes, and items for the home at generally very affordable prices.

SEE ALSO FASHION, P.53; LITERATURE, P.73

Damen and Divison

North of Six Corners, **Damen** ② is actually part of a subset of Wicker Park called Bucktown, so dubbed for the many goats in the area in the 19th

'The Crotch'

Wicker Park may be named after the compact, triangular green space, but the unofficial center of it all is undoubtedly the busy intersection of Damen, Milwaukee, and North avenues, also known as 'The Crotch.' It's a noisy yet exhilarating mishmash of noise from the el station overhead, cars and buses honking, and muted thuds from rock clubs keeping the neighborhood's musical tradition alive.

Milwaukee Avenue

The stretch of Milwaukee from Damen to Ashland probably shows the changing nature of the area more than any other street. On the one hand you've got the upscale shops and sleek lounge/restaurant hybrids such as **Rodan**; on the other there are still a few grubby vintage-clothing stores and cafés, stubborn holdovers from the area's scenester heyday. To load up on reading material

Left: an alternative influence is still felt in Wicker Park.

The blocks of Hoyne Avenue between Potomac and Caton feature drool-worthy gingerbread Victorian mansions built by wealthy German immigrants who settled here in the late 19th and early 20th centuries. Many of them owned breweries, causing the strip to be nicknamed 'Beer Baron Row.' Today it's part of a designated landmark district.

was once the neighborhood's dominant ethnic group. Despite the fountain dedicated to Nelson Algren, the tiny plaza is a little seedy. Better to honor Wicker Park's past with a meal at **Podhalanka**, a family-owned diner that's low on atmosphere but big on authenticity.

SEE ALSO BARS, P.37; CAFÉS, P.39; RESTAURANTS, P.110

Ukrainian Village

Ukrainian immigrants tended to settle in the area between Damen, Western, Division, and Chicago, and the community is still mostly intact despite the forces of gentrification. Try **Saks Ukrainian Village** for a taste of the old country, then head to the **Ukrainian National Museum** ③ for a view of folk art and historical artifacts. There are several churches serving the community, one of them a relatively hidden jewel: the rustic-looking **Holy Trinity Russian Orthodox Cathedral** ④, designed by Chicago architect Louis Sullivan to resemble a Russian provincial church.

SEE ALSO MUSEUMS AND GALLERIES, P.81

century. The stretch up to Webster is shoppers' heaven, being studded with tons of high-end boutiques.

Heading back south, Division Street in Wicker Park was once known as 'Polish Broadway' for all the saloons and taverns serving the local Polish working-class residents in the first half of the 20th century. Of those only a handful still exist, including the **Rainbo Club** – actually just off of Division on Damen. This place was a favorite of

writer Nelson Algren and now serves a bohemian, artistic clientele. These days, like other arteries in the area Division is increasingly given over to upscale retailers and restaurants. However, the friendly **Alliance Bakery** still offers traditional breads and baked treats, including jam- or cream-filled *paczki*, deep-fried Polish doughnuts.

The intersection of Division, Milwaukee, and Ashland marks the Polish Triangle, again honoring what

Left: the busy intersection known as 'The Crotch.'

19

South Loop

Long home to little but students at nearby Columbia College and parking garages, in recent years this formerly desolate area has been transformed by a surge in development, led by savvy builders who recognized the area's proximity to both Loop and lake as a major attraction for homeowners. The many upscale restaurants and pet boutiques attest to the success of their gamble. While not exactly always brimming with energy and excitement, the neighborhood can be a nice respite from the endlessly clogged sidewalks and streets of the Loop, and the attractions tend to have an off-the-beaten-track feel to them as well.

Printers Row

This was once the Midwest's printing center, and while the printing companies are long gone, the enclave still boasts a certain literary cachet and is home to a few bookstores carrying on the tradition. Every summer it's the site of the **Printers Row Book Fair**, featuring stalls of new, rare, and secondhand books as well as readings and seminars. If you've got more dough burning a hole in your pocket, step into **Printers Row Fine & Rare Books**, with its quaintly antiquarian atmosphere. On the south end is the red-brick **Dearborn Station**, a former train depot that now houses retail and office space. On the north end, not technically in Printers Row but just a skip away, is the **Harold Washington Library Center** ①. The massive library, opened in

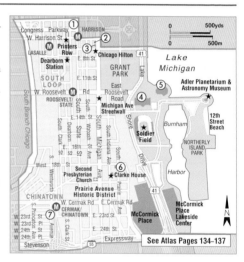

During the War of 1812, a group of about a hundred soldiers, women, and children were ordered to evacuate the Fort Dearborn garrison and head for Indiana. Around what is now 18th and Calumet they were ambushed by Potawatomi Indians allied with British forces This event came to be known as the Fort Dearborn Massacre.

1991, dominates the area – the *Guinness Book of World Records* once listed it as the largest public library building in the world. The top-floor, glass-roofed Winter Garden is an oasis of calm and beauty. SEE ALSO LITERATURE, P.73

South Michigan Avenue

Randolph Street south to 11th Street has been designated the **Michigan Avenue Streetwall**, a cliff-like line of historic buildings, some of them dating back to the 1880s. Although it was awarded Chicago landmark status in

2002, it is under threat by plans for new high-rise buildings that would simply graft the original buildings' facade on front. The wall was recently listed on the National Trust for Historic Preservation's list of most endangered places.

When you're done admiring the outside, head inside, to a couple of lesser-known museums the city has to offer. The **Museum of Contemporary Photography** ②, part of Columbia College, is free and offers rotating exhibits with a unifying theme, such as architecture or portraits, as well as

Left: passing under the South Loop's el tracks.

houses being pulled down or abandoned, but you can still visit the **Glessner House Museum** ⑥, dating from 1886. The imposing granite building houses some 6,000 artifacts, most from the Glessner family's estate. The museum also leads occasional tours of Prairie Avenue and other historically significant buildings. Just steps away is the **Clarke House**, which might just be the oldest building in Chicago, having been built in 1836.

Some Prairie Avenue residents undoubtedly worshiped at the **Second Presbyterian Church**, where you can admire the lovely stained-glass windows. Dating from 1874, it was rebuilt after a 1900 fire by the noted architect Howard Van Doren Shaw. SEE ALSO CHURCHES, SYNAGOGUES, AND TEMPLES, P.43; MUSEUMS AND GALLERIES, P.82, 83

Chinatown

Unsurprisingly, the city's main Asian enclave offers some excellent eating. Non-dining activities include a stop at the **Chinese-American Museum of Chicago** ⑦, which offers temporary exhibits on the immigrant experience, food, and art. The many storefronts offer treasures in the form of obscure Asian foodstuffs, decorative ceramic objects, and silky cheongsams. SEE ALSO MUSEUMS AND GALLERIES, P.82

retrospectives. The **Spertus Museum** ③ focuses on Jewish art and culture all over the world. The gift shop has some lovely jewelry by artisans from Israel and elsewhere.

Irish pubs are a dime a dozen in any city, but **Kitty O'Shea's**, located in the **Hilton Chicago**, is more authentic than most, with employees who hail from the Emerald Isle, Guinness, and Gaelic pub grub. The Hilton itself was the location of a violent confrontation between police and protesters during the tumultuous 1968 Democrat convention, with some civilians being pushed through the hotel's plate-glass windows in the melee. Those images were broadcast soon after at the convention, setting off more riots. The incident haunted the city and the mayor at the time, Richard J. Daley, for years afterward. SEE ALSO BARS, P.37; HOTELS, P.71; MUSEUMS AND GALLERIES, P.82, 83

Prairie Avenue Historic District

At the far east of the South Loop, in the southern stretch of Grant Park *(see p.96)* is the **Field Museum** ④ and **Shedd Aquarium** ⑤. From here, walk south to what is known as the Prairie Avenue Historial District. Before Potter Palmer pulled up stakes and moved north, this area was the most sought-after address among the city's elite. Decades of neglect resulted in many

Right: a mural in Printers Row depicts the area's legacy.

South Side

The vast South Side resists succinct summarization. It has been a center of African-American culture since the days of the Great Migration from the south after the Civil War, resulting in a rich blues and jazz scene that spawned the careers of so many musical legends and inspired many more. It's also known for academics: the University of Chicago is one of the country's most respected academic institutions, while the Illinois Institute of Technology's architecture program is likewise ranked among the best. While large tracts of the area still suffer from the ravages of crime and poverty, there are pockets of middle-class comfort and renewal.

Bronzeville

In some ways, the area once known as the Black Metropolis is a shadow of its former self. This stretch of South State Street was once lined with blues and jazz clubs and dubbed **'The Stroll,'** but the music has long since ceased. However, new development is bringing in new residents, especially African-Americans who appreciate the area's history. At the corner of Martin

Luther King Jr Drive and 26th Street is Alison Saar's 1996 *Monument to the Great Northern Migration* ①, a 15ft (4.5m) -tall sculpture of a man waving with satchel in hand – executed in bronze, of course.

Other historic and cultural spots to check out in the area include the home of civil rights activist Ida B. Wells and the **Harold Washington Cultural Center** ②, which hosts concerts, movies, and other events. The center stands on land that was once home to the Regal Theater, where musical greats including Duke Ellington and Cab Calloway took the stage.

The blocks around State Street are home to the main campus of the **Illinois Institute of Technology**, known for the architectural designs of Ludwig Mies van der Rohe as part of his first American commission. Buildings in his signature Modernist style, which made great use of glass and steel, abound. The one-room **S.R. Crown Hall** ③, now home to the school's College of Architecture, is generally regarded as the finest example of his work here.

Inside the lakefront Jackson Park is one of the city's most underappreciated oases: Osaka Garden, featuring raked gravel paths, an arched bridge, and vegetation native to Japan located on the park's Wooded Island.

In 2003 two new structures were added to the campus: Helmut Jahn's futuristic student dorm and Rem Koolhaas's **Exelon Tube**, a structure of corrugated steel through which the elevated train passes as it makes its way across campus. Architecture students lead tours of the buildings every Tuesday through Friday.

Hyde Park

For families, the **Museum of Science and Industry** ④, located in **Jackson Park**, is one of the main draws to Hyde Park. The building itself is the only existing structure left over from the 200 white plaster buildings constructed for the 1893 World's Columbian Exposition. In Jackson Park itself, the interiors and ballroom of the 1916 South Shore Cultural Center – designed by the architects of the Drake Hotel as a genteel country

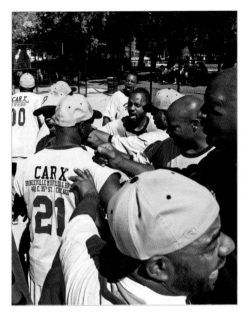

ancient art and artifacts from the Near East. Just behind it, the Gothic **Rockefeller Memorial Chapel**, built between 1925 and 1928, features a 72-bell carillon – the second-largest in the world – that was a gift from university benefactor John D. Rockefeller, for whom the chapel is named.

Walk a block north from the chapel to see where Frank Lloyd Wright made his mark on the South Side with the **Robie House**, which shows the typical features of the pioneering Prairie Style: wide open interiors, a low-lying, horizontal silhouette, and natural materials.

East of here, on the edge of **Washington Park**, is the **DuSable Museum of African American History** ⑦. Named after Chicago's official founder, fur trader Jean Baptiste Pointe DuSable, it presents permanent and temporary exhibits of African and African-American history and culture.

club – hint at the building's distinguished past.

For others, Hyde Park is synonymous with the **University of Chicago** ⑤, which has spawned some 80 Nobel laureates and celebrated alumni, among them Carl Sagan and Susan Sontag. But even if you're not a Mensa member, it's pleasant to take a walk around the largely Gothic campus. The **Smart Museum of Art** ⑥, located in a pretty courtyard, offers a quirky range of temporary exhibits curated by faculty members along with Old Master portraits, 20th-century art, and furniture by Frank Lloyd Wright in its permanent collection. Nearby, the **Oriental Institute Museum** is devoted to

SEE ALSO ARCHITECTURE, P.32; CHILDREN, P.40–1; MUSEUMS AND GALLERIES, P.83, 84, 85; PARKS AND BEACHES, P.99

Below: the elegant grounds and college buildings of the University of Chicago.

Oak Park

Just 20 minutes from downtown Chicago on the el, the western suburb of Oak Park is known mainly for two of its former residents, Frank Lloyd Wright and Ernest Hemingway. Wright, the originator of the groundbreaking Prairie Style, left the village a unique architectural legacy via his own designs and those of his many disciples. Hemingway's influence is fainter, existing mainly in the form of museums dedicated to his early life. Quiet, elegant, and composed, Oak Park makes a pleasant day trip for architecture buffs and the literary. A free shuttle runs a continuous loop around the major sights every day (except major holidays).

Forest Avenue

From 1889 to 1909, Wright lived and worked in the house at the corner of Forest and Chicago avenues, which he designed. The **Frank Lloyd Wright Home and Studio** shows elements of what would later become cornerstones of the Prairie Style: natural materials, spacious interiors, and colors inspired by nature. It was here that he and his colleagues designed more than 120 buildings, some of them incorporating ideas that Wright experimented

with during renovations on the home.

Just down the street from the Home and Studio are many examples of Wright's work. At 318 Forest Avenue is one of his favorites, the **Arthur Heurtley House** ①, from 1902. With its flattened roof and horizontal detailing, the building shows signs of the ground-hugging design that would reach full flower in the Prairie Style. Around the corner on Elizabeth Court is the blocky **Mrs Thomas Gale House** from 1909. Notable here is the second-story bal-

cony projecting from the house, an element that Wright would exaggerate in the 'floating horizontal planes' in later works like Fallingwater in Pennsylvania. Back on Forest, at 238, view Wright's remodeling job on a Gothic cottage at the **Peter A. Beachy House**, while the **Frank W. Thomas House** ② at 210, built in 1901, is considered the architect's first true Prairie Style house in the village.

SEE ALSO ARCHITECTURE, P.30; MUSEUMS AND GALLERIES, P.85

Around Lake Street

Head south on Forest, hang a left, and you'll soon be at **Unity Temple** ③, another of Wright's spectacular works. Naturally, he threw out all of the traditional details of a place of worship – steeples, arches, and so forth – in favor of a shockingly modern Cubist design. Wright intended the poured-concrete structure's intersecting horizontal and vertical planes,

24

Left: one of Wright's creations, the Arthur Heurtley House.

view of village history, head to the second floor, home of the Oak Park River Forest Historical Society. Black-and-white photos from the turn of the century by Philander Barclay, who roved around his hometown on a bicycle, show how Oak Park has both changed and stayed the same.

SEE ALSO CHURCHES, SYNAGOGUES, AND TEMPLES, P.43; MUSEUMS AND GALLERIES, P.85

Harrison Street and South Oak Park

Further east is the **Oak Park Arts District**, an eight-block-long stretch of art galleries, boutiques, bookstores, and the like. Every third Friday there's a gallery walk with new shows and openings.

Just on the other side of the Eisenhower Expressway is the **Oak Park Conservatory** ⑦, an Edwardian-era glass greenhouse dating from 1929. The conservatory nurtures many of the plants and flowers for the village's parks and public areas and also features exotic collections of desert plants, orchids, and begonias.

Other well-known residents of Oak Park include Tarzan creator Edgar Rice Burroughs, Ray Kroc, founder of McDonald's, and mobster Sam Giancana.

open interior flooded with natural light through leaded windows, and many balconies and alcoves to embody 'unity, truth, beauty, simplicity, freedom, and reason.' The church, completed in 1909, still holds regular Unitarian Universalist services and is a popular spot for concerts and other events.

Also near here are two buildings where Ernest Hemingway lived in his youth: the **Hemingway Birthplace Home** ④, a Queen Anne-style residence where the writer was born in 1899 and lived until he was six, and the **Hemingway Museum** ⑤, where he spent the rest of his boyhood. The writer later dismissed his hometown as 'a place of wide lawns and narrow minds,' but clearly the village has not held it against him.

Another stop for devotees of the Prairie School is **Historic Pleasant Home** ⑥, an early example of the genre, dating from 1897 and built by George Washington Maher. For a more comprehensive

Below: from his signature glass panels to plaques commemorating him, Wright's influence can be seen all over Oak Park.

25

Around Chicago

A s beautiful and exciting as the city is, the surrounding areas offer their share of diversions as well. Although suburban growth has largely filled in the wide open spaces of the former prairie, there are plenty of outdoor reserves and institutions devoted to preserving nature and wildlife. Some of the area's loveliest architecture is found in the suburbs, and of course outlying areas offer a fair share of arts and culture as well as other options for entertainment, from nature walks to gambling. That same growth means that highways can be clogged with traffic, so it's a good idea to take advantage of the efficient and reliable Metra train system if at all possible.

As the home of the Women's Christian Temperance Union, Evanston was dry (no alcohol was served or sold) until the early 1970s. Even today there are, strictly speaking, no bars: establishments serving alcohol must also serve food.

North Shore

North of Evanston up to **Lake Bluff** is known as the North Shore ②, where the stunning homes and shiny luxury cars hint at residents' enviable income levels. **Wilmette** is home to the **Baha'i House of Worship**, an arresting domed structure that rises into view over a curvy stretch of Sheridan Road just north of Evanston. One of only seven such temples in the world, it is surrounded by beautifully landscaped gardens. Both the temple and the gardens are open to visitors.

Despite its name, the **Chicago Botanic Garden** is actually located in **Glencoe**. Over its 385 acres (154 hectares) you can find all kinds of landscape gardens, from the formal English walled variety to meditative Japanese ones, splendidly located on a series of small islands. The botanical history and makeup of this area

Evanston

Evanston ① is the home of **Northwestern University** and, as the closest northern suburb to the city, the most urban in nature. Northwestern, founded in 1855, is generally considered one of the top universities in the country, and its beautiful lakeshore campus makes a fine setting for academic reflection. Evanston is more than just a college town, however. Although a recent

redevelopment downtown has brought in more chains, independently owned retailers and restaurants continue to add to the town's liberal air. **Dempster Street** is where you'll find a lot of long-time businesses that are favorites with townies and students alike. They include the Mexican Shop, which offers affordable and exotic jewelry, clothes, and accessories from all over the world.

Baháʾí House of Worship
all are welcome

Left: the Baháʾí House of Worship in Wilmette.

park. Open from approximately May to October, it features both state-of-the-art thrill rides and time-tested ones for kids and roller-coaster fetishists, as well as a water park, parades, and musical shows. For more material thrills, there's **Gurnee Mills Mall**, a truly overwhelming assemblage of over 200 retailers offering outlet and discount shopping for dedicated bargain hunters.
SEE ALSO CHILDREN, P.40

Indiana

Indiana ④, also known as the 'Hoosier State,' offers many diversions within an hour or two of Chicago. The **Indiana Dune National Lakeshore** boasts 18 miles (29km) of shore with several beaches, shifting sand dunes (the tallest, **Mount Baldy**, is 123ft/37m tall), hiking trails along the **Little Calumet River**, and bird- and butterfly-watching. For glitzier entertainment, head to one of the many riverboat casinos in the area to try your luck at the slots or the blackjack table. Among the many options for losing your money are **Majestic Star II** in Gary, a floating casino overlooking Lake Michigan, or the **Horseshow Hammond Casino** in Hammond.

of the Midwest is explored with a section devoted to native prairie plants.

For a free taste of nature, the **Green Bay Trail** is a bike and walking path that wends its way from Wilmette up to Lake Bluff. It is lined with plants and flowers like Queen Anne's Lace and cattails, and you might even stumble on some wildlife in the form of an occasional duck or even a shy deer straying from forest preserves in the area. (The path actually continues north to Wisconsin under another name.)

In Highland Park, the Chicago Symphony Orchestra summers at **Ravinia**, a 36-acre (14.5-hectare) outdoor music venue, which first opened in 1904. Concertgoers spread out with picnics on the lawn in this gracious setting, while more serious fans spring

for tickets in the pavilion. The festival also hosts dance performances and pop acts. A Metra train line from downtown Chicago stops right outside the main entrance.
SEE ALSO CHURCHES, SYNAGOGUES, AND TEMPLES, P.43; PARKS AND BEACHES, P.99; WALKS, TOURS, AND VIEWS, P.129

Gurnee

About halfway between Chicago and Milwaukee is Gurnee ③, home to the **Six Flags Great America** theme

Right: the Northwestern University Wildcats football team.

A–Z

In the following section Chicago's attractions and services are organized by theme, under alphabetical headings. Items that link to another theme are cross-referenced. All sights that are plotted on the atlas section at the end of the book are given a page number and grid reference.

Architecture

Great buildings, from soaring, iconic skyscrapers to residential homes, are a Chicago trademark. This is due in part to the Great Chicago Fire of 1871, which provided a clean slate for the architects charged with helping the city to rise from the ashes. Residents are proud of the subsequent contributions of Daniel Burnham – who called the city his 'Paris on the Prairie' – and Frank Lloyd Wright. Balancing the preservation of historic structures and the dreams of 21st-century architects is sometimes tricky, but a spate of new projects will ensure that the city's bold architectural legacy continues apace.

History

1800s–1871
Chicago's early buildings were mostly wooden structures – which turned out to be disastrous during the Great Chicago Fire. The few buildings that survived were made of limestone, including the historic **Water Tower** and its pumping station downtown.

1870s–1880s
Advances in engineering paved the way for the construction of steel-framed commercial high-rises. Such buildings, clad in masonry with a grid of distinctive

Below: the Beaux Arts Museum of Science and Industry.

three-paneled windows and a minimum of exterior ornamentation, became known as examples of the Chicago School of architecture. Examples include Daniel Burnham's **Reliance Building** and the **Sullivan Center** (formerly the Carson Pirie Scott Building) by Louis Sullivan.

1890s
Daniel Burnham, charged with designing and constructing the facilities for the 1893 World's Columbian Exposition on his own after the death of his business partner, transformed Jackson Park into a landscape of stunning neoclassical buildings. What became known as the White City touched off a revival of interest in classical and Beaux Arts design worldwide. The only extant buildings from the fair are the **Art Institute** and the **Museum of Science and Industry**.

1900s–1910s
In suburban **Oak Park**, Frank Lloyd Wright started experimenting with and refining what would become one of the country's first distinctly

American architectural styles. His Prairie School buildings reflected the flat landscape and open spaces of the Midwest with their horizontal planes and open floor plans. Hyde Park's **Robie House** is the best example in the city limits of his groundbreaking theories and principles.

1920s
A booming economy in the 1920s led to a spate of building downtown, resulting in many of the most recognizable structures on Michigan Avenue, including the Gothic Revival **Tribune Tower** (whose design was chosen via an international competition) and the Art Deco **Carbide and Carbon Building**, designed by Daniel Burnham's sons, Daniel and Hubert.

1930s
Unrest in Europe and worldwide economic woes led Ludwig Mies van der Rohe to leave Germany for Chicago, where he headed the architecture school of what would later be called the **Illinois Institute of Technology**. It

Left: the architectural playground that is Chicago.

walking/bus tours year-round, boat tours May–Nov
Offers dozens of walking, bus, and boat tours of the city and suburbs organized by neighborhood, historical era, style, or architect. The skyscraper tour is also available in French, German, and Italian. The river cruise, which is really the definitive version, is extremely popular, and reservations are advised in summer.

River Tours

Chicago Line
465 North McClurg Court, North Side; tel: 312-527-2002; www.chicagoline.com; Mar–Nov; el: Red line to Grand, then free trolley (in season); bus: 65; map p.133 D4

Shoreline Sightseeing
Ogden Slip, 455 East Illinois Street, North Side; tel: 312-222-9328; www.shorelinesight seeing.com; Mar–Oct; el: Red line to Grand, then free trolley (in season); bus: 65; map p.133 D4

Wendella Boats
Southwest cnr of Michigan Avenue and Wacker Drive, Loop; tel: 312-337-1446; www.wendellaboats.com; Apr–Nov; el: Brown, Orange, Green, Pink line to State/Lake; map p.133 C4

Iconic Buildings

Auditorium Building
430 South Michigan Avenue, Loop; tel: 312-341-3500; bus: 3, 145, 147, 151; map p.135 C2
Engineer Dankmar Adler and architect Louis Sullivan designed the 1889 Auditorium Building as an opera house. The granite and limestone Romanesque Revival exterior is impressive, but it is the lavish, stately interior – adorned with the opulent, nature-inspired ornamentation of the sort Sullivan was famous for – that is most

One of the cheapest architectural tours in town is a ride on the el lines that circle around the Loop (Brown, Purple, Orange, and Pink). The elevated tracks provide an up-close-and-personal view of many cool architectural details and ornamentation, such as ornate stonework and masonry, that aren't visible from street level. The circular trip takes about 20 minutes, and you can go around several times if you hop on and off the different lines.

was the beginning of a long and fruitful career in the city.

1950–70S

Mies continued making his mark on Chicago's architectural landscape, perhaps most notably with two glass-and-steel residential high-rises on Lake Shore Drive, known as the **Glass Houses**, that would prove hugely influential in future skyscraper design. During this time the firm also was responsible for two major additions to the Chicago skyline, the **John Hancock Center** and the **Sears Tower**.

1980S–1990S

In 1985, Helmut Jahn made a strong postmodern statement with his controversial **James R. Thompson Center**, whose massive, curving design had residents comparing it to a spaceship or a wedding cake. New condo buildings sprouted up all over the city, to the dismay of preservationists mourning the often architecturally or historically significant lower-rise buildings they replaced.

2000S

The city continues to distinguish itself with striking skyscrapers; the **Trump International Hotel and Tower** on the Chicago River will break the Hancock's record for having the highest residences off ground level, and plans for Spanish architect Sergio Calatrava's twisting 150-story **Chicago Spire** are moving forward.

Architectural Tours

Chicago Architecture Foundation
Various locations; tel: 312-922-3432; www.architecture.org;

31

Above: Art Deco style at the Chicago Board of Trade.

breathtaking. The theater itself, with its four elliptical arches rising over the stage like a rainbow, features excellent acoustics.

Chicago Board of Trade

141 West Jackson Boulevard, Loop; tel: 312-435-3590; www.cbot.com; Mon–Fri 8am–4pm; el: Blue, Red line to Jackson; map p.134 C2

The firm of Holabird and Root designed this iconic example of Art Deco architecture, located at the foot of the LaSalle Street 'canyon' and dating from 1930. At its top is an aluminum statue of Ceres, the goddess of grain, a symbol of the agricultural goods traded here. The story goes that the statue has no facial features because the sculptor thought the building's extreme height at the time (45 stories) would make it unlikely anyone would ever see it up close.

Chicago Federal Center and Plaza

219 South Dearborn Street, Loop; el: Red, Blue line to Jackson or Monroe; map p.134 C2

The center, designed by Ludwig Mies van der Rohe, is made up of two towers and a low-rise freestanding post office, all of which showcase Mies's signature style in glass and steel. The austere buildings, painted in flat black and featuring bronze-tinted glass,

lend an aura of contemporary urban grandeur. The structures' grid pattern is even integrated into the granite plaza, insuring each component interacts harmoniously.

Inland Steel Building

30 West Monroe Street, Loop; el: Blue, Red line to Monroe; map p.134 C2

Built in the mid-50s, this was the first high-rise structure built in the Loop after the Great Depression. The design firm Skidmore, Owings, & Merrill placed all the structural columns around the building's perimeter, maximizing the interior space, and used steel cladding as a nod to its original owners.

John Hancock Center

875 North Michigan Avenue, North Side; tel: 312-751-3681, www.johnhancockcenter.com; daily 9am–11pm; admission charge; el: Red line to Chicago; bus: 144, 145, 146, 147, 148, 151; map p.133 C3

One of the city's most recognizable architectural landmarks, the John Hancock Center building was completed in 1970 and houses offices and residences. Its most striking feature are the X-shaped braces that replace traditional supports. The observatory includes a mesh-protected area where visitors can feel the high winds. Alternatively, have a drink in the Signature Lounge, which also offers spectacular views.

SEE ALSO BARS, P.34; RESTAURANTS, P.105; WALKS, TOURS, AND VIEWS, P.129

Lake Point Tower

505 North Lake Shore Drive, North Side; Red line to Grand, then free trolley (in season); bus: 29, 65; map p.133 D4

The designers took the architect's glass-and-steel skeleton and gave it three curving wings. The only skyscraper east of Lake Shore Drive, it is

a striking presence. The rooftop restaurant, Cite, offers panoramic views.

Marina City

300 North State Street, North Side; el: Red line to Grand; bus: 29, 36; map p.132 C4

Designed by Bertrand Goldberg (yet another of Mies's students) and completed in 1959, these two rounded structures are known around town as 'the corncobs.' Concrete was used instead of steel because it was the only way to create the distinctive 'petal' shapes of the individual apartments, which are built around a 35ft (10.5m) diameter core that houses the elevators and heating and cooling systems.

Robie House

5757 South Woodlawn Drive; tel: 773-834-1847; www.gowright. org; tours Mon–Fri 11am, 1pm, 3pm, Thur also 4pm, 5pm, also 6pm in summer, Sat–Sun every 30 minutes 11am–3.30pm; charge; bus: 6; train: Metra to 59th Street; map p.139 C3

The landmark house, built in 1910, still impresses for Frank Lloyd Wright's grasp of modern design and seemingly intuitive sense of space. Its long, low silhouette, dramatically overhanging eaves, and art-glass windows are just a few of the details that make the building the archetype of the Prairie School. Note that an ongoing restoration means that parts of the building may

Left: the John Hancock Center on the North Side.

acteristic touches include the three-paneled Chicago windows and the stunning cast-iron scrollwork with motifs of berries and flowers around the curving corner entrance, which was intended to literally attract customers with its beauty. Home to a Carson Pirie Scott department store from 1904 until 2007, there are plans to redevelop it into an office building.

333 West Wacker
333 West Wacker, Loop; el: Brown, Purple line to Merchandise Mart; map p.134 B1
The sweeping, curving glass facade of this 1983 building, which hugs a bend in the Chicago River, makes it a local favorite. The arc of green glass, often tinged blue by the sky, reflects other iconic buildings across the river and blazes with light as it catches rays from the setting sun in the evening. The structure looks particularly impressive when viewed from one of the river tours.

be closed to the public.

Rookery Building
209 South LaSalle Street, South Side; el: Brown, Orange, Pink, Purple line to Quincy; map p.134 C2
Another product of the firm of Holabird and Root, the Rookery, built in 1885, is considered perhaps the finest example of their talents. The ornate red-granite exterior, with its turrets and five horizontal layers, shows influences of Romanesque, Islamic, Venetian, and even Moorish styles. The interior, which was remodeled in 1907 by Frank Lloyd Wright, features light streaming down from a domed skylight, which highlights the iron cantilevered stairway and the white marble lobby. The building's name is

a leftover from the previous building on the spot, a favorite nesting place for pigeons.

Sears Tower
233 South Wacker Drive, Loop; tel: 312-875-96960; www.thesky deck.com; May–Sept: daily 10am–10pm, Oct–Apr: daily 10am–8pm; admission charge; el: Brown, Orange, Pink line to Quincy; map p.134 B2
When the 110-story Sears Tower was completed in 1973 it was the tallest building in the world; it's still the tallest office building in North America and dominates the city's skyline. The building's nine square 'tubes' at different heights give it its signature silhouette. On a clear day, the visibility can run from 40 to 50 miles (65–80km) – all the way into the neighboring states of Michigan, Indiana, and Wisconsin.

Sullivan Center
1 South State Street, Loop; el: Brown, Green, Orange, Pink line to Madison/Wabash; map p.135 C2
This stately structure, built in 1899, is a classic example of Louis Sullivan's work. Char-

Left: the distinctive balconies of Marina City.

One common residential style in the area – accounting for one-third of all Chicago single-family homes – is the 'Chicago bungalow,' squat, one-and-a-half-story brick homes that were built from around 1910 to 1940 and aimed at middle- and working-class families. The homes, which show elements of the Arts and Crafts and Prairie School styles in their many windows and pitched roofs with dormers, are officially recognized as architectural assets through an association that offers incentives and loans for their restoration. The Chicago Architecture Foundation *(see p.31)* offers tours of the 'Bungalow Belt' around the city.

Bars

As befits a town known for its bootlegging in the days of the Prohibiton, Chicago has nearly limitless options for imbibing, from dingy 'old man' bars to chic lounges. Once you could find neighborhood bars tucked away in side streets all over the city; some still exist but are now enjoyed by a younger crowd looking for 'authenticity.' Different crowds tend to self-segregate, each colonising their own favored taverns. In the past ten years wine bars have become extremely popular, and more recently a resurgence of interest in cocktail culture has emerged. For bars that offer live music and dancing, see Nightlife, p.92–3.

The Loop

Exchequer Pub

226 South Wabash Avenue; tel: 312-939-5633; www.exchequerpub.com; Mon–Thur 11am–11pm, Fri–Sat 11am–midnight, Sun noon–9pm; el: Brown, Purple, Green, Orange, Pink line to Adams/Wabash; map p.135 C2

There's probably no better place to get a sense of the Loop in the old days than this bar and restaurant, which opened in 1969 and hasn't changed much since, judging from the fern-bar decor in back. Fortunately a decent beer menu has kept up with the times, which pleases the motley but easygoing mix of office workers, students, and tourists. The deep-dish pizza at the restaurant in back is considered some of the city's best by those in the know.

Manhattan's

415 South Dearborn Street; tel: 312-957-0460; Mon–Sat 11.30am–2am; el: Red, Blue line to Jackson; map p.134 C2

Despite the name, this divey bar (with two floors) is pure Chicago: friendly, inexpensive, and attitude-free. Expect to hobnob with corporate suits as well as students from downtown colleges. Sports fans can gaze at any of a dozen flat-screen TVs, while those wanting more interaction can take advantage of darts or videogames.

Whiskey Blue

172 West Adams Street (inside W Hotel); tel: 312-782-4933; daily 4pm–2am; el: Brown, Purple, Orange, Pink line to Quincy; map p.134 C2

As you might expect from a nightspot owned by Cindy Crawford's husband, this place draws in the beautiful people – not least the servers, many of whom are moonlighting models. It's most bustling after work, when the place is crawling with professional types kicking back in the leather sofas and chairs. Crisp Martinis, in a giant glass that won't make the hefty price tag seem so bad, are poured tableside.

North Side

Coq d'Or

Drake Hotel, 140 East Walton Place; tel: 312-787-2200; www.drakehotel.com; Mon–Sat 11am–2am, Sun 11am–1am; el: Red line to Chicago; bus: 66, 3, 145, 146, 151; map p.133 C3

This clubby, low-ceilinged bar on the lower level of the Drake Hotel is the proud owner of the first liquor license to be issued in Chicago after the repeal of Prohibition, which is displayed on the front door. The vibe hearkens back to a more genteel time when people dressed up to have a drink. The dim, hushed atmosphere makes it perfect for romantic assignations.

Signature Lounge

875 North Michigan Avenue; tel: 312-787-7230; www.

If you fancy a drink on the water but tend to get seasick on boats, head to **Castaway's**, on North Street Beach, a basic bar and grill located on the top level of a boathouse shaped like a steamship (1603 North Lake Shore Drive; tel: 773-281-1200). You can also hit the **Oak Street Beachstro** at Oak Street Beach further south (1001 North Lake Shore Drive; tel: 312-915-4100), but to sit down you'll have to order something to eat.

Left: cocktails at a trendy Wicker Park bar *(see p.37)*.

Clark/Division; bus: 22 , 36, 70; map p.132 C2

It's been around since the original swinging days in the 1970s, and other than the clothes and the prices, not much has changed: there are still plenty of hookups, especially in the frenetic back room, where patrons get down to Top 40 hits.

Lincoln Park and Old Town

Delilah's

2771 North Lincoln Avenue; tel: 773-472-2771; www.delilahs chicago.com; daily 4pm–2am, Sat until 3am; el: Brown line to Diversey

This punk rock bar (note the black walls) seems a little out of place in upscale Lincoln Park but makes itself welcome with literally hundreds of varieties of whiskey and a beer menu worthy of a brewpub. Daily specials offer some great deals, and an eclectic assortment of DJs spin nightly.

Jake's Pub

2932 North Clark Street; tel: 773-248-3318; www.jakes pub.net; Mon–Fri 3pm–2am, Sat noon–3am, Sun noon–2am; el: Red line to Belmont; bus: 22

This 75-year-old watering hole is a nicely low-key alternative to the raucous pickup joints endemic to the area. The impressive beer selection includes Belgian ales and

---

signatureroom.com; daily 11am–12.30am, Fri–Sat until 1.30am; el: Red Line to Chicago, bus: 66, 3, 145, 146, 151; map p.133 C3

Yes, you'll pay top dollar for your cosmopolitan and will probably be surrounded by tourists at this elegant bar on the 96th floor of the John Hancock Center, but who cares? The views are amazing, particularly in the early evening, and the cost of a drink isn't much more than the fee for the viewing deck a couple of floors below.

Gold Coast

Cru Café and Wine Bar

25 East Delaware Place; tel: 312-337-4001; www.cru winebar.com; daily 11.30am–2am, Sun–Mon until midnight; el: Red line to Chicago; map p.132 C3

It's easy to pretend you're in Paris at this wine bar, where you can enjoy your choice of glass, half-bottle or bottle outside on the sidewalk in summer and watch the

Right: Delilah's is a local punk-rock institution.

---

well-dressed denizens of the upscale neighborhood go by. In winter, stay warm in a comfortable chair by the fireplace.

Elm Street Liquors

12 West Elm Street; tel: 312-337-3200; www.elmstreet liquors.com; Wed–Fri 8pm–2am, Sat 8pm–3am; el: Red line to Clark/Division; map p.132 C2

More sleek and upscale than the watering holes on nearby Division Street, this bar/club/lounge hybrid attracts a well-dressed crowd of all ages looking for some meet-and-greet. Cocktails sport amusing names like 'The Pre-nup' and 'Arm Candy.'

The Original Mother's

26 West Division Street; tel: 312-642-7251; daily 5pm–4am, Sat until 5am; el: Red line to

Midwestern brews as well as the usual cheapies for the light of wallet.

Old Town Ale House

219 West North Avenue; tel: 312-944-7020; www.oldtownale house.net; Mon–Fri 8am–4am, Sat 8am–5am, Sun noon–4am; bus: 72; map p.132 B1

Although there's been a smoking ban in effect since the beginning of 2008, a yellowish haze still seems to permeate this long-time hangout for **Second City** performers and neighborhood denizens. The jukebox plays only jazz – the original owner didn't care for rock, and her preferences are still honored. SEE ALSO COMEDY, P.44–5

Webster Wine Bar

1480 West Webster Avenue; tel: 773-868-0608; www. websterwinebar.com; Sun–Fri 5pm–2am, Sat 4pm–3am; el: Brown, Red line to Diversey, then bus: 74

One of the first wine bars to open in Chicago, the dim candlelit space is romantic for couples and just plain cozy for everyone else. The menu offers a changing list of 35 wines by the glass (which are also available for smaller 'tastes') and over 500 bottles from all over the globe, as well as sophisticated nibbles.

Lakeview to Andersonville

Big Chicks

5024 North Sheridan Road; tel: 773-728-5511; www.big chicks.com; Mon–Fri 4pm–2am, Sat 3pm–3am, Sun 11am–2pm; el: Red line to Argyle; bus: 36, 151

Whether it's a hetero-friendly gay bar or a gay-friendly straight bar, everyone is made to feel welcome at this neighborhood hangout. Highlights include the owner's art collection on the walls and, often, free shots at midnight.

Carol's Pub

4659 North Clark Street; tel: 773-334-2402; Mon–Tue 9am–4am, Wed–Fri, Sun 11am–4am, Sat 11am–5am; el: Red line to Wilson; bus: 36, 151

Southern transplants and country-music fans congregate at Carol's, possibly the city's only honky-tonk bar. Regulars line up for the country karaoke, and the house band pounds out tunes from Johnny Cash and Dwight Yoakam. Don't expect much hipster irony here – these people take their music seriously.

Ginger Man Tavern

3740 North Clark Street; tel: 773-549-2050; Mon–Fri 3pm–2am, Sat noon–3am, Sun noon–midnight; el: Red line to Addison; bus: 22

It's just blocks away from Wrigley Field, but the low-key Ginger Man is no sports bar. You'll find clean-cut neighborhood residents, tough-looking bikers, and hipsters playing board games or shooting some pool in the triangle-shaped back room.

Simon's Tavern

5210 North Clark Street; tel: 773-878-0894; Mon–Fri 11am–2am, Sat 11am–3am, Sun 11am–midnight; el: Red line to

Below: friendly Big Chicks in Andersonville.

Berwyn; bus: 22, 92

This neighborhood institution honors the area's Swedish community with Viking paraphernalia strewn around the bar and a truly awful Scandinavian liqueur, Malort, behind it. The bar attracts an indie, down-to-earth crowd in their 20s and 30s. If Scott, the owner, isn't too busy, he'll show you quirky features like the bulletproof booth where the original owner cashed paychecks for bootleg liquor during Prohibition.

West Side

The Continental

2801 West Chicago Avenue; tel: 773-292-1200; Mon–Fri 5pm–4am, Sat 5pm–5am, Sun 6pm–4am; bus: 66

It looks a little sleek, but make no mistake: this is a dive bar gussied up as a lounge. Still, it's a cleaner, nicer alternative to most of the other 4am bars in town, and the largely young, hip, and tattooed crowd makes it more attractive as well. Drive or get a ride – it can be tough to hail a cab around here late at night.

Skylark

2149 South Halsted Street; tel: 312-948-5275; daily 4pm–2am, Sat until 3am; el: Orange line to Cermak; bus: 8; map p.136 A2

Located on a near-desolate corner by the highway, Skylark is a beacon to the chicly dishevelled artists and musicians living in the Pilsen neighborhood for the reasonable prices and good beer selection. The vintage photobooth

The city's no-smoking ordinance, which went into effect at the beginning of 2008, bans smoking in bars and restaurants. In many cases smokers may not puff within 15ft (4.5m) of the entrance. Look for posted signs for guidance.

Right: sports fans gather to watch the Cubs game.

inspires a lot of drunken giggling behind the curtain. Music varies according to the bartenders' tastes – you might hear anything from Black Sabbath to the Stone Roses.

Wicker Park

Danny's Tavern

1951 West Dickens Avenue; tel: 773-489-6457; daily 7pm–2am, Sat until 3am; el: Blue line to Damen

Located in a house on a side street in Bucktown – look for the neon Schlitz sign – Danny's feels like a discovery even when it's packed. Hang out in front rooms, with their adjoining alcoves, to watch DJs spin almost every night, or head to the secluded back room for more privacy.

Map Room

1949 North Hoyne Avenue; tel: 773-252-7636; www.map room.com; daily 11am–2am, Sat until 3am; el: Blue line to Damen, then bus: 50

Not surprisingly, travel is the theme of this bar and influences everything from the decor – the walls are festooned with maps and bookcases, hold guides and travel narratives – to the international beer selection. Every Tuesday is international night, featuring a buffet meal from a different ethnic restaurant, which is free with a two-drink minimum.

Rainbo Club

1150 North Damen Avenue; tel: 773-489-5999; daily 4pm–2am, Sat until 3am; el: Blue line to Division

Reportedly the Chicago writer Nelson Algren was known to tipple here back in the day, but today the Rainbo is a mecca for members of the city's independent music scene (members of which may be working

behind the bar). Low prices appeal to a young crowd, and the red leather booths along the back wall are a good vantage point to watch all of the posing and flirting.

Violet Hour

1520 North Damen Avenue; tel: 773-252-1500; www.theviolet hour.com; daily 6pm–2am, Sat until 3am; el: Blue line to Damen

At this swanky lounge (which inside conveys a convincingly twilit aura), cocktails are taken very seriously. Drinks on the menu, which changes seasonally, are inspired by everything from barbecues to classic mixes and may incorporate house-made bitters, obscure liqueurs, or egg whites. Even the ice – made with twice-filtered water – comes in different shapes to suit specific drinks. Light appetizers and sandwiches with a similarly creative bent are available to sop up the booze.

South Loop

Kitty O'Shea's

720 South Michigan Avenue; tel: 312-294-6860; daily 11am–1am; el: Red line to Harrison; map p.135 C3

Kitty O'Shea's strives for authenticity with staffers from Ireland and live Celtic music – not bad for what is essentially a hotel bar (it is located in the Hilton – see

p.71). In summer, the outdoor patio offers fun people-watching on Michigan Avenue.

Tantrum

1023 South State Street; tel: 312-939-9160; Mon–Fri 5pm–2am, Sat 5pm–3am; el: Red line to Roosevelt; bus: 29, 62; map p.135 C3

No one's having a meltdown here – this loungey, chic bar is so named because of the hoops the owner had to go through to secure a liquor license. A mostly professional, neighborhood crowd hangs out here, especially after work.

South Side

Woodlawn Tap

1172 East 55th Street; tel: 773-643-5516; Mon–Fri 10.30am–2am, Sat 11am–3am, Sun 11am–2am; bus: 55; Metra: Electric Line to 55th; map p.138 C2

Technically it's just the Woodlawn Tap. You don't come here for great ambience or fancy drinks but to honor the generations of Hyde Parkers who have been here before you, notably some of the greatest minds from the University of Chicago. There's no word on whether it's possible to soak up some smarts along with your suds. Also known as Jimmy's, for the long-time owner who manned the bar until his death in 1999.

Cafés

L ike most major metropolitan areas, at times Chicago seems to run on caffeine like a car runs on gas. From nine-to-fivers, grabbing their morning fix to go, to moody art students lingering over a double espresso, everyone has a favorite spot. Some cafés specialize in pastries, other in light bites, while a few are practically restaurants in their own right – there are few hard and fast rules about the definition of a coffeehouse. An increasing sophistication and appreciation of good coffee means that you won't have to suffer the the insipid offerings that coffee connoisseurs have complained of in the past.

The Loop

Intelligentsia Millennium Park

53 East Randolph Street; tel: 312-920-9332; www. intelligentsiacoffee.com; Mon–Thur 6am–8pm, Fri 6am–9pm, Sat 7am–9pm, Sun 7am–7pm; el: Blue, Red line to Washington; map p.135 C1

This local company imports green coffee beans with an eye toward environmentally and responsible growers, and roasts them in town. The company also employs 'cuppers,' who test the brews for aroma, body, and acidity. Free Wi-fi, and the central location means this place is always bustling, but the independent vibe remains strong.

North Side

L'Appetito

875 North Michigan Avenue; tel: 312-337-0691; www.lappetito. com; winter: Mon–Fri 7.30am–6.30pm, Sat 8.30am–6.30pm, Sun 8.30am–5.30pm, summer: Mon–Sat until 10pm, Sun until 6.30pm; el: Red line to Chicago; bus: 151; map p.133 C3

Office workers and Italian expats crowd in at lunch for the

Tipping in cafés can be confusing. In general, if your order is extremely large or complicated, it's nice to leave something in the tip jar at the counter. The same goes if your food or drink is brought to you and the table cleaned up afterward. If you're just getting a quick drink to go or everything is self-service, you can leave a little change if you like, but it's not required.

delicious grilled *tostino* sandwiches and fresh pasta and seafood salads. Located on the sunny sunken plaza in front of the John Hancock Center, everyone eats alfresco in the summer. Also at: 30 East Huron Street; tel: 312-787-9881; Mon–Fri 7.30am–6.30pm, Sat 9.30am–6.30pm; el: Red line to Chicago or Grand; map p.132 C3

Sarah's Pastries and Candies

70 East Oak Street; tel: 312-664-6223; www.sarahs candies.com; Mon–Sat 8am–6pm, Sun 10am–6pm; el: Red line to Chicago; bus: 151; map p.132 C2

The coffee's good and reasonably priced, but the real rea-

son to stop by this tiny gem is for the sweets. The cupcakes and chocolate-covered Oreos are guilty pleasures, while the elegant Oak Street ladies might opt for truffles and petit-fours to lend an air of French elegance to their indulgence.

Lincoln Park and Old Town

Bourgeois Pig

738 West Fullerton Avenue; tel: 773-883-5282; www.bpig cafe.com; Mon–Sat 7am–11pm, Sun 8am–11pm; el: Red, Brown line to Fullerton; map p.133 D1

The vintage brick storefront, worn wooden tables, and old-fashioned upholstered furniture make this a place where people stop to sip their coffee, hang out, and browse through the books scattered about.

Lakeview to Andersonville

Southport Grocery and Café

3552 North Southport Avenue; tel: 773-665-0100; www.south portgrocery.com; Mon–Fri 8am–7pm, Sat 8am–5pm, Sun 8am–3pm; el: Brown line to Southport

This trendy, upscale gourmet deli is nearly always crowded

Left: lunch at Earwax.

This modern, open space painted in muted shades draws a mix of families, shoppers trawling nearby boutiques, and arty types for a quick fix of caffeine or the homemade granola and specialty sandwiches.

South Loop

Hi Tea

14 East 11th Street; tel: 312-880-0832; www.hiteachicago.com; Mon–Fri 7am–7pm, Sat–Sun 8am–8pm; el: Red, Orange, Green line to Roosevelt; map p.135 C3

Tea-drinkers get equal time at this chic new spot, where some 60 different types of loose-leaf teas are on offer. Co-owned by long-time Chicago mayor Richard M. Daley's nephew, it fittingly honors city traditions by airing old local TV programs.

South Side

Third World Café

1301 East 53rd Street; tel: 773-288-3882; Mon–Thur 7am–8.30pm, Fri 7am–10pm, Sat 8am–10pm, Sun 9am–8.30pm; train: Metra to Hyde Park/53rd Street; map p.139 C2

Mellow spot conducive to reading, web surfing, or a light lunch, that is one of few independent cafés in Hyde Park.

Below: a sweet treat at Sarah's Pastries and Candies.

with nearby residents enjoying a light meal or browsing the exotic olive oils. The coffee is a special blend made by local coffee company Intelligentsia (*see left*).

West Side

Café Jumping Bean

1439 West 18th Street; tel: 312-455-0019; Mon–Fri 6am–10pm, Sat–Sun 8am–8pm; el: Pink, Blue line to 18th Street

Truly the apotheosis of the neighborhood coffeeshop, this brightly painted spot reflects the many faces of the Pilsen area. Long-time Latino residents, artists, professionals, and high-school students come together for Mexican hot chocolate mixed with espresso and café carmela.

Pan Hellenic Bakery

322 South Halsted Street; tel: 312-454-1886; Mon–Thur 9am–8pm, Fri 9am–9pm, Sun noon–6pm; el: Blue line to UIC-Halsted; map p.134 A2

A refreshingly old-school, family-run alternative to corporate cafés, the coffee here is strong and sweet, a perfect complement to syrupy baklava or other Greek pastries.

Wicker Park

Alliance Bakery and Café

1736 West Division; tel: 773-278-0366; www.alliance-bakery.com; Mon–Sat 6am–9pm, Sun 9am–9pm; el: Blue line to Division

This long-time neighborhood spot has gone a bit upscale in recent years, adding decadent macaroons and pastries to the menu alongside the kolachy and butter cookies. Still, patrons are welcome to hang out for hours in the comfortable café space next door.

Earwax

1561 North Milwaukee Avenue; tel: 773-772-4019; www.earwax cafe.com; Mon–Thur 9am–11pm, Fri–Sun 8am–midnight; el: Blue line to Damen

A scruffy, bohemian holdout in a gentrified area, Earwax is a favorite among the young tattooed and pierced set for its healthy veggie options, although a few meat dishes and sweet treats are available.

Milk and Honey Cafe

1920 West Division; tel: 773-395-9434; www.milkandhoney cafe.com; Mon–Fri 7am–4pm, Sat 8am–5pm, Sun 8am–4pm; el: Blue line to Division

Children

There's no end of things for kids to do in Chicago outside, from running around parks to renting paddleboats and building sandcastles. Even in winter or inclement weather, there are plenty of activities to keep little ones amused and entertained. Ice-skating rinks offer hours of fun, and for indoor options there are several museums, game centers, and even theaters – they might even just learn something if they're not careful. Navy Pier, Lincoln Park Zoo, and gazing at skyscrapers are all great options, too, for both kids and their parents. See also *Museums and Galleries, p.76–85*, and *Parks and Beaches, p.96–9*.

Amusement Parks and Entertainment

ESPN Zone
43 East Ohio Street, North Side; tel: 312-644-3776; www.espn zone.com; daily 11am–11pm, Fri–Sat until midnight; free; el: Red Line to Grand; bus: 151 (24hrs), 157; map p.132 C4

The sports-themed arcade is full of old-school games like pinball and air hockey as well as videogames and the latest in virtual-reality sports. A great rainy-day option.

Navy Pier
600 East Grand Avenue, North Side: tel: 312-595-7437; www.navypier.com; free; daily

Below: a resident of the popular Lincoln Park Zoo.

10am–8pm, Fri–Sat until 10pm, later closing times in summer; bus: 29, 65, 66, 124; free trolley from State and Illinois Street in summer; map p.133 E4

There's good reason this is the Midwest's most popular attraction – the kid-friendly options are seemingly endless. The 150ft (45m) Ferris wheel is the pier's crown jewel and provides great views of the city's skyline. Tamer rides include an old-fashioned carousel and whirling swings. Visual and audio effects amp up a Chicago-themed funhouse maze, while the state-of-the-art Imax theater offers both popular and special releases. There's also a fireworks display every Wednesday and Saturday night from late May to early September.

Six Flags Great America
542 North Route 21, Gurnee; tel: 847-249-4636; June–Aug: daily 10am–10pm, Sept–May: Sat–Sun 10am–7pm; charge; by car

This huge amusement park is a definite day trip. Hi-tech roller coasters and milder rides are scattered across eight themed areas. Daring youngsters can choose from

high-tech looping coasters or the slightly more sedate variety, including one of the last wooden roller coasters in the country, while there are plenty of kiddie rides, including special play areas. When the lines get too long, escape to one of the live shows or take a turn in the arcade area.

Museums

Chicago Children's Museum
700 East Grand Avenue, North Side; tel: 312-527-1000; www.chicagochildrens museum.org; daily 10am–5pm, Thur, Sat until 8pm; charge; bus: 29, 65, 66, 124; map p.133 E4

The quintessential museum for toddlers to preteens. Interactive exhibits include a facsimile of an archeological excavation and a three-story-high schooner, which encourage age exploration and play.
SEE ALSO MUSEUMS AND GALLERIES, P.76

Museum of Science and Industry
57th Street and South Lake Shore Drive, South Side; tel: 773-684-1414; www.msi chicago.org; Mon–Sat 9.30am–

Left: kids splash about in Crown Fountain.

line to Washington or Lake; map p.135 C2

In summer **Crown Fountain** is teeming with kids splashing in the water that flows down from its two towers. General hilarity ensues when one of the 'mouths' of the faces projected on the towers sprays water onto the platform below. In winter there's an ice rink in the McCormick Tribune Plaza.

SEE ALSO PARKS AND BEACHES, P.96; PUBLIC ART, P.100

Theater

Chicago's Children Theatre
Various locations; tel: 773-227-0180; www.chicagochildrens theatre.org

The only theater group in the city devoted exclusively to family-friendly productions, many of them based on children's books. Plays are staged at various locations, including the Chicago Cultural Center and the Goodman Theatre.

Noble Horse Theatre
1410 North Orleans Street, Old Town; tel: 312-266-7878; www.noblehorsechicago.com; admission charge; el: Brown line to Sedgwick; map p.132 B1

Older kids with an interest in horses will enjoy shows here, which incorporate jumping, balancing, and synchronized movements with horse and rider decked out in traditional costumes. There are also special seasonal shows at Halloween and Christmas.

4pm, Sun 11am–4pm; charge; bus: 2, 6, 10, X28; train: Metra to 57th Street; map p.139 E3

Older children will enjoy the more technical exhibits, but there are plenty of fun things to see here, such as the massive train set, the Fairy Palace dollhouse, and baby chicks hatching in an incubator.

SEE ALSO MUSEUMS AND GALLERIES, P.84

Peggy Notebaert Nature Museum
2430 North Cannon Drive, Lincoln Park; tel: 773-755-5100; www.chias.org; Mon–Fri 9am–4.30pm, Sat–Sun 10am–5pm; charge; bus: 77, 151, 157; map p.133 E1

Children learn about the natural world and the importance of the environment via large-scale interactive exhibits, such as an installation about the crawling creatures that live in the average American lawn.

SEE ALSO MUSEUMS AND GALLERIES, P.80

Parks

Brookfield Zoo
3300 Golf Road, Brookfield; tel: 708-688-8000; www.brookfield zoo.org; daily 10am–5pm, spring–summer also Sat–Sun

until 6pm; charge; Metra train: Burlington North line to Zoo

This 216-acre (87-hectare) zoo 14 miles (22.5km) west of downtown Chicago features several state-of-the-art animal enclosures that mimic creatures' natural habitats in the desert, rain forest, and savanna as closely as possible, complete with sounds and smells. A new exhibit highlights the relationship between rays, which visitors can touch, and sharks.

Lincoln Park Zoo
2200 North Cannon Drive, Lincoln Park; tel: 312-742-2000; www.lpzoo.com; daily 9am–6pm, winter until 5pm, summer Sat–Sun until 7pm; free; el: Red line to Fullerton; bus: 151, 156; map p.133 E2

The city's zoo is a perennial pleaser, filled with lions, tigers, and bears, as well as gorillas, penguins, and snakes. The Farm-in-the-Zoo offers the opportunity to pet animals as well as see cows milked.

Millennium Park
55 North Michigan Avenue, Loop; tel: 312-742-1168; www.millenniumpark.org; daily 6am–10pm; free; el: Blue, Red

While some of the more high-minded architectural boat tours might be over kids' heads, there are plenty of options for a simple boat ride. Visit Navy Pier for lake tours, and the intersection of Wacker Drive and Michigan Avenue for river tours. *See also Architecture, p.31.*

Churches, Synagogues, and Temples

Churches in the Chicago area are most famous for their architecture and design. Many prominent Midwestern architects lent their expertise to the design of houses of worship, resulting in unusual structures. Although etiquette about appropriate dress is not as strictly enforced as in many other countries, visitors should try to be as respectful as possible, especially during services.

The Loop

Chicago Temple
77 West Washington; tel: 312-236-4548; www.chicago temple.org; visitors welcome daily at 2pm; el: Green, Brown, Orange lines to Randolph/Wabash; map p.134 C2

This skyscraper, built by the firm of Holabird and Roche in 1924, is the tallest church building in the world and also the home of the oldest congregation in Chicago. There are three sanctuaries, two on the first and second floors and the tiny 'Sky Chapel' just below the steeple, some 400ft (120m) above the ground.

North Side

Fourth Presbyterian Church
126 East Chestnut Street; tel: 312-787-4570; www.fourth church.org; daily 7.30am–9pm;

> In 1979 Pope John Paul II became the first pope to say mass at Holy Name Cathedral. His visit included performances by Luciano Pavarotti and the Chicago Symphony Orchestra in the cathedral's nave.

free; el: Red line to Chicago; bus: 10, 144, 146, 151; map p.133 C3

The most striking feature of this church is the lovely courtyard surrounded by covered cloisters, a serene haven from the bustle of Michigan Avenue. Free concerts are held here every Friday in the summer. Inside the main building, designed by architect Ralph Adams Cram in 1914, an intricately carved wooden ceiling resembles a ship's hull. The Tudor-style buildings around the courtyard are the work of Midwestern architect Howard Van Doren Shaw.

Holy Name Cathedral
735 North State Street; tel: 312-787-1544; www.holyname cathedral.org; Mon–Fri 6am–7pm, Sun 7am–7pm; free; el: Red line to Chicago; map p.132 C3

This grand limestone building, built in 1875, is the seat of the Chicago diocese of the Catholic Church, one of the country's largest. Abstract stained-glass windows hand-crafted in Milan and massive bronze doors worked with a Tree of Life theme add a contemporary touch to the traditional cathedral design.

St James Cathedral
5 East Huron Street; tel: 312-787-7360; www.saintjames cathedral.org; Mon–Fri 9am–4pm; free; el: Red line to Chicago; map p.132 C3

The bell tower and bits of the facade date back to 1857, when Abraham Lincoln worshiped here; the rest was rebuilt after the Great Chicago Fire in 1871. An outdoor walking labyrinth, used to calm the mind and soothe the spirit, is located on the upper level of the plaza between the cathedral and 65 East Huron Street, and is available to the public 24 hours a day.

West Side

Holy Trinity Russian Orthodox Cathedral
1121 North Leavitt Street; tel: 773-486-6064; www.holytrinity cathedral.net; Sat 11am–4pm; free; bus: 65, 66

A little treasure by celebrated Chicago architect Louis Sullivan. Built in 1903 (and partially financed by the Russian Czar Nicholas II), its octagonal dome and front bell tower were inspired by the provincial Russian churches of the era.

Left: visiting Unity Temple in Oak Park.

Jewish temple unearthed in Galilee. Motifs of clusters of grapes, foliage, vials of oil, and menorahs appear throughout the ornate interior.

Oak Park

Unity Temple
875 Lake Street, Oak Park; tel: 708-383-8873; www.unity temple-utrf.org; Mon–Fri 10.30am–4.30pm, Sat–Sun 1–4pm; charge; Green Line to Oak Park

Considered Frank Lloyd Wright's greatest work in his hometown, the temple is a testament to the architect's forward-minded design. Instead of steeples and Gothic windows, he created a blocky, almost cubist design out of concrete, which emphasizes the intersection of vertical and horizontal planes that are a trademark of his work. Inside, the effect is surprisingly delicate, with leaded windows providing soft natural light to illuminate the geometric wood trim and balconies and ledges.

Around Chicago

Baha'i House of Worship
100 Linden Avenue, Wilmette; tel: 847-853-2300; auditorium: daily 7am–10pm; free; Purple line to Linden

One of seven Baha'i temples around the world, the Wilmette location is the largest and oldest. It was begun in 1921 but was not completed until 1953 due to the Great Depression and World War II. The nine-sided structure, with its 90ft (30m) diameter dome, resembles a mosque, with its lacy designs incorporating symbols of the world's major religions – the Baha'i faith emphasizes 'the oneness of God.' Gardens featuring nine fountains surround the structure.

Above: traditional mosaics feature at Orthodox churches.

South Loop

Second Presbyterian Church
1936 South Michigan Avenue; tel: 312-225-4951; www.2nd presbyterian.org; Tue–Sat 9am–1pm; bus: 3, 4; map p.136 C1

In the late 19th century this was *the* place of worship for the families living around Prairie Avenue, then a very smart address. The original Gothic Revival building was designed in 1874; it was restored after a fire by Howard Van Doren Shaw, who built the sanctuary in the English Arts and Crafts style. The walls feature murals by the Chicago-born artist Frederick Clay Bartlett. Among the church's splendid 20 stained-glass windows are several by Tiffany and two extremely rare specimens by Sir Edward Burne-Jones from the 1880s.

South Side

Eighth Church of Christ, Scientist
4359 South Michigan Avenue; tel: 773-373-4126; open for services: Sun 10.15am–noon, Wed 5.45–8pm; free; bus: 2, 6, 10, 14

Built between 1910 and 1911, the Classical Revival style of the church – its temple front, grand dome, and interior layout – was modeled after that of temples in ancient Rome.

KAM Isaiah Israel Synagogue
1100 East Hyde Park Boulevard; tel: 773-924-1234; www.kamii. org; visitors welcome 8.30am–4.30pm (call for appointment); train: Metra to Hyde Park/55th; map p.138 C1

The congregation, dating from 1847, forms the oldest synagogue in the Midwest. The squat Byzantine-style building, built in 1924, was inspired by fragments of a second-century

43

Comedy

Most professional laughs in Chicago come via the robust improvisation scene, which has been an entertainment powerhouse here since the creation of Second City in the late 1950s. It's hard to overstate its influence: aspiring funnymen and women come here from all over the country to study at the city's celebrated improvisation programs, and the ranks of graduates include not only internationally famous actors, but plenty of writers and directors cracking wise behind the scenes. Stand-up here has always run a distant second, but there are signs of a renaissance in the form of an emerging underground comedy scene.

Improv and Sketch Comedy

Some would say that Chicago comedy really began with **Second City**, which began when a bunch of University of Chicago students started horsing around together in the 1950s. Some members would go on to success in both comedy and drama, such as **Alan Alda** and the directors **Mike Nichols** and **Paul Mazursky**. The group gradually received increasing exposure throughout the 60s, during which time they moved to their current home in Piper's Alley in the Old Town neighborhood.

The nation really became aware of Second City in the mid-70s, when several of its members moved to New York

> It's a little-known fact that the Marx Brothers lived in Chicago for several years starting in 1910, when the entire family relocated from New York to try their luck on the Chicago stages. The family even owned a farm in suburban LaGrange for a while before returning to New York and entering into comedy history.

to star in the phenomenally successful sketch TV show *Saturday Night Live (SNL)*, including **John Belushi** and **Bill Murray**. Second City has been sending them down the production line ever since, and its list of famous alums is very long. A few of the famous names include **George Wendt** (TV's *Cheers*), **Mike Myers** (*Saturday Night Live* and the *Austin Powers* movies), **Dan Castellaneta** (the voice of Homer on *The Simpsons*), **Steve Carell** (the American version of *The Office*), **Tina Fey** (*SNL* and *30 Rock*), and **Stephen Colbert** (*The Daily Show* and *The Colbert Report*).

The city's other prominent improvisation venue and training center, **IO** (formerly Improv-Olympic), founded in 1981, is built around long-form improvisation, dubbed 'The Harold' by **Del Close**, the director and performer who refined the process and how to teach it. Close, who was also involved with Second City throughout his career, was a mentor to many performers who have gone on to success in film and

TV and was somewhat of a local legend for his drug habits and contentious personality.

Improv Venues

Annoyance Theatre
4830 North Broadway Street, Andersonville; tel: 773-561-4665; www.annoyanceproductions. com; shows nightly, check website for listings; el: Red line to Lawrence; bus: 144, 148

Apollo Theater
2540 North Lincoln Street, Lincoln Park; tel: 773-935-6100; www.apollochicago.com; 'musical improv comedy': Fri 10.30pm; el: Red, Brown line to Fullerton

Chemically Imbalanced Theatre
1420 West Irving Park, Lakeview; tel: 773-865-7731; www.cico comedy.com; Fri–Sat 8pm, 10.30pm; el: Red line to Sheridan

ComedySportz Theatre
929 West Belmont Avenue, Lakeview; tel: 773-549-8080; www.comedysportzchicago.com; Thur 8pm, Fri 8pm, 10pm, Sat 6pm, 8pm, 10pm; el: Red, Brown line to Belmont

Cornservatory
929 West Belmont Avenue, Lakeview; tel: 312-409-6435; www.cornservatory.org; check

Left: Steve Martin does stand-up in Chicago in 1978.

Note that clubs may not offer shows on a regular schedule and that venues for comedy shows may change, so check the website or local listings for the most current information.

The Edge Comedy Club
Chicago Center for the Performing Arts, 777 North Green Street, River North; tel: 312-733-6000; www.theedgecomedyclub.com; Fri–Sat 10.30pm; bus: 66; map p.132 A3

Jokes and Notes
4641 South King Drive, South Side; tel: 773-373-3390; www.jokesandnotes.com; Sat–Sun, check website for listings; el: Green line to 47th Street

Lakeshore Theater
3175 North Broadway Street, Lakeview; tel: 773-472-3492; www.lakeshoretheater.com; check website for listings; el: Red, Brown lines to Belmont

Pressure Billiards and Comedy Café
6318 North Clark Street, Westridge; tel: 773-743-7665, www.pressurebilliards.com; improv showcase: Fri 8pm, live comedy: Sat 9pm; el: Red line to Thorndale; bus: 36,151

Zanies
1548 North Wells Street, Old Town; tel: 312-337-4027; www.chicago.zanies.com; check website for listings; el: Red line to Sedgwick; map p.132 B1

Festivals

Many of the festivals bring graduates of the city's improv schools back for fun, informal performances.

Chicago Comedy Fest
www.chicomfest.com; fall

Chicago Improv Festival
tel: 773-935-9810; www. chicagoimprovfestival.org; June

Chicago Sketchfest
www.chicagosketchfest.com; Jan

website for listings; el: Brown line to Irving Park

IO
3541 North Clark Street, Wrigleyville; tel: 773-880-0199; www.ioimprov.com; shows nightly; Red line to Addison

Playground Theater
3209 North Halsted Street, Lakeview; tel: 773-871-3793; www.the-playground.com; check website for listings; el: Red line to Belmont

Second City, Second City ETC, Second City Training Center
1608, 1616 North Wells Street, Old Town; tel: 312-337-3992; www.secondcity.com; shows

Below: Mike Myers performing in improv at IO.

nightly; el: Brown line to Sedgwick; map p.132 B1

Stand-Up

The roster of famous stand-up comedians who got their start here is significantly shorter, perhaps because the improvisation scene is so influential. However, one of the best-known and most beloved is **Bob Newhart**, an Oak Park native. Gigs on Chicago radio stations led to a couple of very successful TV shows, most notably the seminal sitcom *The Bob Newhart Show*, which ran from 1972 to 1978 and was set in Chicago.

More recently, the late comedian and actor **Bernie Mac**, who costarred in the *Ocean's Eleven/Twelve/Thirteen* movies, got his start doing stand-up in local clubs.

Stand-Up Venues and Shows

Chicago Underground Comedy
Beat Kitchen, 2100 West Belmont Avenue, Lakeview; tel: 312-719-5476; www.chicagounderground comedy.com; Tue 9.30pm; el: Red, Brown line to Belmont

45

Environment

It may come as a surprise to find that this brash, no-nonsense city in the Midwest is on its way to becoming one of the greenest cities in the US. Besides a successful urban beautification program that has increased the number of trees and greenery, the city has been actively working to lessen the impact of pollution and run-off from industry, not to mention the waste and carbon emitted by its millions of residents and their cars. Some of the most immediate results can be seen in the ongoing recovery of the Chicago River, once a sludgy toxic nightmare, and the profusion of 'green' buildings downtown and in residential communities.

Lake Michigan

The lake is the source of the city's drinking water (treated, of course) as well as entertainment during warm weather. There is always a certain amount of industrial run-off released into the lake, although a 2007 announcement by BP that it would increase the amount of certain contaminants from its refinery in northwest Indiana created widespread opposition and protests. However, the water is considered safe to swim in, except after large amounts of rainfall, when high E.coli levels cause beaches to be closed, usually for just a day or two. Most fish from the lake are safe to eat in moderate amounts.

Chicago River

For years the Chicago River and other area waterways were used as dumping grounds for garbage and sewage from private homes and effluent from the city's stockyards. But as a result of the Clean Water Act and government initiatives for habitat restoration and long-term

Many hotels have instituted practices to limit their businesses' impact on the environment, such as recycling 'gray' water or giving guests the option of reusing their towels and sheets throughout their stay. Websites such as **www.environmentallyfriendly hotels.com** offer information about the practices of many hotels in Chicago and around the world.

planning over the last several decades, the river is in the midst of a comeback. Wildlife such as herons and turtles (and the ever-present ducks and geese) glide by, and the river is a frequent destination for kayakers. Still, there are advisories against eating fish from the river, especially carp, due to high levels of PCB and mercury contamination.

Cycling

Like most major urban areas, Chicago suffers from some serious traffic problems, which are compounded by an aging public transportation infrastructure and a system that periodically cuts service due to lack of adequate funding. That, plus concerns about health and the impact of cars on the environment, have spurred the city to encourage bicycles as a form of transportation. Guided by a long-ranging plan, dedicated bike lanes have been added all over the city, there are some 10,000 new bike racks, many city buses offer bike racks, and el riders are permitted to bring bicycles aboard trains during non-rush hours. To encourage biking as an alternative to cars, the city hosts an annual 'Bike to Work' day and maintains a center in Millennium Park with 300 secure spaces for bicycles, showers, lockers, and bike rental and repair services.

The Greening of the City

The shining example of the city's commitment to improving the environment is the **Center for Green Technology**, which is located on the site of a former illegal dumping ground. The 40,000-sq-ft (3,700-sq-m) building, which was revamped in 1999, was

Left: the Chicago River is steadily being cleaned up.

The **Center for Green Technology** is open for self-guided tours (445 North Sacramento Boulevard; tel: 312-746-9642; Mon–Fri 9am–5pm, Tue, Thur until 8pm, Sat 9am–4pm). Guided tours for groups larger than 10 are available by appointment. Call for information about seminars and events.

designed according to strict environmental guidelines, features solar panels, a green roof, and a geothermal exchange system for heating and cooling. The site houses offices for a few businesses but is open to the public for tours *(see box, right)*. It also hosts several seminars per week on green topics and includes a library with resources on incorporating environmentally friendly and energy-saving processes and products into homes and businesses.

Among many other city initiatives is the Green Roof Program, in which owners of houses and buildings may receive grants to build rooftop gardens, which help reuse rainwater, lessen the urban heat island effect, and help reduce the costs of heating and cooling. The most prominent example is on top of City Hall, but to date there are some 4 million sq ft (370,000 sq m) of green roofs in the city, more than in all other American cities combined. The city has also created a framework for green construction known as the Chicago Standard, which will guide the design of city-funded facilities and help save 15 to 20 percent in energy costs per year, save water, and result in healthier indoor environments. There are also resources available to help owners of existing structures retrofit their buildings to become more environmentally friendly.

Recycling

For a city with so many initiatives targeted toward preserving the environment, Chicago has lagged behind in providing a comprehensive residential recycling program. A 'blue bag' system, in which recyclables were collected with the regular trash and sorted at city facilities, was dogged by accusations that the actual recycling rate was much lower than reported. It was finally scrapped in 2008 in favor of a more traditional curbside pickup program, which is expected to be fully implemented by 2011. Meanwhile, there are plenty of receptacles set up in public places to recycle newspapers and magazines, and many cafés offer bins for plastics, glass, and aluminum cans.

Below: the city is working to encourage more people to cycle.

Essentials

Having been planned with a grid system, Chicago is pretty easy to navigate once you get your bearings. Residents, true to their reputation for Midwestern-style friendliness, are generally happy to help set you on the right path if you get lost. Hotel concierges are incredibly helpful with directions as well as things to do, and there are plenty of resources, such as tourist information counters and local publications, for ideas on events and excursions. As in any large city, exercise caution with your valuables and your person in large crowds and in certain areas at night, but in general the city is quite safe.

Consulates

Australia: tel: 312-419-1480
Britain: tel: 312-970-3800
Canada: tel: 312-616-1860
France: tel: 312-327-5200
Ireland: tel: 312-337-1868
New Zealand: tel: 773-714-8669
South Africa: tel: 312-939-7929

Emergencies

For police, ambulances, and fire, dial **911**.

Health

The quality of health care in Chicago is very good, although as in the rest of the country it is extremely expensive, and the costs can be devastating. The US has no national health program, so it is essential to check with your insurance provider about coverage before you leave.

MAJOR HOSPITALS
John H. Stroger Jr Hospital of Cook County
901 West Harrison Street, West Side; tel: 312-864-6000; map p.134 A3

Northwestern Memorial Hospital

Addresses in Chicago are conveniently organized according to a grid system, the epicenter of which is at State (which runs north–south) and Madison (east–west). From here, addresses start at '1' and go in ascending order in all four directions. The numbering system is based on approximately eight blocks to every mile (with some exceptions in the Loop). So if an address is at 200 North Michigan, you know it is approximately two city blocks north of Madison.

251 East Huron Street, North Side; tel: 312-926-2000; map p.133 C3
Rush University Medical Center
1653 West Congress Parkway, West Side; tel: 312-942-5000

Internet Access

Internet cafés are few and far between in Chicago. Your best bet is to head to the library, where there are computers set aside for the public. You may have to wait when it's busy.
Harold Washington Library Center

400 South State Street, Loop; tel: 312-747-3147; map p.134 C2
If you have a laptop or a phone with browsing capability, there are plenty of free Wi-fi hotspots all over the city (including public libraries, bookstores, and cafés). Others may charge for it. Free public hotspots include the **Chicago Cultural Center**, **Millennium Park**, and **Daley Plaza**.

Media and Local Listings

Dozens of newspapers and magazines offer listings of music, theater, performance, and other events on in the city.
The Chicago Collection
www.chicagocollection.com
A free quarterly magazine that has an extensive overview of shopping and art galleries. It is found in many shops and hotels.
The Chicago Reader
www.chicagoreader.com
The city's leading free 'alternative' weekly newspaper is known for its extensive arts coverage. It is available in the vestibules of many bookstores, cafés, and other businesses around the city and comes out every Thursday.

lobby, and stamps are also sold at many drugstores such as Walgreens and CVS.

Public telephones take coins (quarters, dimes, and nickels), or you may use a prepaid phone card, also widely available at drugstores and occasionally newspaper stands. Some phones may accept standard credit or debit cards, but the cost can be exorbitant.

Tourist Information

The Chicago Convention and Tourism Bureau's website, www.choosechicago.com, is an excellent and wide-ranging resource. There are two main centers to stop in at:
Chicago Cultural Center Visitor Information Center
77 East Randolph Street, Loop; tel: 312-744-8000; Mon–Thur 10am–7pm, Fri 10am–6pm, Sat 10am–5pm, Sun 11am–5pm; map p.135 C1
Chicago Water Works Visitor Information Center
163 East Pearson Street, North Side; tel: 877-244-2246; daily 7.30am–7pm; map p.133 C3

Visa Information

To enter the US you need a valid passport. In January 2009, the US government announced that visitors from countries formerly covered by the Visa Waiver Program, including Australia, Ireland, New Zealand, and the United Kingdom, will need to fill out an online form with details of their visit at least three days in advance of their departure. This Electronic Travel System will provide a valid visa for two years. Go to https://esta.cbp. dhs.gov for more information and to apply online. Exceptions will be made for last-minute trips and emergencies.

Gapers Block
www.gapersblock.com
For a quirky, local perspective, this website offers information on readings, gatherings, and off-the-beaten-path events.
Time Out Chicago
www.timeoutchicago.com
The quintessential listings magazine has arts and events coverage, but also a service-oriented bent, with information about various lifestyle-related happenings.
WHERE Magazine
www.chicago.wheretraveler.com
Found in hotels, this offers information on major sights, exhibitions, and shops.

Money

The US unit of currency is the dollar ($), divided into 100 cents (¢). Currency can be exchanged at major branches of banks for free and at many American Express offices, which charge a small fee. Confusingly, storefronts labeled 'currency exchange' are used mostly for cashing checks and sending money abroad, not foreign exchange. Exchange rates are available online at www.xe.com.

Major credit cards (Visa, MasterCard, American Express) are widely accepted, although some smaller businesses require a minimum purchase, usually $10–15. ATMs are another convenient option as long as you have a PIN number.

Post and Telephones

Post office hours vary, but they are generally open from early morning to early evening during the week, with short-ened hours on Saturday morn-ing. Stamps for letters and smaller packages are available at automatic machines in the

Below: the Harold Washington Library Center.

Fashion

Chicago has a thriving local fashion scene, with new independent boutiques that showcase unique styles seeming to open every week, as well as dozens of accessories and clothing designers, many of them graduates of one of the many college-level fashion programs here. Over the last 10 years the scene here has exploded, due in no small part to new programs and events intended to spotlight the city as a major capital for fashion talent. These listings focus on the best individual stores for clothes and accessories; see also *Shopping, p.112–15*, for further retail outlets.

Building an Industry

Although not quite yet a player on the international style scene, Chicago has the beginnings of a strong fashion industry, fed in large part by graduates from the fashion programs at the School of the Art Institute and Columbia College. The most obvious manifestation is **Fashion Focus Chicago** (www.fashionfocuschicago.com), an annual weeklong event sponsored by the city every fall that showcases local designs via runway shows, shopping tours, and other programs – and is open to the public.

Meanwhile, in an attempt to encourage designers to stay in Chicago and to build up the industry's infrastruc-

ture, there are various programs intended to pool resources for designers and help them with the financial and marketing aspects of their businesses. **Macy's** offers a program called Fashion Incubator, in which a few designers each year are given office space and work equipment on the top floor of the State Street location to give them a leg up toward meeting their goals. A handful of local designers have even opened their own shops, such as **Michelle Tan** *(see right)* in Bucktown and jeweler **Erin Gallagher** *(see right)* in the West Loop, while **Habit** *(see right)* makes a point of stocking work by emerging designers, including lots of Chicagoans. Many high-end boutiques also feature a few lines by Chicago fashion designers, including **Hejfina** *(see right)* and **p45** *(see p.52)*.

Chicago Style

Chicagoans have a reputation for being less daring in their dress than their urban counterparts on either coast, but that is hardly the case across

the board, especially as residents become ever more fashion-conscious. You'll see the most creative looks in the arty neighborhoods, such as Wicker Park and Bucktown, while sleek, upscale designer wear is de rigueur downtown. Given that Midwesterners have a bent toward thriftiness, people here delight in augmenting their wardrobes with cheap finds from inexpensive retailers such as **H&M**.

Perhaps due to the presence of a strong art community, vintage-inspired, 'crafty' looks also have a strong fol-

Below: Wicker Park is home to many quirky boutiques.

Popular fashion chains such as **H&M**, **Banana Republic**, and of course, **The Gap**, can be found on Michigan Avenue, while there are branches of shops like **Anthropologie**, **Urban Outfitters**, and **American Apparel** in the Gold Coast; the latter two cool brands are also found in Wicker Park.

Left: covetable and chic wares on display at Pivot *(see p.52)*.

Habit
1951 West Division Street, Wicker Park; tel: 773-342-0093; www.habitchicago.com; Tue–Sat 11am–7pm, Sun noon–5pm; el: Blue line to Division

This whitewashed boutique is dedicated to women's fashion from emerging designers, many of them local, including the owner's line of easy separates, Superficial. Because the clothes are made in small batches the prices can be a little high, but it's a fair trade-off for a unique piece. Especially charming are the quirky accessories, such as a brass octopus pendant and bags appliquéd with fabric in the shape of internal organs.

Hejfina
1529 North Milwaukee Avenue, Wicker Park; tel: 773-772-0002; www.hejfina.com; Sun–Mon noon–6pm, Tue–Sat 11am–7pm; el: Blue line to Damen

The owner of this men's and women's 'lifestyle clothing boutique' modeled it after similar shops she admired in Paris and Tokyo. Not surprisingly, the uber-cool, pricey clothes draw a sophisticated, international crowd, as well as neighborhood hipsters during the excellent sales. Pieces from hard-to-find designers like Opening Ceremony hang alongside looks from perennial fashion-insider favorites Isabel Marant, Vanessa Bruno, and Helmut Lang.

Michelle Tan
1872 North Damen Avenue, Wicker Park; tel: 773-252-1888; www.michelletan.com; Mon noon–7pm, Tue–Sat 11am–7pm, Sun noon–5pm; el: Blue line to Damen

This local designer loves to play with textures and unusual fabrics while sticking with a basic color scheme.

---

lowing here, particularly anything that looks homemade and one-of-a-kind. For men, there's a strong liking for anything smacking of streetwear, such as limited-edition T-shirts and sneakers, perhaps topped with a cap.

Accessories
Erin Gallagher Jewelry
1017 West Lake Street, West Side; tel: 312-492-7548; www.egjewelry.com; Mon–Fri 11am–7pm, Sat noon–7pm, Sun noon–5pm; el: Green line to Clinton; map p.134 A1

The front of this romantic-looking shop features local designer Gallagher's dazzling 'couture' creations of gems and semi-precious stones displayed in vintage vitrines. The back half houses the 'studio,' featuring pieces that are just as eye-catching at lower prices. Customers can mix and match stones and metals to customize Gallagher's elegant designs, each of which is named after a Hollywood star.

Boutiques
Eskell
1509 North Milwaukee Avenue,

Macy's carries clothing and accessories by local designers at the historic State Street store, at 111 North State Street *(see Shopping, p.113).*

Wicker Park; tel: 773-486-0830; www.eskell.com; Tue–Sat 11am–7pm, Sun noon–6pm; el: Blue line to Division

Run by the two designers, this women's clothing and accessories shop features their own line (also called Eskell) as well as other independent designers. Everything is funky with a slightly bohemian twist. The small selection of vintage pieces sold here perfectly complements the overall look.

Gamma Player
2035 West Division Street, Wicker Park; tel: 773-235-0755; www.gammaplayer.com; Tue–Sat 11am–7pm, Sun noon–6pm; el: Blue line to Division

The internationally savvy owners scour Europe and South America for avant-garde garb from little-known designers. Expect statement pieces for daring men and women, from knitted wool hoods to jewelry made with lace.

Pieces have a sharp urban edge softened by frayed hems or fringed details. Prices are high, but there's satisfaction in the limited numbers – you won't see these items at every turn.

p45

1643 North Damen Avenue, Wicker Park; tel: 773-862-4523; www.p45.com; Mon–Sat 11am–7pm, Sun noon–5pm, Nov–Dec: Thur until 8pm; el: Blue line to Damen

When it opened in 1997, this sleek, spare store was a retail pioneer. It's still known for unabashedly contemporary designs from smaller labels (Ulla Johnson, 3.1 Philip Lim) that appeal to a cosmopolitan, style-savvy clientele. Even basics such as black pants and white shirts feature unusual details or a modern fit. You can also find pieces by some of the more fashion-forward local designers here.

Pivot

1101 West Fulton Market, West Side; tel: 312-243-4754; www.pivotboutique.com; Tue–Sat 11am–7pm, Sun noon–6pm; el: Green line to Clinton

Wicker Park and Bucktown are home to funkier, more fashion-forward boutiques, while Armitage Avenue in Lincoln Park generally offers more classic, mainstream garb. A mix of affordable and high-end boutiques makes Southport Avenue an interesting destination, while downtown, Oak Street is the city's version of Rodeo Drive, with plenty of haute designer boutiques like **Yves Saint Laurent**, **Jil Sander**, and **Prada**. The newest shopping district, the West Loop, is where anything goes, from $300 handbags to surprisingly inexpensive separates, depending on the store.

Set among the meatpacking plants of the newly hip Fulton Market area, Pivot is the city's first eco-conscious boutique. But there are no shapeless burlap caftans here: the women's clothes and accessories are stunningly edgy and urban, as if they just happen to be made of organic cotton, bamboo, and other environmentally sustainable materials. As with everything else carrying the label 'organic,' be prepared to pay a premium for them.

Robin Richman

824 West Armitage Avenue, Wicker Park; tel: 773-281-5655; www.robinrichman.com; Tue–Thur 11am–7pm, Fri 11am–6pm, Sat 10am–6pm, Sun noon–5pm; el: Blue line to Damen

Richman originally opened her shop to stock her own designs, but it's now mainly known for arty women's clothes by European and American designers such as Hussein Chalayan and Gary Graham that tend to be challenging than conventionally 'pretty.' Unusual jewelry is another big draw, as are the shoes by Chie Mihara from Spain and Marsell from Italy.

TK Men

1909 West North Avenue, Wicker Park; tel: 773-342-9800; www.tkmen.com; Tue–Sat 11am–8pm, Sun noon–6pm, Mon by appointment only; Blue line to Damen

This spot is indisputably a guys' haven, from the beer on tap to the sports on the flat-screen TV. But the bachelor-pad atmosphere is only part of the appeal: the clothes are basics with a knowing rock-star undercurrent. Look for accessories like belt buckles that double as pocket knives (just remember not to wear them on the plane home).

Tula

3738 North Southport Avenue, Lakeview; tel: 773-549-2876;

www.tulaboutique.com; Mon–Fri 11am–7pm, Sat 10am–5pm, Sun noon–5pm; el: Brown line to Southport

You'll feel like you stumbled onto a treasure in this small, cozy boutique, which stocks colorful, modern-classic women's clothes and accessories from hard-to-find lines, as well as chunky cocktail rings and a smattering of slouchy handbags.

Discount and Vintage

Beta Boutique

2016 West Concord Place, Wicker Park; tel: 773-276-0905; www.betaboutique.com; Thur–Fri 11am–7pm, Sat 11am–6pm, Sun noon–5pm; el: Blue line to Damen

Bargain prices in a boutique setting. The store stocks samples and overstock from local shops and designers as well as larger manufacturers. Happily, unlike actual sample sales, there is a wide size range and private dressing rooms, although the changing stock means this place can be hit or miss.

Silver Moon Vintage

1755 West North Avenue, Wicker Park; tel: 773-235-5797; www.silvermoonvintage.com; Tue–Sat noon–7pm, Sun noon–5pm; el: Blue line to Damen

Vintage collectors swear by this long-time presence in Chicago. No mothball-scented rags or ugly 70s polyester

Left: Lindsey Boland in her boutique, Habit *(see p.51)*.

9pm, Sat 11am–9pm, Sun 11am–7pm, el: Blue line to Damen

The pumping music hints at the clothes inside: colorful clubwear-inspired styles for women, at very affordable prices – and of a corresponding quality. The trends will only last for a season or two anyway, so it's a great place to find a gauzy summer dress or a hip plaid fedora. Conveniently down the street are other outposts of the Akira empire, including a men's boutique and a shoe store.

Belmont Army
855 West Belmont Avenue, Lakeview; tel: 773-549-1038; www.belmontarmy.com; Mon–Sat 11am–8pm, Sun noon–6pm; el: Brown, Red, Purple line to Belmont

Alongside army surplus, like combat boots, camouflage jackets, and military hats, as well as a selection of vintage items, there's a good selection of reasonably priced new women's and men's clothing. The store attracts a younger clientele from the area, but many items are suitable for nearly any age – and there are four huge floors to explore.

Clandestine Industries
952 West Newport, Lakeview; tel: 773-857-3525; www.clandestine industries.com; Wed–Fri 2–8pm, Sat–Sun noon–6pm; el: Red line to Addison

The brainchild of musician Pete Wentz of the band Fall Out Boy, the company's flagship store is here in Chicago. The co-ed styles cross hip-hop with Goth-rocker chic: lots of T-shirts with cool graphics, skinny jeans, and hoodies. If nothing seems quite spot-on to your taste, there's a design station at which to create your own tee with various logos and images.

dresses here: the owner, who styles the band Aerosmith, offers only the best pieces from the 1900s up to the 1960s (Victorian tea gowns, white 1930s dinner jackets), restoring them in-house by experts when necessary.

Footwear

City Soles/Niche
1566 North Damen Avenue, Wicker Park; tel: 773-489-2001; www.citysoles.com; Mon–Sat 10am–7pm, Thur–Fri until 8pm, Sun 11am–6pm; Blue line to Damen

Men and women with a penchant for funky shoes make a beeline here for extremely stylized shoe designs, from sneakers to pumps. Essentially two shoe stores in one,

City Soles features more recognizable brands, while on the Niche side you'll find contemporary designs from imported labels. There's always a huge sale rack to check out too.

Lori's Designer Shoes
824 West Armitage Avenue, Lincoln Park; tel: 773-281-5655; www.lorisshoes.com; Mon–Thur 11am–7pm, Fri 11am–6pm, Sat 10am–6pm, Sun noon–5pm; el: Brown line to Armitage; map p.133 D2

This hugely popular shoe store is inundated on weekends, when women prowl the stacks of boxes on the sales floor looking for the perfect shoes in their size while their bored boyfriends suffer in the aisles. Prices run from about $50 and rarely top $300, and there's a great selection of handbags as well. Best of all, all sizes are out on the sales floor so you don't have to wait for a salesperson to bring them to you.

Streetwear

Akira
1837 West North Avenue, Wicker Park; tel: 773-489-0818; www.akirachicago.com; Mon–Fri noon–

Left: a detail on an item at men's emporium, TK Men.

53

Festivals and Events

Chicagoans love their festivals – especially in summer, when it seems like streets all over the city are blocked off every weekend in an attempt to cram in all of the alfresco fun. Consequently, this is a only a representative sampling of the most popular and well-known happenings throughout the year. Many take place downtown and near the lakefront, but smaller festivals offer a chance to explore outlying neighborhoods, discover ethnic cuisines, and experience other unusual or lesser-known aspects of the city.

January

Chicago Winter Delights
www.choosechicago.com
Winter-long celebration with a focus on arts-oriented indoor activities, such as concerts and play readings.

March

Chicago Flower and Garden Show
www.chicagoflowerand garden.com
Gorgeous gardens and blooms among other greenery-related exhibits on display at Navy Pier.

St Patrick's Day Parade
www.cityofchicago.org
The city gets into the Celtic spirit by dyeing the Chicago River green, and everyone is Irish at this heavily attended event downtown.

May

Artropolis
www.artropolis.com
Huge international show devoted to arts, antiques, and culture, with exhibits, performances, and parties.

Great Chicago Places and Spaces
www.cityofchicago.org

Free outdoor and indoor tours of area architecture, including many spaces not normally open to the public.

June

Chicago Blues Festival
www.cityofchicago.org
Top blues musicians as well as lesser-known favorites perform at Grant Park for several days and nights.

Chicago Gospel Music Festival
www.cityofchicago.org
Voices are raised in praise in Millennium Park in this unique choral tradition.

Grant Park Music Festival
www.grantparkmusicfestival.com
The Grant Park Orchestra and Chorus performs a series of free outdoor classical concerts over several weeks.

Old Town Art Fair
www.oldtownartfair.org
Prestigious juried art fair, one

> The staffers at the help desk at the Cultural Center downtown have a wealth of information about daily happenings all over the city. *(See Essentials, p.49).*

of the country's oldest. A garden walk and architecture tour of the historically significant neighborhood are also part of the festivities.

Printers Row Book Fair
www.chicagotribune.com/about/custom/events/printersrow/
Browse through thousands of rare tomes and first editions as well as secondhand finds and new books. Includes readings and author signings.

Ribfest
www.northcenterchamber.com
Thousands of pounds of barbecued ribs – and hundreds of varieties of sauces – are sampled at this fest, a favorite among hungry locals.

SummerDance
www.cityofchicago.org
Free dance lessons and live music in a variety of styles in Grant Park's Spirit of Music Garden Thursday through Sunday for 11 weeks.

July

Bughouse Square Debates
www.newberry.org
Speakers continue the tradition of soapbox oratory in Washington Square Park, pontificating on anything

Left: the Taste of Chicago is huge in a city of foodies.

October

Chicago International Film Festival
www.chicagofilmfestival.org
Competitive film festival, one of the oldest in North America.

Chicago Marathon
www.chicagomarathon.com
Thousands of amateur runners and professional athletes follow a route that winds around the city.

November–December

Chicago Humanities Festival
www.chfestival.org
Concerts, lectures, and exhibits built around an annual theme celebrate the uplifting qualities of the liberal arts.

Magnificent Mile Lights Festival
www.themagnificentmile.com
A procession on North Michigan Avenue follows the illumination of more than a million holiday lights to kick off the season, followed by a fireworks display.

Christkindlmarkt
www.christkindlmarket.com
German-style holiday market on Daley Plaza featuring seasonal merchandise as well as food and warm drinks.

Below: a brass band heralds the Christmas season.

Expect massive crowds at major events like **Taste of Chicago** and **Chicago Blues Festival**, which occur during the height of the summer. Bring your own water to avoid the high prices.

---

from politics to pet peeves. Heckling is encouraged.

Chicago Outdoor Film Festival
www.cityofchicago.org
For six weeks, the city screens movie classics on Tuesday evenings in Grant Park.

Old St Pat's World's Largest Block Party
www.worldslargestblock party.com
The name says it all. The annual benefit for the West Loop church draws lots of well-known musical acts.

Pitchfork Music Festival
www.pitchforkmusicfestival.com
One of the year's highlights for the independent music fan. Two stages, two full days, and the run of Union Park.

Taste of Chicago
www.cityofchicago.org
Dozens of stalls featuring food from all types of restaurants in the Chicago area: pizza, eth-

nic cuisines, even fine dining.

Venetian Night
www.cityofchicago.org
Boat owners decorate their craft with lights for a water parade along the lakefront, followed by fireworks.

August

Chicago Air and Water Show
www.cityofchicago.org
The lakefront planes and boats bonanza features stunt flying by military pilots, vintage planes, and water-skiing.

Chicago Jazz Festival
www.cityofchicago.org
One of the longest-running music festivals in the city, with free outdoor shows from big names and local jazz stars.

Lollapalooza
www.lollapalooza.com
The three-day pop and rock fest dreamed up by Perry Farrell has grown to a half-dozen stages in Grant Park, with familiar and unfamiliar acts.

North Halsted Market Days
www.northhalsted.com
One of the largest street fairs in the city, with performances, food and drink, and alfresco shopping.

Food and Drink

Several years ago, a skit on a popular late-night TV show featured a group of overweight, middle-aged men dressed in Chicago sports jerseys and gorging on Polish sausage and pizza as they talked about 'da Bears' in flat nasal tones. The city's pride in such gut-busting cuisine continues, but it is becoming increasingly better-known for its more sophisticated offerings, especially since the city's many well-regarded and experimental eateries have put it on the international gourmand radar. The best way to get acquainted with the fantastic and varied local cuisine is to sit down and start eating. See also *Restaurants, p.104–11*.

Classic Chicago Eats

Deep-dish pizza – a thick, almost fried-like crust with copious amounts of cheese and chunky tomato sauce – is probably still the city's most famous gastronomic export, and while it's not always the first choice among residents, people still have very definite ideas of what should go on top of it. Sausage, pepperoni, mushrooms, even spinach are all OK; pineapples or anything too exotic are definitely not. Thin-crust pizza is often sliced into squares, a habit that pizza enthusiasts from other regions view with puzzlement.

Hot dogs are another Chicago specialty, as the proliferation of hot-dog stands all over the city testifies. Offerings range from the classic Chicago dog (an all-beef frankfurter topped with mustard, relish, tomato, pickle spear, celery salt, and peperoncini) to all sorts of variations with different types of sausage and toppings. **Barbecued ribs** and **Italian beef sandwiches** are other examples of the type of down-home, hearty fare

enjoyed by everyone – in moderation, of course.

Sweet Stuff

Once the candy capital of the country, Chicago still has a sweet tooth. Several candy companies were headquartered or had major factories here, including **Brach's**, **Fannie May**, and **Wrigley**. **Frango Mints**, chocolates that were once sold exclusively at department store Marshall Field's, are still considered one of the city's iconic foods, even though they are no longer produced here and Field's is no more, having been bought by Macy's. Still, the scent of chocolate still wafts from the near West Side location of the **Blommer Chocolate** factory, and a host of entrepreneurs and family-owned businesses have sprung up to fill the gap with exquisitely handcrafted chocolates, locally made ice cream, and other treats.

Ethnic Influences

The city's long history of immigration has also sweetened the gustatory pot. Name almost any country or

The bulletin board and chat site LTH Forum (www.lthforum.com; the name honors the initials of a Chinatown restaurant) was started by Chicago foodie Gary Wiviott in 2004 for lively discussions and tips on everything from where to find obscure ingredients to the best place in the city for a bowl of Vietnamese *pho*. It's an especially good source of information for visitors interested in hunting down lesser-known ethnic restaurants.

ethnicity and there's probably at least one place that specializes in its cuisine. Devon Avenue on the far North Side offers some of the best Indian and Pakistani fare you'll have in the Western Hemisphere, while the city's Polish population (and fans of its meaty dishes) head to Wicker Park or the Northwest Side for sausage and pierogi.

Chinatown is a well-known destination for Asian food and ingredients, while the area on the north side around Broadway and Argyle streets caters to a growing Vietnamese com-

Left: a classic Chicago dog.

pierogi, a traditional butcher, and a bakery specializing in Polish pastries.

Patel Brothers
2610 West Devon Avenue, Westridge; tel: 773-262-7777; daily 9.30am–9pm; bus: 155

All sorts of foods and spices essential to South Asian food are found here. Be sure to check out the bins of salty and spicy snack mixes.

Farmers' Markets

From May to October there's a farmers' market somewhere in Chicago every day of the week. Some carry just the basics, while others feature flower stands, heirloom vegetables, pastries, and more.

Green City Market
1750 North Clark Street, Lincoln Park; tel: 773-435-0280; www.chicagogreencitymarket.com; May–Oct: Wed, Sat 7am–1.30pm; bus: 22, 151; map p.133 E2

The gold standard of farmers' markets, this is where many chefs forage for ingredients – and you can usually find at least one giving a cooking presentation or offering tips. It's also one of the few year-round markets (it moves to the nearby Peggy Notebaert Nature Museum in winter; *see Museums and Galleries, p.80*). The emphasis is squarely on sustainable, locally produced

munity. And of course the large Latino population means you have your pick of Mexican (in fact, you can choose from several regions of the country), Ecuadorian, Cuban, Puerto Rican, and Argentine cuisine, to name but a few.

Sophisticated Palates

Thanks to prominent chefs whose names (or at least their restaurants) are known to foodies around the country and even the world, as well as a growing general awareness and sophistication about food, there is renewed appreciation for fresh ingredients, artisanal techniques, and organic and sustainable foodstuffs. This is reflected in the increasing popularity of farmers' markets and foods made and grown locally in necessarily limited batches. The availability at farmers' markets varies wildly – some may carry basic fruit and vegetables, such as corn, peaches, and the like, while larger markets get fancier, with area dairies offering fresh

cheese and small growers selling heirloom vegetables. There is even a local honey made from city beehives.

Ethnic Markets and Groceries

Bobak's Sausage Company
5275 South Archer Avenue, South Side; tel: 773-73-5334; www.bobak.com; Mon–Sat 8am–8pm, Sun 8am–6pm; bus: 62

A beloved institution among lovers of Polish cuisine and other Eastern European fare. There's a massive deli counter with seemingly endless supplies of kielbasa and

Right: fresh, local produce on offer at the Green City Market.

Above: Chicago has a long beer-brewing tradition.

food, of which there is a dizzying array. There are several stands for sandwiches and snacks if you can't wait to eat.

Nettelhorst French Market
3252 North Broadway Street, Lakeview; tel: 312-502-5603; www.bensidounusa.com; Sat 8am–2pm; el: Red, Brown, Purple Line to Belmont

It's a little bit of France in Chicago, what with the jams and preserves, delectable pastries, and fresh-cut flowers to give your shopping bag a stylish twist.

Gourmet Groceries

Fox & Obel
401 East Illinois Street, North Side; tel: 312-410-7301; www.foxandobel.com; CTA bus: 29, 65, 66, 120, 121, 129; daily 6am–midnight; el: Red line to Grand; map p.133 D4

Only the best of the best pates, smoked fish, olive oils, and prosciuttos are stocked here. Conveniently located near Navy Pier, it's a good place to load up for a picnic on the grounds or a boat ride.

Treasure Island
75 West Elm Street, Gold Coast; tel: 312-440-1144; www.tifoods.com; Mon–Fri 7am–10pm, Sat–Sun 7am–9pm; el: Red line to Chicago or Division; map p.132 B2

Julia Child once called Treasure Island 'America's most European supermarket,' and in fact you can almost imagine yourself in one of the Continent's grand food halls as you browse aisles filled with Italian cantuccini, French confit, and Spanish sardines.

Microbreweries and Brewpubs

Chicago has a long history of beer brewing, starting with German immigrants in the mid-19th century, and the industry once had a huge impact on the culture here, from architecture to politics. The industry largely died out after the challenges of Prohibition and the advent of canned beer. However, today a handful of smaller, upscale breweries offer ales and beers of nuanced flavors, continuing the tradition for a contemporary audience.

Goose Island
3535 North Clark Street, Wrigleyville; tel: 773-832-9040; www.gooseisland.com; Apr–Sept: Mon–Thur 11am–midnight, Fri–Sun 11am–midnight, Oct–Mar: Mon–Wed 4–11pm, Thur 4pm–midnight, Fri 4pm–2am, Sat 11am–2am, Sun 11am–11pm; el: Red line to Addison

The city's best-known local beer. Honker's Ale, an amber pale ale, and 312, a refreshing wheat ale, are favorites. Seasonal offerings range from a light fruity summer quaff to a super-dark Guinness-like beer in winter.

Piece
1927 West North Avenue, Wicker Park; tel: 773-772-4422; www.piecechicago.com; Mon–Thur 11.30am–1.30am, Fri 11.30am–2am, Sat 11am–3am, Sun 11am–1am; el: Blue line to Damen

Half the fun at this casual pizzeria-cum-brewpub are the names of the handcrafted beers, which speak to the angst and longings of the largely young crowd. Choose from Dysfunctionale, a pale ale; Worryn Ale, an unusual rye beer; and Dark-n-Curvy Dunkelweizen, a wheat ale.

Specialty Shops

Canady le Chocolatier
824 South Wabash Avenue, Loop; tel: 312-212-1270; www.canadylechocolatier.com; daily 11am–9pm; el: Red line to Harrison; map p.135 C3

All of the chocolates here are made in-house under the direction of master chocolatier Michael Canady. Each one is a little piece of art, molded into shapes such as pharaoh's heads and little tuxedoes.

Conte di Savoia
1438 West Taylor Street, West Side; tel: 312-666-3471; www.contedisavoia.com; Mon–Fri 9am–7pm, Sat 9am–6pm, Sun 9am–4pm; el: Blue line to Racine

This little shop is one of the few genuine articles left in the now-generic Little Italy neighborhood. Here you can pick up biscotti, some of the rarer forms of pasta, vintage wine, and salumi, as well as ready-to-eat sandwiches.

Garrett's Popcorn

26 West Randolph Street, Loop; tel: 312-201-0511; www.garrett popcorn.com; Mon–Sat 10am–8pm, Sun 11am–7pm; el: Red, Blue line to Washington or Lake; map p.134 C1

Garrett's best marketing tool may be the scent of its popcorn, which comes in caramel, cheese, and 'buttery,' and is impossible to resist, despite the line snaking out the door.

Kasia's Deli
2101 West Chicago Avenue, West Side; tel: 773-486-6163; www.kasiasdeli.com; Mon–Sat 9am–6pm, Sun 10am–6pm; bus: 66

Polish-born Kasia Bober's award-winning pierogi – in flavors from blueberry to mushroom – are legend around these parts. Other traditional favorites include potato pancakes, Ukrainian borscht, and homemade Polish sausage.

Pasticceria Natalina
5406 North Clark Street, Uptown; tel: 773-989-0662; www.pasticcerianatalina.com; Wed–Sun 9am–7pm; bus: 22

The light and airy Sicilian pastries here – crisp cannoli filled with real ricotta cheese, cream puffs, and custardy cakes laced with rose water – are the best you can get without getting on a plane to Palermo.

Pastoral
2945 North Broadway Street, Lakeview; tel: 773-472-4781; www.pastoralartisan.com; Tue–Fri 11am–8pm, Sat–Sun 11am–6pm; el: Red line to Belmont, or Brown line to Wellington

Everything here, from French cheese to jam made in Wisconsin, is lovingly crafted in small batches and of artisanal quality. Fresh bread is available every day, and the fancy sandwiches come in some delicious combinations.

The Spice House
1512 North Wells Street, Old Town; tel: 312-274-0378; www.thespicehouse.com; Mon–Sat 1am–7pm, Sat–Sun 10am–5pm; el: Brown line to Sedgwick; map p.132 B1

Nearly every kind of spice, no matter how obscure, is available here, from arrowroot powder to zaatar. If you thought salt was something that just came in a big container from the grocery store, the offerings here – including fleur de sel and Himalayan pink salt – will open your eyes.

Trotters to Go
1337 West Fullerton Avenue, Lincoln Park; tel: 773-868-6510; www.charlietrotters.com/togo; Mon–Sat 11am–8pm, Sun 11am–6pm; el: Red, Brown line to Fullerton; map p.133 D1

A much less pricey option to eating at Charlie Trotter's, this food shop/deli offers the high quality and elegant recipes the chef is known for in takeaway form. The company specializes in organic meat and seasonable produce.

Vosges Haut Chocolat
951 West Armitage Avenue, Lincoln Park; tel: 773-296-9866; www.vosgeschocolate.com; Mon–Thur 10am–7pm, Fri–Sat 10am–8pm, Sun 11am–6pm; el: Brown line to Armitage; map p.133 D2

Vosges is known for terribly addictive truffles infused with exotic ingredients such as cardamom, chili pepper, and even Taleggio cheese, which come in beautiful royal-purple boxes. The flavors come in other forms as well, including bars, ice cream, and hot cocoa.

There are a number of breweries around the Midwest that supply some of the city's most popular beers, such as **Three Floyds** in Indiana and **New Glarus** in Wisconsin. Disappointment reigned when a favorite, **Bell's** in Kalamazoo, Michigan, discontinued sales in Illinois in 2006 after problems with its distributor. However, the company maneuvered around legal loopholes by creating new beers especially for the Chicago market, making local beer drinkers extremely grateful – and loyal.

Left: making the quintessential deep-dish pizza at Pizzeria Uno *(see p.105).*

Gay and Lesbian

Chicago is largely a gay-friendly city, as evidenced by the official rainbow-bedecked pylons dotting the Boys Town neighborhood – not to mention the crowds swelling the many bars and clubs in the area. Further north, Andersonville is another gay hub, although with a stronger lesbian presence; it tends to be a little more sedate than raucous Boys Town. In both neighborhoods, there are plenty of centers, businesses, and restaurants that cater to the gay, lesbian, bisexual, and transgender community. For more listings of bars and nightclubs, see *Bars, p.34–7*, and *Nightlife, p.92–3*.

UPER JESUS

Organizations and Helplines

Center on Halsted
3656 North Halsted Street, Boys Town; tel: 773-472-6469, 24-hour crisis line: 773-871-2273; www.centeronhalsted.com; daily 8am–10pm; el: Red line to Addison
Community center that offers social and recreational programs, counseling and support, and legal services.

Gerber/Hart Library
1127 West Granville Avenue, Uptown; tel: 773-381-8030; www.gerberhart.org; Wed–Thur 6–9pm, Fri–Sun noon–4pm; el: Red line to Granville
Circulating library with some 14,000 volumes relating to the LGBT experience, hosting events, book groups, and occasional exhibits.

Howard Brown Health Center
4025 North Sheridan Road, Lakeview; tel: 773-388-1600; www.howardbrown.org; Mon–Thur 9am–9pm, Fri 9am–5pm, Sat 9am–3pm; bus: 151; el: Red line to Sheridan
Long-time, respected organization offering health services, workshops, and support.

Bars and Cafés

Joie de Vine
1744 West Balmoral Avenue, Uptown; tel: 773-989-6846; Mon–Thur 5pm–midnight, Fri–Sat 5pm–2am, Sun 2pm–midnight; bus: 22
Yummy wines and light bites draw a laid-back lesbian crowd to this cozy wine lounge, as well as straight folk.

Roscoe's
3356 North Halsted Street, Boys Town; tel: 773-281-3355; www.roscoes.com; Mon–Fri noon–2am, Sat noon–3am, Sun 11am–midnight; el: Red, Brown, Purple line to Belmont
One of the city's most popular gay bars, the mood here ranges from relaxed during the week, with workers stopping by during happy hour to shoot some pool or drink on the patio, to weekend high energy.

Star Gaze
5419 North Clark Street, Uptown; tel: 773-561-7363; www.stargazechicago.com; Tue–Fri 6pm–2am, Sat 5pm–3am, Sun 11.30am–2am; bus: 22
There's a dance floor here, but this mainly lesbian bar is mostly a low-key, no-frills spot for shooting some pool,

Above: a girls' night out at popular lesbian bar, Star Gaze.

maybe singing some karaoke, and just hanging out.

Nightclubs and Dancing

Berlin
954 West Belmont Avenue, Boys Town; tel: 773-348-4975; www.berlinchicago.com; Sun–Mon 8pm–4am, Tue–Fri 5pm–4am, Sat 5pm–5am; el: Red, Brown, Purple line to Belmont
One of the oldest dance clubs in Chicago, this non-stop party hub with a retro-futuristic decor caters to a largely gay crowd but welcomes anyone with an open mind and nostalgia for 80s-style decadence.

Gentry of Chicago
440 North State Street, North

MEDUSA

Left: Berlin nightclub.

There are plenty of free local newspapers and magazines offering news with a gay perspective as well as listings of events. Among the weekly newspapers, *Windy City Times* edges toward the liberal side, while the *Chicago Free Press* is a bit more to the center. Pick up *Gay Chicago* and *Nightspots* for coverage of what's happening at the bars and clubs around town.

The community-wide celebration includes a parade with hundreds of floats and participants through Boys Town.

Side; tel: 312-836-0933; www.gentryofchicago.com; daily 4pm–2am, Sat until 3am; el: Red line to Grand; map p.132 C4
This elegant, romantic cabaret club features jazzy live music most nights in the main Martini bar, with its huge Swarovsky crystal chandelier. In the downstairs lounge things are a little more playful, with karaoke and comedy on offer.

Restaurants

HB Home Bistro
3404 North Halsted Street, Boys Town; tel: 773-661-0299; www.homebistrochicago.com; Wed–Thur 5.30–10pm, Fri–Sat 5–10.30pm, Sun 10am–3pm, 5–9pm; $$$; el: Red, Purple, Brown line to Belmont
This elegant but friendly little BYOB bistro is run by the Hearty Boys, who were catapulted to fame with their own

Prices for an average three-course meal with a glass of wine, beer, or a cocktail:
$$$$ – over $60
$$$ – $45–$65
$$ – $20–$45
$ – under $20

show on the Food Network. The menu leans toward classics with twists, such as pork chops accompanied by rhubarb jam.

Tweet Let's Eat
5020 North Sheridan Road, Andersonville; tel: 773-728-5576; www.tweet.biz; Wed–Mon 9am–3pm; $; bus: 151
A cheerful brunch spot where you'll find all the typical American breakfast standards, as well as many veggie options. On the first and third Tuesday of the month, the restaurant hosts performances by gay and lesbian artists.

Festivals and Events

Chicago Lesbian and Gay International Film Festival
c/o Chicago Filmmakers, 5243 North Clark Street; tel: 773-293-1447; November
Also known as Reeling, this film fest, billed as the second-oldest of its kind, screens documentaries, short and feature films that speak to the LGBT experience and lifestyle.

Pride Chicago
3712 North Broadway Street; tel: 773-348-8243; www.chicago pridecalendar.org; last Sat in June

Shopping

Beatnix
3400 North Halsted Street, Boys Town; tel: 773-281-6933; Sun–Thur noon–9pm, Fri–Sat 11am–11pm; Red, Brown, Purple line to Belmont
The store stocks everything a drag queen or a glamour girl could desire, from candy-colored wigs to outrageously high platform shoes, in addition to vintage and new items for more mainstream tastes.

Gay Mart
3457 North Halsted Street, Boys Town; tel: 773-929-4272; Mon–Sat 11am–7pm, Fri until 8pm, Sun noon–7pm; Red, Brown, Purple line to Belmont
If it's got a gay theme, you'll find it here, from birthday cards for kids with two dads, to the anatomically correct 'Billy' doll, who's much more out of the closet than Ken.

Unabridged Bookstore
3251 North Broadway, Lakeview; tel: 773-883-9119; Mon–Fri 10am–9pm, Sat–Sun 10am–7pm; Red, Brown, Purple line to Belmont
Independent store stocking a large and varied section of LGBT titles, including comics, erotica, and travel guides.

61

History

Pre-1600

Native Americans term the area 'Chicagou,' which refers to a wild leek growing in the swampy area.

1672

Missionary and explorer Father Pierre Charlevoix mentions 'Chicagou' in a written report to the French court.

1673

Jacques Marquette and Louis Jolliet, French-Canadian explorers, arrive on what is to become the city, the first recorded Europeans to set foot there.

1683

French Jesuits found the Fort de Chicago, the area's first European settlement.

1696

The Jesuits build the Mission of the Guardian Angel, probably around where the Merchandise Mart stands today.

1705

Fort de Chicago is abandoned after skirmishes between French traders and the Fox tribe.

1763

Great Britain takes control of the Chicago area after the end of the French and Indian War.

1779

Haitian immigrant Jean Baptiste Pointe DuSable arrives, establishing the city's first permanent settlement near the mouth of the Chicago River.

1795

The Treaty of Greenville gives the government 'one piece of land six miles square at the mouth of the Chicago River,' ceded from the tribes in the area.

1803

Fort Dearborn is constructed.

1812

After conflicts with area tribes, Fort Dearborn is evacuated. On their way to safety in Fort Wayne, Indiana, a group of women, children, and soldiers are attacked. Many are killed, their bodies mutilated, and the survivors are sold as slaves to the British, who free them. Fort Dearborn is burned to the ground. The event becomes known as the Fort Dearborn Massacre.

1818

Illinois becomes a state.

1837

With 4,170 residents, Chicago is incorporated as a city.

1847

The first edition of the *Chicago Tribune*, still one of the city's major newspapers, is printed.

1860

The city hosts its first political convention, at which Abraham Lincoln is nominated for president.

1871

The Great Chicago Fire rages for two and a half days in October. About 4 sq miles (10 sq km) of the city are destroyed, an estimated 200 to 300 people perish, and some 30,000 are left homeless.

1885

The Home Insurance Building, at nine stories tall, becomes the world's first 'skyscraper.'

1886

At a Haymarket Square rally of workers protesting strike-related violence at a factory the day before, someone throws a bomb at police officers. Seven police officers and many civilians are killed in the ensuing melee.

1891

Elevated trains run for the first time.

1893

The World's Columbian Exposition opens. The fair attracts 27 million visitors.

1900

The flow of the Chicago River is reversed, reducing pollution in Lake Michigan.

1907–8

The Cubs win the World Series two years in a row.

1914

Wrigley Field – then called Weeghman Park – opens in Lakeview.

1929

Seven people are murdered in what becomes known as the St Valentine's Day Massacre. Gangland boss Al Capone is widely believed to be behind the crime.

1930

The Merchandise Mart is built for the Marshall Field company. At this time it is the largest commercial building in the world.

1934

John Dillinger, a bank robber at the top of the FBI's Most Wanted list, is shot by federal agents near the Biograph Theater in Lincoln Park.

1942

Physicist Enrico Fermi produces the first controlled nuclear chain reaction at the University of Chicago.

1955

Richard J. Daley is elected mayor of Chicago, a post he will hold for the next 21 years until his death. His 'political machine' will have an indelible influence on the way the city works.

1958

The last streetcar line is shut down, marking the end of what was formerly the largest such system in the world.

1959

Comedy group Second City is founded.

1960

Hugh Hefner opens the first Playboy Club downtown, featuring waitresses dressed in bunny costumes.

1968

The Democratic Convention takes place downtown, accompanied by riots and protests.

1969

The John Hancock Center is built.

1973

The Sears Tower, the tallest building in the world for the next 30 years, is completed.

1978

An extremely heavy snowstorm paralyzes the city. The slow response to clearing and cleanup leads to the downfall of Mayor Michael Bilandic.

1983

Harold Washington becomes the city's first African-American mayor.

1984

Michael Jordan joins the Chicago Bulls. He eventually leads the basketball team to six of its eight championships during the 90s.

1989

Richard M. Daley is elected mayor of the city, a post formerly held by his father, Richard J. Daley.

1992

The 'Great Chicago Flood' occurs when a wall in the river cracks and thousands of gallons of water wash through a series of tunnels under the city.

2003

Millennium Park opens.

2006

Beloved, historic department store Marshall Field's becomes a Macy's after being bought by its parent company. Locals arrange protests and petitions, to no avail.

2008

Chicago is named one of four finalists to host the 2016 Olympic Games.

Hotels

Chicago offers a lot of options to suit every lifestyle and budget, from bare-bones hostels to grand historical landmarks. Hotels closer to downtown's major attractions tend to be pricey, although there are budget options here and there, and there are some good options in outlying neighborhoods, from B&Bs to small hotels that provide a respite from the noise and crowds in the center. One note of caution: Chicago's central location in the US makes it a popular choice for national conventions, making rooms scarce on weekends, especially during the high season. Booking ahead is essential during these times.

The Loop

Fairmont Hotel

200 North Columbus Drive; tel: 312-565-8000; www.fairmont. com; $$$$, el: Red line to Lake, or Orange, Brown, Purple Express, Green, Pink to Randolph/Wabash; map p.135 C1
The Fairmont, a favorite with stars and visiting dignitaries, sets the standard for luxury hotels. There's a car and driver at your service should the need arrive, and a Bath Sommelier will draw the perfect perfume-infused soak.

Hard Rock Hotel

230 North Michigan Avenue; tel: 312-345-1000; www.hardrock hotelchicago.com; $$$, el: Red, Blue line to State/Lake; bus: 3, 145, 147, 151; map p.135 C1
Located in the dramatic Carbide and Carbon Building, the rooms here are aggressively fashionable and

Prices per night for a standard double room in high season, exclusive of breakfast, taxes (15.4 percent), or parking:
$$$$ – over $300
$$$ – $175–$300
$$ – $125–$175
$ – under $125

include state-of-the-art home-theater systems – all the better to live that rock-star fantasy.

HI-Chicago

24 East Congress Parkway; tel: 31-360-0300, www.hichicago. org; $; el: Blue line to LaSalle, or Orange, Purple, Brown line to Library; map p.134 C2
The clean, modern facility in a vintage building offers easy access to downtown sites and transportation. Rooms are dorm-style, with six to 10 beds per room, but there's no curfew.

Hotel 71

71 East Wacker Drive; tel: 312-265-3386; www.hotel1-px.trvl click.com; $$$, el: Orange, Brown, Purple Express, Green, Pink line to State/Lake or Clark/Lake, or Red line to Lake; bus: 3, 29, 145, 147, 151; map p.135 C1
Located in a 1950s high-rise, the 400 rooms are spread out over some 30 stories. Large rooms feature linens in an oversize bright-yellow check and furniture upholstered in animal-print fabrics. The central location makes it attractive to business travelers and those in town for short visits.

Many hotels offer special packages that can include discounts at shops, deals at spas, theater tickets, free museum admission, and more. Winter is an especially good time to save. Check with hotels about their offerings, or go to **www.choosechicago.com** for a listing of the tourism bureau's deals.

Hotel Allegro

171 West Randolph Street; tel: 312-236-0123; www.allegro chicago.com; $$$, el: Blue, Orange, Purple, Brown, or Pink line to Clark/Lake; map p.134 C1
This boutique hotel recently underwent a $40 million renovation, which included a new eco-friendly water system. The 483 guest rooms are all done in contemporary, cool decor, especially the hyper-modern bathrooms.

Hotel Burnham

1 West Washington Street; tel: 312-782-1111; www.burnham hotel.com; $$$$; el: Red, Blue line to Washington, or Orange, Brown, Purple Express, Green, Pink to Madison/Wabash; bus: 22; map p.135 C2

Left: fabulous views over Chicago from a glamorous Hard Rock Hotel room.

Jeweler's Row. Rooms are bright and airy, and bathrooms are surprisingly spacious.

Swissotel
323 East Wacker Drive; tel: 312-565-0565; www.swissotel.com; $$$; el: Red, Orange, Brown, Green line to Randolph; bus: 3, 145, 147, 151; map p.135 D1
There are great wraparound views of the city – including Grant Park and the lake – from this glass triangular-shaped building, which can also be enjoyed from one of the exercise machines in the 42nd-floor fitness center. Large rooms are done in soothing, muted tones.

North Side

Allerton Hotel
701 North Michigan Avenue; tel:

A former office building designed by the architect Daniel Burnham, this place features original details like mosaic floors and marble staircases that will warm the hearts of history buffs. Many rooms and floors feature the original wooden doors with a pane of Florentine glass (complete with an opening for letters) and gilded hardware. The **Atwood Café** in the lobby is a convivial place for lunch or dinner.
SEE ALSO RESTAURANTS, P.104

Hotel Monaco
225 North Wabash Avenue; tel: 312-960-8500, www.monaco-chicago.com; $$$; el: Pink, Brown, Green, Blue, Purple Express, Orange line to Clark/Lake or State/Lake, or Red line to Lake; bus: 29; map p.135 C1
Some of the sumptuous French Art Deco rooms at this luxurious hotel come in tall sizes, with extra-long beds and taller showerheads. A portion of the cost of the packages for pet-friendly rooms goes to a local animal welfare organization.

Palmer House Hilton
17 East Monroe Street; tel: 312-

726-7500; www.hilton.com; $$$; el: Red, Blue line to Monroe, or Green, Orange, Brown line to Madison/Wabash; bus: 3, 29, 145, 147, 151; map p.135 C2
One of the oldest and grandest hotels in the city with an astonishing 1,639 rooms. Executive rooms are decorated in a French Empire style and are assigned a special concierge. The ceiling mural of classical Greek mythology in the two-story lobby gets touched up every once in a while by workers who handled the restoration of the Sistine Chapel.

Silversmith Hotel & Suites
10 South Wabash Avenue; tel: 312-372-7696; www.silversmith chicagohotel.com; $$$; el: Orange, Brown, Purple Express, Green, Pink line to Madison/Wabash, or Red, Blue line to Washington; bus: 3, 145, 147, 151; map p.135 C2
Often called a gem, and not just for the diamond-in-the-rough quality of its semi-anonymous location: the building is located on a stretch of Wabash known as

Right: the Hard Rock Hotel.

65

Above: boutique style at the James.

312-440-1500; www.theallerton
hotel.com; $$$, el: Red line to
Chicago; bus: 3, 145, 147, 151;
map p.133 C3

Each of the 443 rooms in
this historic hotel features a
unique layout, the legacy of
its past as a 'club hotel' for
extended stays. The rooms'
decor is a touch above stan-
dard, but the location – and
views of Michigan Avenue
from the top-floor ballroom –
can't be beaten.

> Budget chains such as **Best
> Western** (www.bestwestern.
> com), **Red Roof Inn** (www.red
> roof.com), and **Super 8**
> (www.super8.com), while
> extremely basic, can offer good
> value for location, and the
> standardization of such busi-
> nesses means you know what
> you are getting for the price.

Amalfi Hotel

20 West Kinzie Street; tel: 877-
262-5341; www.amalfihotel
chicago.com; $$$, el: Red line to
Grand, or Orange, Brown, Purple
Express, Green, Pink line to
State/Lake or Clark/Lake; map
p.132 C4

Stays here include a compli-
mentary happy hour with
antipasti and 'Amalfitinis.'
The sunny guest rooms are
filled with curved lines and
Mediterranean hues.

Avenue Hotel

160 East Huron Street; tel: 312-
787-2900; www.avenue
hotelchicago.com; $$$, el: Red
Line to Chicago; bus: 66; map
p.133 C3

The design here is the last
word in urban cool, espe-
cially the signature
ergonomic zebra chairs in
every room. The 40th-floor
Sky Lounge is a futuristic,

sleek space in which to
enjoy breakfast or drinks
with a view.

Cass Hotel

640 North Wabash Avenue; tel:
312-787-4030; www.cass
hotel.com; $$$, el: Red line to
Grand; bus: 65, 29, 66; map
p.133 C3

Although part of the Holiday
Inn Express chain, the Cass
is more boutique hotel than
generic motel. Bright rooms
with green headboards,
upholstered furniture in
cheerful prints, and modern-
hip light fixtures no doubt
appeal to visitors heading to
the nearby River North
design district.

Conrad

521 North Rush Street; tel: 312-
645-1500; www.conrad
hotels.com; $$$$, el: Red line to
Chicago; bus: 65; map p.132 C3

The location is great for shop-
aholics: just downstairs is an
upscale mall. Rooms feature
luxurious Pratesi linens and
deep soaking tubs in the bath-
room. Head to the terrace for
alfresco dining and movies.

Drake Hotel

140 East Walton Place; tel: 312-
787-2200; www.thedrake
hotel.com; $$$, el: Red line to
Chicago; bus: 66, 3, 145, 146,
151; map p.133 C2/3

Ask for a room along the
north side of this 535-room
hotel for unparalleled views of
the lake and Oak Street
Beach. Afternoon tea in the

sumptuous Palm Court off the gilded lobby (accompanied by a live harpist) is a must.

Four Seasons
120 East Delaware Place; tel: 312-280-8800; www.four seasons.com; $$$$; bus: 145, 147, 151; el: Red line to Chicago; map p.132 C3
Rooms here combine European grandeur with clean lines, and the windows actually open. Hidden on the upper floors of a vertical shopping mall, it's a favorite among celebrities hiding out from the paparazzi.

Hotel Sax
333 North Dearborn Street; tel: 312-245-0333; www.loews hotels.com; $$$; el: Red line to Grand, or Blue line to Clark/Lake, or Green, Orange, Brown line to State/Lake; map p.132 C4
The 353 rooms, lobby, and bar were redone recently to feature such luxuries as Italian marble floors. Select rooms feature mp3 players and Xbox consoles; for those without there's an entertainment lounge sponsored by Microsoft outfitted with entertainment technology.

InterContinental
505 North Michigan Avenue; tel: 312-944-4100; www.inter continental.com; $$$; el: Red line to Grand; bus: 3, 145, 147, 151, 65; map p.133 C4
There are actually two sections of this hotel: the historic tower, built in 1929, where the rooms have a more traditional look, and a later addition, with a modern urban decor. The junior Olympic-size pool on the top floor of the tower is surrounded by ornate mosaic tiles.

James
16 West Ontario Street; tel: 877-526-3755; www.james hotels.com; $$$; el: Red, Brown

line to Chicago; bus: 65, 66, 3, 145, 147, 151; map p.132 C3
One of the city's first boutique hotels, with a modern-Zen aesthetic and high-design furniture. It's set in the middle of a lively nightlife scene, which includes the hotel's own low-lit bar.

Millennium Knickerbocker
163 East Walton Street; tel: 312-751-8100; www.millennium hotels.com; $$$; el: Red line to Chicago; bus: 3, 145, 147, 151; map p.133 C3
This is a hotel with a past: Al Capone was rumored to do business here, and later Hugh Hefner turned it into the Playboy Towers. (Peek into the Crystal Ballroom to see the lighted dance floor.) Rooms tend to be small, but as of writing are undergoing restoration.

Ohio House Motel
600 North LaSalle Street; tel: 312-943-6000; www.ohiohouse motel.com; $; el: Red line to Grand, or Brown, Purple line to Merchandise Mart; bus: 65; map p.132 B4
Generic rooms offer basic comfort, but the 50s aesthetic can be fun, as is the old-school coffeeshop. For the location, the price is hard to beat.

Omni Chicago
676 North Michigan Avenue; tel:

312-944-6664; www.omni hotels.com; $$$$; el: Red line to Chicago; bus: 3, 65, 66, 145, 147, 151; map p.133 C3
Part of the Omni chain, the luxuriously appointed suites here are par for the course, but kids are welcome here too and receive a 'goodie bag' on arrival.

Peninsula Hotel
108 East Superior Street; tel: 312-337-2888; www.chicago. peninsula.com; $$$$; el: Red line to Chicago; bus: 3, 66, 145, 147, 151; map p.133 C3
Each of the 339 guest rooms at this ultra-high-end, award-winning hotel comes with a system that allows for features to be accessed with the touch of a button. The Shanghai Terrace, one of the four full-service restaurants, features a terrace overlooking Michigan Avenue.

Raffaello
201 East Delaware Place; tel: 312-235-6312; www.chicago raffaello.reachlocal.net; $$$; el: Red line to Chicago; bus: 3, 66,

> Prices per night for a standard double room in high season, exclusive of breakfast, taxes (15.4 percent), or parking:
> $$$$ – over $300
> $$$ – $175–$300
> $$ – $125–$175
> $ – under $125

Right: afternoon tea at the sumptuous Drake Hotel.

Left: the trendy W offers both
nightlife and pampering.

147, 151; map p.132 C3
The Gallic flair on exhibit
here extends to the building,
a striking triangular edifice
by French architect Jean-
Paul Viguier. The wood-and-
chrome-accented rooms
feature large windows, all
the better to enjoy the view.
The downstairs bar features
a fireplace and is a cozy
place to hide out on cold or
rainy days.

Talbott
20 East Delaware Place; tel:
312-944-4970; www.talbott
hotel.com; $$$; el: Red line to
Chicago; bus: 3, 29, 66, 70, 145,
147, 151; map p.132 C3
A pretty traditional
European-style hotel, with
antiques, carved wood furni-
ture, and half-canopies over
the beds. But the technology
is anything but staid: the
hotel purchases wind-
produced energy to offset its
electrical use and features a
high-efficiency heating and
cooling system.

Tremont Hotel
100 East Chestnut Street; tel:
312-751-1900; www.starwood
hotels.com; $$$, el: Red line to
Chicago; bus: 3, 66, 145, 147,
151; map p.132 C3
European-style hotel with
unremarkable decor, but a
homey vibe. The lobby, with
its wood-beam ceiling and
fireplace, is a pleasant place
to relax after a busy day of
sightseeing.

W Hotel Lakeshore
644 North Lake Shore Drive; tel:

145, 147, 151; map p.133 C3
The prevailing hue here is a
warm golden beige, the aesthetic urban and sleek.
Bathrooms feature luxurious
rain showers, and there's a
spa for more intense pam-
pering. The rooftop deck is
a splendid spot to catch
some rays.

Ritz-Carlton
160 East Pearson Street; tel:
312-266-1000; www.four
seasons.com; $$$$; el: Red line
to Chicago; bus: 3, 66, 145, 147,
151; map p.133 C3
The Ritz-Carlton is the last
word in luxury, and although
now part of the Four Sea-
sons chain, this location
doesn't disappoint. Rooms
are splendidly furnished in
classic French style. Some-

what surprisingly, the atmosphere is extremely friendly
and laid-back, with a special
welcome extended to chil-
dren, who enjoy special gifts
and pool hours.

Seneca Hotel
200 East Chestnut Street; tel:
312-787-8900; www.seneca
hotel.com; $$$; el: Red line to
Chicago; bus: 3, 66, 145, 147,
151; map p.132 C3
The rooms here, most of
which have full kitchens, rep-
resent good value for the
location, which is just steps
from Michigan Avenue.

**Sofitel Chicago
Water Tower**
20 East Chestnut Street; tel:
877-813-7700; www.
sofitel.com; $$$$; el: Red line to
Chicago; bus: 3, 29, 66, 145,

Prices per night for a standard
double room in high season,
exclusive of breakfast, taxes
(15.4 percent), or parking:
$$$$ – over $300
$$$ – $175–$300
$$ – $125–$175
$ – under $125

For a more personal experience, some travelers like to swap their homes with another traveler or family for a short period. There are plenty of websites with listings of available homes in the Chicago area (and all over the world), such as **www.exchangehome.com**, **www.exchangeplaces.com**, and **www.intervacus.org**. **www.craigslist.com** is another option, with occasional listings located in the 'swap' section of the Chicago site.

312-943-9200; www.whotels.com; $$$; el: Red line to Grand or Chicago; bus: 3, 65, 66, 145, 147, 151; map p.133 D3
As the name says, it's right on the lake, although separated from the water by Lake Shore Drive. The rooms are slick and feature top amenities, but you might want to spend more time at the Whiskey Sky bar on the top floor, with it great views outside and eye candy inside. The Bliss Spa offers dozens of delightful ways to detox if you overdo it.

Whitehall Hotel
105 East Delaware Place; tel: 312-944-6300; www.thewhite hallhotel.com; $$$; el: Red line to Chicago; bus: 3, 66, 145, 147, 151; map p.132 C3
Patrician and refined, with marble bathrooms, mahogany furnishings, and sparkling chandeliers, the Whitehall has won a loyal clientele. Hallways can be narrow in this older building, but the rooms are relatively spacious.

Gold Coast

Ambassador East
1301 North State Parkway; tel: 312-787-7200; www.the ambassadoreasthotel.com; $$$; el: Red line to Chicago or Clark/Division; bus: 29, 70; map p.132 C2
This was once the preferred hotel of celebrities like Frank Sinatra and Dean Martin, who now have suites named after them. Rooms are elegantly turned out with dark cherry-wood furniture and floral accents. The old-school glamour of the location can be best felt in the opulent **Pump Room** restaurant.
SEE ALSO RESTAURANTS, P.107

Flemish House
68 East Cedar Street; tel: 312-664-9981; www.innchicago.com; $$$; el: Red line to Clark/Division; bus: 70; map p.132 C2
The seven rooms in this 1892 row house – three one-bedrooms, four one-room studios – feature private baths and full kitchens, and are occasionally available for long-term stays. Original architectural details like wood paneling and decorative molding provide vintage charms.

Gold Coast Bed and Breakfast
113 West Elm Street; tel: 312-337-0361; www.bbchicago.com; $$; el: Red line to Clark/Division; bus: 22, 70; map p.132 B2
With just four guest rooms in an 1873 Victorian townhouse, each with its own en suite bathroom, this B&B offers lots of privacy. The lush backyard garden, visible through tall windows on two floors, is a good place to take advantage of the free Wi-fi.

Hotel Indigo
1244 North Dearborn Street; tel: 312-787-4980; www.goldcoast chicagohotel.com; $$$; el: Red line to Clark/Division; bus: 22, 29, 70; map p.132 C2
Everything in this hotel is designed to approximate a soothing getaway – from the scents in the lobby (which change every 90 days) to the blue-and-green color scheme. The rooms have a cabana-like feel as well, with brightly polished wood floors and white-painted furniture. Set in a largely residential neighborhood, it's a nice option for those who prefer to escape from the noise and bustle further downtown.

Sutton Place
21 East Bellevue Place; tel: 312-266-2100; www.chicago.sutton place.com; $$$; el: Red line to Clark/Division; bus: 3, 29, 70, 145, 147, 151; map p.132 C2
Notable here are the Robert Mapplethorpe photographs hanging in the rooms (don't worry, they aren't the naughty ones). Downstairs is the Whiskey Bar & Grill, which attracts refugees from the nightlife on nearby Rush Street. Thoughtfully, the rooms are soundproofed.

Lincoln Park and Old Town

Arlington House International Hostel
616 West Arlington Place; tel: 773-929-5380; www.arlington house.com; $; el: Red, Purple, Brown line to Fullerton; bus: 8,

Below: classic style at the Ambassador East.

74; map p.133 D1
Budget-priced and basic, the accommodations here are about what you'd expect, but the largely youthful clientele doesn't mind, especially given the upscale location.

Belden-Stratford Hotel
2300 North Lincoln Park West; tel: 773-281-2900; www.belden stratford.com; $$; el: Red, Purple, Brown line to Fullerton; bus: 22, 74; map p.133 E2

A great option for longer stays, the Belden-Stratford offers 70 rooms and apartments, all with kitchen facilities. Lincoln Park Zoo is right outside, and many rooms have fantastic views of the park and the lake, and even the skyline downtown.

China Doll
738 West Schubert Avenue; tel: 866-361-1819; www.chinadoll guesthouse.com; $$$; el: Brown, Purple line to Wellington; bus: 8, 22, 76

The apartments in this ivy-clad brownstone are warmly furnished with all of the comforts of home, as well as the office requirements for the business traveler.

Days Inn
644 West Diversey Parkway; tel: 773-525-7010; www.daysinn chicago.net; $; el: Brown, Purple line to Diversey; bus: 22, 36, 76; map p.133 D1

This place is also known as the 'Rock & Roll Days Inn' for all of the bands and musicians that have stayed here over the years. The rooms here are pretty standard, but there are fun art pieces by the entrance and in the courtyard, which also hint at the management's lighter side.

Windy City Urban Inn
607 West Deming Place; tel: 773-248-7091; www.windycity inn.com; $$; el: Red, Brown, Purple line to Fullerton; bus: 8, 74, 76; map p.133 D1

The five guest rooms and three apartments in this Victorian mansion on a quiet street are named after notable Chicago writers (Carl Sandburg, Gwendolyn Brooks) and include working fireplaces. One suite even boasts a Jacuzzi tub. Guests have access to two sitting rooms and the garden, where they might spend some time reading up on the history and culture of the city in the books and other materials provided throughout the B&B.

Lakeview to Andersonville

Majestic Hotel
528 West Brompton Avenue; tel: 773-404-3499; www.city inns.com; $$$; el: Red line to Addison; bus: 36, 152

The gracious English country-estate style of this quiet hotel is lovely, but baseball fans will appreciate the proximity to Wrigley Field more.

Villa Toscana
3447 North Halsted Street; tel: 773-404-2643; www.thevilla toscana.com; $$; el: Red line to Addison; bus: 8, 152

A large front yard leads to this 1890s B&B, where the rooms are ornately furnished in various European styles: Venetian, French, Empire, Moroccan.

Many upscale hotels offer concierge services, which can range from explaining the best way to get to a particular museum to arranging dinner reservations. The service is free, although it's customary – and appreciated – to tip for extraordinary services, such as securing hard-to-get theater tickets or special requests.

Below: make good use of your concierge.

Left: a light and airy retreat from the busy city.

Forget flowery quilts and canopy beds – this is a B&B for the 21st century. There's a sauna and steam room for relaxation after taking calls in the business center or meetings in the conference room. Wicker Park clubs and nightlife are just steps away, but there's a projected television and HDTV for those who just want to veg out. Breakfast is cooked to order.

Wicker Park Inn

1329 North Wicker Park Avenue; tel: 773-486-2743; www.wicker parkinn.com; $$; el: Blue line to Damen; bus: 50, 56

Although smack in the middle of the lively Wicker Park neighborhood, this gracious B&B is surprisingly sedate, except for the el rumbling by in back of the main building (some rooms are sound-proofed, and ear plugs are provided).

South Loop

Essex Inn

800 South Michigan Avenue; tel: 312-939-2800; www.essex inn.com; $$$; el: Red, Orange, Green line to Harrison, or Orange, Brown, Purple, Pink line to Library; map p.135 C3

The plain exterior is not encouraging, but the interior has recently been remodeled in minimalist-modern style. The hotel is very popular with families for amenities like the rooftop swimming pool and deck with views of Grant Park and the lake, the free shuttle along Michigan Avenue, and nearby access to several major museums.

Hilton Chicago

720 South Michigan Avenue; tel: 312-922-4400, www.chicago hilton.com; $$$; el: Orange, Purple, Brown, Pink line to Library/

Willows Hotel

555 West Surf Street; tel: 773-528-8400; www.cityinns.com; $$; el: Brown, Purple line to Diversey; bus: 8, 76

A vintage elevator and comfortable rooms with French doors give this hotel a certain charm, as does the location, tucked away on a leafy side street.

Wicker Park

House of Two Urns

1239 North Greenview Avenue; tel: 773-235-1408; www.two urns.com; $$$; el: Blue line to Division; bus: 9, 70

This inviting B&B, in a building that once housed a Polish bakery, specializes in personal touches such as breakfasts cooked with fruit from the garden.

Ray's Bucktown Bed and Breakfast

2144 North Leavitt; tel: 773-384-3245; www.raysbucktown bandb.com; $$; el: Blue line to Western; bus: 49, 50

State/Van Buren; bus: 3, 29, 62, 145, 157, 151; map p.135 C3

Built in 1927 and located right across the street from Grant Park, a lot of history has been made here, from visits by heads of state to the riots of the contentious 1968 Democrat Convention. These days you're more likely to run into convention visitors as well as families, brought here by perks like rooms with two bathrooms and policy that lets children under 17 stay free with their parents.

Hotel Blake

500 South Dearborn Street; tel: 312-986-1234; www.hotel blake.com; $$$; el: Blue line to LaSalle, or Red line to Harrison, or Orange, Brown, Purple, Pink line to Library/State/Van Buren; bus: 29; map p.134 C3

It's carved out of three vintage buildings (including the former headquarters for Morton Salt), but inside the feel is totally-of-the-moment. Rooms, decorated in a deluxe, contemporary style, boast floor-to-ceiling windows.

South Side

Wheeler Mansion

2020 South Calumet Avenue; tel: 312-945-2020; www.wheeler mansion.com; $$$; train: Metra to 18th Street or McCormick Place; bus: 34; map p.137 D1

Staying in this Italianate mansion is a peek into the past of this once elite area, with its wooden paneling, high ceilings, and antique wardrobes. Modern touches include cable TV and Egyptian cotton linens.

> Prices per night for a standard double room in high season, exclusive of breakfast, taxes (15.4 percent), or parking:
> $$$$ – over $300
> $$$ – $175–$300
> $$ – $125–$175
> $ – under $125

Literature

While lacking the publishing infrastructure of New York, Chicago has a long literary tradition and a love of reading. Many writers have taken the city's neighborhoods as inspiration for their fiction, while others have unearthed forgotten bits of the city's history and presented them in thrilling yet historically accurate detail. With a history of dynamic journalism as well as literature, the writing scene continues to evolve; today, a new generation even uses comics as a literary medium. See *Festivals and Events, p.54–5* and *Gay and Lesbian, p.60–1*, for more bookstores and event listings.

Early 20th Century

Writers have always used the city's historical rough-and-tumble character to tell larger stories about the nature of what would become modern urban life. **Theodore Dreiser's** *Sister Carrie* followed a naive young girl who ditches mind-numbing menial work in the factories for a more glamorous life as a mistress of wealthy men, while the journalist **Upton Sinclair** decried the corruption and ghastly working conditions of the Chicago meatpacking industry in his novel *The Jungle* – which led to a large public outcry and, eventually, new federal legislation.

Mid-20th Century

The city's blustery, brash character was explored – and perhaps cemented – by writers such as **Nelson Algren**, who explored the doings of the Polish working class around Wicker Park in his classic novel *The Man with the Golden Arm*. A generation after Algren, oral historian and writer **Studs Terkel** gathered the thoughts and opinions of

residents from different ethnic backgrounds and economic classes in some of the same areas Algren haunted for his seminal book *Division Street: America*. **Saul Bellow**, widely considered one of the greatest novelists of the 20th century, set many of his cerebral works in Chicago, with themes built around modern Jewish life. The poet **Gwendolyn Brooks**, who hails from the South Side, illustrates the joy and despair of the city's African-American community in her lyrical yet unmistakably modern verse.

Contemporary Literature

Many of the current crop of writers who spent formative years in Chicago still use the city's ethnic divisions and history as a backdrop on which to project tales of the human condition in the late 20th and early 21st centuries. Short-story writer **Stuart Dybek** explores the ramifications of gentrification and community change in his work, while **Angela Jackson** uses themes of African heritage as filtered through the rural American south as well as well as the

> Chicagoans don't just like to read books – they like to write about them, too. Local writer Jessica Crispin's website and blog, **Bookslut** (www.bookslut.com), has a large national following for its extensive reviews, author interviews, and ruminations on literature.

urban north in her prose and poetry. **Don De Grazia's** disturbing novel *American Skin* takes place among anti-racist punks and skinheads in the Lakeview neighborhood around the late 1980s.

The city has also spawned a number of talented comic-strip artists, such as **Lynda Barry**, who illustrates themes of adolescent alienation and confusion (albeit in a hilarious manner) in her books and comic strips; **Jessica Abel**, whose influential 1990s comic *Artbabe* chronicled Chicago twentysomethings wrestling with love and fulfillment; and **Chris Ware**, who uses the architecture and landscape of the city almost as a silent character in his epic, intricately detailed graphic novels.

Left: Chicagoan author Sandra Cisneros at a book-signing.

10am–8pm; el: Red line to Lake; map p.134 C1
Wide selection of general fiction and non-fiction, as well as music, dvds, and magazines.

Printers Row Fine & Rare Books
715 South Dearborn Street, South Loop; tel: 312-583-1800; www.chicagorarebooks.com; Tue–Fri 10am–7pm, Sat–Sun 11am–5pm; el: Red line to Harrison; map p.134 C3
The interior, with its glass-fronted bookcases, holds only a small selection of the first editions and arcane available.

Quimby's Bookstore
1854 West North Avenue, Wicker Park; tel: 773-342-0910; www.quimbys.com; Mon–Fri 10am–10pm, Sat 11am–10pm, Sun noon–6pm; el: Blue line to Damen; bus: 72, 50, 56
Comics, art books, erotica – anything a bit subversive.

Women and Children First
5233 North Clark Street, Andersonville; tel: 773-769-9299; www.womenandchildrenfirst.com; Mon–Sat 11am–7pm, Wed–Fri until 9pm, Sun 11am–6pm; bus: 22, 50, 92
Excellent gay and feminist offerings, as well as general popular titles.

Further Reading

Boss
Mike Royko (1971)
Devil in the White City
Erik Larson (2003)
The House on Mango Street
Sandra Cisneros (1984)
Jimmy Corrigan, the Smartest Kid on Earth
Chris Ware (2000)
Native Son
Richard Wright (1940)
Sin in the Second City
Karen Abbott (2007)
Studs Lonigan: A Trilogy
James T. Farrell (1932–5)

Bookstores

57th Street Books
1301 East 57th Street, South Side; tel: 773-684-1300; www.semcoop.booksense.com; Mon–Fri 10am–9pm, Sat–Sun 10am–8pm; train: Metra to 57th Street; map p.139 C3
This Hyde Park bookstore caters to the academic tastes of students and professors, but also stocks general titles.

Barbara's Bookstore
1218 South Halsted Street, West Side; tel: 312-413-2665; www.barbarasbookstore.com; Mon–Fri 9am–10pm, Sat 10am–10pm, Sun 10am–8pm; el: Blue line to UIC; bus: 8, 12; map p.134 A4
Good selection of popular titles as well as Chicago-centric ones. Also at: 111 North State Street, Lower Level, Loop; tel: 312-781-3033; Mon–Sat 9am–8pm, Sun 11am–6pm; el: Red line to Lake; map p.135 C1

Barnes and Noble
1441 West Webster Avenue, Lincoln Park; tel: 773-871-3610; www.barnesandnoble.com; Mon–Sat 9am–11pm, Sun 10am–10pm; bus: 9, 74
You'll find virtually anything you want here, from bestsellers to books on Chicago. Also at: 1130 North State Street, Gold Coast; tel: 312-280-8155; Mon–Sat 9am–10pm, Sun 10am–10pm; el: Red line to Clark/Division; bus: 70; map p.132 C2

Borders
150 North State Street, Loop; tel: 312-606-0750; www.borderstores.com; Mon–Fri 8am–9pm, Sat 9am–9pm, Sun

Every Sunday wordsmiths converge at the **Green Mill** *(see Music, p.87)* in Uptown for the no-holds-barred verse and performance competition known as the **Uptown Poetry Slam**.

Below: vintage books on offer in the Printers Row district.

Movies

T he relative affordability of Chicago makes it an attractive destination for filmmakers, and the small industry is an important – and exciting – part of the local economy, with residents lining up to be cast as extras and the media breathlessly reporting where celebrities have been spotted around town. Meanwhile, many well-known actors have gotten their start in the performing arts departments of area universities or by treading the boards at one of the local theater companies. There are plenty of venues at which to enjoy their work, from small art-house cinemas to downtown multiplexes.

Chicago-set Movies

***North by Northwest* (1959)**
Alfred Hitchcock's thriller, starring Cary Grant, was filmed in part at the Ambassador East hotel.

***The Blues Brothers* (1980)**
Perhaps the ultimate Chicago movie, this action-comedy used dozens of locations around the city, including Daley Plaza, Wrigley Field, and of course the famous car chase on Lower Wacker Drive.

***Ordinary People* (1980)**
The drama about a family undone by a son's suicide was filmed in various locations in the Chicago suburbs.

***Risky Business* (1983)**
Naive North Shore teenager

The Chicago Film Office occasionally casts for extras to appear in background scenes for local productions. It's usually low-paying and tedious, but for many that's a small price to pay for a chance to be on film (or catch a glance of a favorite celebrity). The office's extras casting hotline (tel: 312-814-9605) provides information on current opportunities.

Tom Cruise and sultry call-girl Rebecca De Mornay have a romantic interlude on an el train and sip drinks at the top of the John Hancock Center.

***About Last Night* (1986)**
Demi Moore and Rob Lowe fall in love and break up against the backdrop of Lincoln Park and Rush Street area nightlife.

***Ferris Bueller's Day Off* (1986)**
High school student Ferris plays hooky with friends by gallivanting around Chicago, including the Art Institute, Wrigley Field, and the top of the Sears Tower.

***The Untouchables* (1987)**
Prohibition-era Chicago was recreated for this movie about Eliot Ness fighting gangsters. The Chicago Cultural Center was used as a location, and the movie's final shoot-out takes place in Union Station.

***High Fidelity* (2000)**
Romantic comedy-drama (starring Chicago native John Cusack) follows the owner of a Wicker Park record store around the area.

***Chicago* (2002)**
This Oscar-winning musical

adaptation is based loosely on real-life Chicago murders in the 1920s.

***Batman Begins* (2005), *The Dark Knight* (2008)**
Lower Wacker Drive, the Franklin Street Bridge, and various downtown areas stand in for gloomy Gotham City in the latest Batman movies.

***Public Enemies* (2009)**
Locations for this film starring Johnny Depp as notorious bank robber and gangster John Dillinger include the Biograph Theater, where Dillinger was fatally shot.

Actors and Directors

When dramatic actors here hit the big time they necessarily move to New York or LA for work, but many times they owe the refinement of their performing skills to one of the many respected theater programs here or years spent on the stage as part of one of the city's theater companies.

Evanston natives **John Cusack**, **Joan Cusack**, and **Jeremy Piven** all studied at the Piven Theater Workshop, run by Piven's parents. **David Schwimmer** studied at North-

Left: Dan Aykroyd and John Belushi as the *Blues Brothers*.

For showtimes, check local listings or the venue's website.

with second- and third-run movies as well as cult hits.

Chicago Filmmakers
5243 North Clark Street; Andersonville; tel: 773-293-1447; www.chicagofilmmakers.org; bus: 9, 22
Features art-house movies that will appeal to the auteur.

Chicago Outdoor Film Festival
Grant Park; summer
SEE ALSO FESTIVALS AND EVENTS, P.55

Facets Cinematheque
1517 West Fullerton Avenue, Lincoln Park; tel: 773-281-4114; www.facets.org; el: Red, Brown, Purple line to Fullerton; bus: 74, 9
Art-house in Lincoln Park.

Gene Siskel Film Center
164 North State Street, Loop; tel: 312-846-2600; www.artic.edu; el: Blue, Purple, Brown, Green, Orange line to Clark/Lake; map p.135 C1
Run by the Art Institute School.

Music Box Theatre
3733 North Southport Avenue, Lakeview; tel: 773-871-6604; www.musicboxtheatre.com; el: Red, Brown line to Southport; bus: 22, 9, 80, 152
Art Deco beauty from the 1920s features a working organ.

Navy Pier
600 East Grand Avenue, North Side; tel: 312-595-5629; www.imax.com/chicago; bus: 29, 65, 66, 120; map p.133 E4
IMAX theater hosts first-run movies as well as 3D films.

University of Chicago Doc Films
1212 East 59th Street, South Side; tel: 773-702-8575; www.docfilms.uchicago.edu; bus: 4, 128, 59, 171; train: Metra to 59th Street; map p.139 C3
Student-run film society.

western University and is a co-founder of the Lookingglass Theater, which is headquartered in downtown Chicago. Other notable Northwestern alums in the film business include **Charlton Heston**, **Warren Beatty**, and director and producer **Garry Marshall** *(Pretty Woman, The Princess Diaries)*.

Other locals include **Gillian Anderson**, and **John C. Reilly** studied at DePaul University's drama program. Siblings **Virginia Madsen** *(Sideways)* and **Michael Madsen** *(Pulp Fiction, Kill Bill)* grew up in suburban Winnetka.

Below: Chicago native John Cusack stars in *High Fidelity*.

Steppenwolf Theatre has also seen several of its ensemble members go on to success in movies, such as **Gary Sinise** and **John Malkovich**. **Jennifer Hudson**, a native of the city's South Side, won an Oscar for her role in the movie of *Dreamgirls*.
SEE ALSO THEATER AND DANCE, P.122

First-Run Movie Theaters

AMC Loews 600 North Michigan
600 North Michigan Avenue, North Side; tel: 312-255-9347; www.amctheatres.com; el: Red line to Grand; bus: 65, 147, 151; map p.133 C3

Landmark's Century Center
2828 North Clark Street, Lakeview; tel: 773-509-4949; www.landmarktheatres.com; Red line to Belmont; bus: 22, 36, 76

Foreign Films, Independent Cinema, and Revivals

Brew and View at the Vic
3145 North Sheffield Avenue, Boys Town; tel: 773-472-0366; www.brewview.com; el: Red line to Belmont; bus: 77, 22
Drinks are on offer to enjoy

Museums and Galleries

As a major American city, Chicago has a large number of high-profile museums that are on most first-time visitors' lists, many of which supplement their exhibitions with a full roster of concerts, lectures, performances, and social events. The many smaller institutions scattered around the city can offer a more closely focused view on subjects from local history and the immigrant experience to surgical science and sports. The only problem is winnowing down which ones to visit.

The Loop

ArchiCenter

224 South Michigan Avenue; tel: 312-922-3432; www. architecture.org; Tue–Sun 9.30am–4pm; free; el: Red, Blue line to Jackson; map p.135 C2

The Chicago Architecture Foundation is known mainly for its exceptional tours *(see Architecture, p.31)*, but the two small gallery spaces at its headquarters are worth a look as well. A permanent exhibit provides an overview of Chicago's major spaces and sights, while temporary shows look at architecture both within and beyond the city.

Art Institute of Chicago

111 South Michigan Avenue; tel: 312-443-3600; www.artic.edu/ aic; Mon–Fri 10.30am–4.30pm, Thur until 8pm, Sat–Sun 10am–5pm; charge; free Thur evening; el: Brown line to Adams/Wabash,

Together, the Adler Planetarium, Field Museum, and Shedd Aquarium make up the Museum Campus, a 57-acre (23-hectare) lakefront park with walking paths and outdoor sculptures and art installations.

or Red, Blue line to Monroe; map p.135 C2/D2

One of the world's greatest art museums, the Art Institute's collection includes more than 300,000 pieces from the ancient to the modern day. is probably best-known for its collection of paintings, especially the Impressionist and Post-Impressionist holdings, including six of Claude Monet's *Haystacks*, Georges Seurat's pointillist masterpiece *Sunday Afternoon on the Island of La Grande Jatte*, and Gustave Caillebotte's *Paris Street; Rainy Day*. Among the many iconic American works on view are Edward Hopper's eerie *Nighthawks* and Grant Wood's *American Gothic*. The photograph collection, though less extensive, includes impressive work by Diane Arbus and Richard Avedon.

Save some time to explore the institute's lower-profile exhibits, such as fearsome examples of weapons and armor from the medieval period and the Thorne Miniature Rooms, small-scale versions of typical European and American interiors from the late 13th century to the 1930s. As of press time a new wing is under construction, and some exhibits are temporarily closed.

North Side

Chicago Children's Museum

700 East Grand Avenue; tel: 312-527-1000; www.chicago childrensmuseum.org; daily 10am–5pm, Thur, Sat until 8pm; charge; bus: 29, 65, 66, 124; map p.133 E4

Family-friendly Navy Pier *(see p.40)* seems the perfect location for this museum, housed in a neoclassical structure with two towers that once held water tanks for the pier's sprinkler systems. Intended for kids under 10 (several exhibits cater specifically to pre-schoolers), the museum promotes learning with inter-activity and play. Children are 'shrunk' to ant-size beings in a giant urban backyard alive with huge insects and toad-stools, while they can learn about the power of water by changing the flow of a river with locks and dams. For pure fun there's a maze with

simple brick and limestone exterior, which except for a loggia-like balcony is free of extraneous detail. The building's horizontal planes fore-shadow the birth of the Prairie School, and in fact Frank Lloyd Wright worked on the project as Sullivan's drafts-man. Fittingly, it's now home to the Society of Architectural Historians and is open for tours, during which visitors can view the Arts and Crafts-influenced oak woodwork and mosaic fireplace tiles up close.

International Museum of Surgical Science

1524 North Lake Shore Drive; tel: 312-642-6502; www.im ss.org; Tue–Sun 10am–4pm, Tue–Sat in winter; charge; bus: 151; el: Red line to Clark/Divi-sion; map p.132 C1

This collection of oddities is housed in a Howard Van Doren Shaw-designed build-ing, in the style of the Petit Tri-anon, Marie Antoinette's hideaway at Versailles. Original features like the gilded stair-case and marble fireplaces provide a fitting context for the

Below: Pierre-Auguste Renoir's *Acrobats at the Cirque Fernando*, at the Art Institute.

Best Chicago museums for

...Art
Art Institute
See p.76.

...History
Chicago History Museum
See p.80.

...Science
Museum of Science and Industry
See p.84.

---

toddler-sized gas stations, buses, and other urban phenomena.

Museum of Contemporary Art

220 East Chicago Avenue; tel: 312-280-2660; www.mca chicago.org; Tue 10am–8pm, Wed–Sun 10am–5pm; charge; el: Red line to Chicago; bus: 10, 66; map p.133 C3

The museum opened in 1996 in its limestone and aluminum home, focusing on art since 1945 with a special interest in minimalism, surrealism, con-ceptual photography, and Chicago artists. While the col-lection includes works by Andy Warhol and Alexander Calder, those coming hoping to see specific pieces could end up disappointed, as only

a small selection of the collec-tion of 2,345 pieces is on view at one time, and they're often moved around to take part in themed or temporary exhibits – making a detailed plan for a visit impossible. But on any one day you might be treated to one of Andreas Gursky's giant photographs (including one of the floor of the Board of Trade), Claes Oldenburg's playful *Sculpture in the Form of a Fried Egg*, or Jenny Holzer's *Truisms*, in which one-line sayings flit past on an electronic sign. The terrace, overlooking the sculpture gar-den, hosts performances and concerts in summer.

Gold Coast

Charley-Persky House

1365 North Astor Street; tel: 312-915-0105; www.charnley house.org; tours Apr–Nov: Wed noon, Sat 10am, 1pm, Dec: Sat 10am; charge; el: Red line to Clark/Division; bus: 151, 22, 36; map p.132 C2

One of the few residences designed by Louis Sullivan that has remained largely unchanged, the Charnley-Per-sky House is notable for its

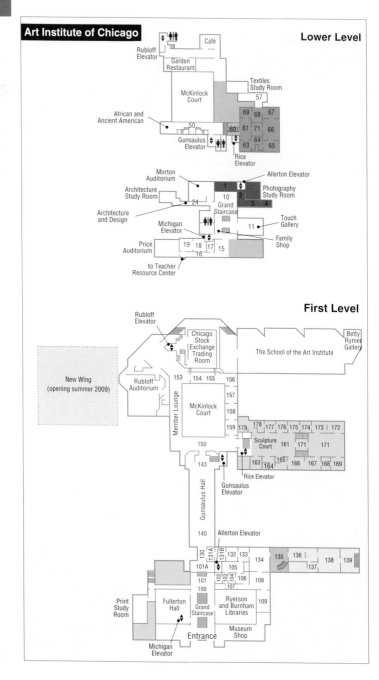

Art Institute of Chicago

Lower Level

Café

Rubloff Elevator

Garden Restaurant

McKinlock Court

Textiles Study Room

57

69 68 67

African and Ancient American

50

60

61 71 66

Gunsaulus Elevator

64 65

63

Rice Elevator

Morton Auditorium

Allerton Elevator

Architecture Study Room

Photography Study Room

1

2

10

24

Grand Staircase

3 4

Architecture and Design

Michigan Elevator

11

Touch Gallery

Price Auditorium

Family Shop

19 18 17

16

15

to Teacher Resource Center

First Level

Rubloff Elevator

Chicago Stock Exchange Trading Room

Betty Rymer Gallery

The School of the Art Institute

New Wing (opening summer 2009)

Rubloff Auditorium

153

154 155

156

Member Lounge

McKinlock Court

157

158

159

179

178

177 176 175 174

173 | 172

150

Sculpture Court

161 171

171

143

163

165

Gunsaulus Hall

164

166 167 168 169

Gunsaulus Elevator

Rice Elevator

140

Allerton Elevator

130

131A

131B

132 133

134

135 136 |

138 139

101A

105

137

101

102

103

104

106 108

100

107

Print Study Room

Fullerton Hall

Grand Staircase

Ryerson and Burnham Libraries

109

Museum Shop

Entrance

Michigan Elevator

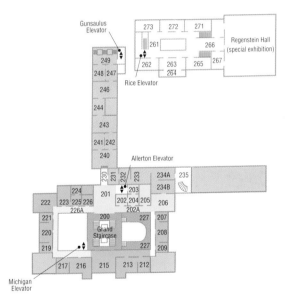

Art Institute of Chicago

Second Level

New Wing
(opening summer 2009)

Millennium Park Room

Rubloff Elevator

Rubloff Auditorium

Gunsaulus Elevator

273 | 272 | 271

261

266

Regenstein Hall
(special exhibition)

262 | 263 | 265 | 267
264

249

248 | 247

Rice Elevator

246

244

243

241 | 242

240

Allerton Elevator

230 | 231 | 232 | 233 | 234A | 235

234B

224

201

203

202 | 204 | 205 | 206

222 | 223 | 225 | 226

226A

200

227

207

221

220

Grand Staircase

208

219

227

209

Michigan Elevator

217 | 216 | 215 | 213 | 212

American to 1890

American Decorative Arts 1901 onward

Ancient Egyptian, Greek, Etruscan and Roman

Contemporary

Indian and Southeast Asian

Chinese, Japanese and Korean

Impressionism / Postimpressionism

Photography

European Decorative Arts 1600-1900

Modern / Contemporary

European Prints / Drawings

European

Architecture

ℹ️ Information Center

↕ Elevator

🚻 Restrooms

✐ Escalator

Cloakroom

79

Left: the Museum of Contemporary Art *(above)* features work such as *Cindy* by Chuck Close *(below)*. *(See p.77.)*

10am–5pm; charge; bus: 77, 151, 157; map p.133 E1

Although definitely geared toward the under-7 crowd, this museum has a way of charming adults as well – especially the 2,700-sq-ft (250-sq-m) butterfly haven, a 'tropical forest' that's home to some 75 species of butterflies and moths. The Marsh exhibit features a lab where you can watch scientists study insects like water scorpions and praying mantises, while the two-story Hands-on Habitat reaches new heights in inter-activity, with a treehouse, binoculars that simulate insect vision, and a wind tunnel to blow seed pods away.

museum's holdings, like drills used by ancient Incas to bore holes in patients' skulls (to release evil spirits), an iron lung, and paintings of various gruesome surgeries. One room is fitted out as an old-fashioned apothecary, complete with patent medicines, and an early 20th-century dentist's office is nearby. But it's not all snake oil and blood-letting; other exhibits explore discoveries in pain manage-ment and medical imaging, while 'Anatomy in the Gallery' showcases contemporary art with a medical theme.

Lincoln Park and Old Town

Chicago History Museum
1601 North Clark Street; tel: 312-642-4600; www.chicagohistory.org; Mon–Sat 9.30am–4.30pm, Thur until 8pm, Sun noon–5pm; charge; bus: 11, 22; map p.133 E3

The recently renovated Chicago History Museum could be called the city's attic – albeit a well-organized, state-of-the-art one. Its holdings include some 22 million artifacts, such as household items scavenged after the Great Chicago Fire and Michael Jordan's basketball jersey. Permanent exhibits trace the growth of the city from the days of a small fron-tier town to the metropolitan center it is today, with particular emphasis on the devastating Great Chicago Fire of 1871, while special presentations focus on spe-cific aspects of the city's cul-ture, such as a study of the classic Chicago hot dog.

Peggy Notebaert Nature Museum
2430 North Cannon Drive; tel: 773-755-5100; www.chias.org; Mon–Fri 9am–4.30pm, Sat–Sun

Lakeview to Andersonville

Swedish American Museum Center
5211 North Clark Street; tel: 773-728-8111; www.samac.org; Tue–Fri 10am–4pm, Sat–Sun 11am–4pm; charge; bus: 22, 92

This small museum maintains a collection of art and artifacts related to Swedish immigra-tion to America on the second floor. Of more interest are the temporary exhibits of both established and up-and-coming Scandinavian artists on the main floor, as well as the third-floor children's museum, where kids can pre-tend to be Vikings aboard a ship or learn about household chores in a replica of a *stuga*, or traditional farmhouse.

West Side

The Hellenic Museum and Cultural Center
801 West Adams Street, 4th floor; tel: 312-655-1234; www.hellenicmuseum.org;

Outside the Chicago History Museum is a sign of Lincoln Park's grim beginnings: a lone mausoleum. It's the tomb of Ira Couch, left over from when the park area was the city cemetery. Allegedly, the family didn't want to pay to move it when the cemetery was relocated.

Tue–Fri 10am–4pm, Sat 11am–4pm; charge; train: Blue line to UIC/Halsted; map p.134 A2
Though small, this institution is unique in that exhibits about the Greek immigrant experience in Chicago come directly from locals' personal histories and recollections. Many items in the museum's collection, from tapestries to pottery, were also donations from the community. Exhibits have illustrated the Greeks' entry into the restaurant business, the myth of Atlantis, and Greek contemporary art.

Jane Addams Hull-House Museum

800 South Halsted Street; tel: 312-413-5353; www.uic.edu/jaddams/hull; Tue–Fri 10am–4pm, Sun noon–4pm; free; bus: 7, 60; el: Blue line to UIC/Halsted; map p.134 A3
In 1889 social activist Jane Addams bought this mansion and transformed it into Hull-House, a settlement that offered educational programs and other resources to the poor and new immigrants in this West Side neighborhood. The holdings include some original furnishings, including Addams's desk, but the focus is on the rotating exhibits that use personal letters and photographs to show how Addams equipped members of the community with the tools to survive in the city.

National Museum of Mexican Art

1852 West 19th Street; tel: 312-738-1503; www.nationalmuseum ofmexicanart.org; Tue–Sun 10am–5pm; free; el: Pink line to 18th Street
The largest Latino arts institution in the United States, the museum presents Mexican culture *sin fronteras* (without borders), including art created on both sides of the border. The permanent collection includes pieces like an 18th-

century painting of an allegory of St Francis's life, colorfully woven textiles, and artifacts from ancient Mayan, Toltec, and Mezcala civilizations.

Wicker Park

Polish Museum of America

984 North Milwaukee Avenue; tel: 773-384-3352; www.polish museumofamerica.org; Fri–Wed 11am–4pm; charge; el: Blue line to Chicago
Highlights of the museum, reportedly the largest ethnic museum in the US, include items from the Polish exhibit at the 1939 World's Fair, an area devoted to the life of Pope John Paul II, and furnishings from the New York hotel room where the famous pianist Ignacy Paderewski lived.

Ukrainian Institute of Modern Art

2320 West Chicago Avenue; tel: 773-227-5522; www.uima-chicago.org; Wed–Sun, noon–4pm; free; bus: 66
The institute focuses on abstract and minimalist work in a variety of media – even digital – by Ukrainian and Ukrainian-American as well as local artists, with viewpoints ranging from playful to resolutely political. In addition, the Institute organizes five or six temporary shows per year.

Ukrainian National Museum

2249 West Superior Street; tel:

Although Hull-House eventually grew to encompass 13 buildings, the mansion and the adjoining dining hall are all that remain, the other structures having been razed to make room for expansion at the University of Illinois at Chicago. The existing structure was also moved 200yds (180m) from the original location for the same reason.

312-421-8020; www.ukrainian nationalmuseum.org; Mon–Wed by appointment only, Thur–Sun 11am–4pm; charge; bus: 66
The often suppressed history and culture of the Ukrainian people is shown with folk arts like *pysanky* (ornately colored Easter eggs), religious items, and letters from prisoners of war in Ukraine during WWII. A special exhibit explains the suffering of Ukrainian peasants during the same war, when an estimated 10 million died as a result of famine.

South Loop

Adler Planetarium

1300 South Lake Shore Drive; tel: 312-922-7827; www.adler planetarium.org; daily 9.30am–4.30pm, summer until 6pm, first Fri of month until 10pm; charge; bus: 146, 12; map p.135 E4
The planetarium dates from 1930, when it was built it to house the Zeiss planetarium projector, donated by Sears, Roebuck executive Max Adler. The two main attractions are the Sky Theater, where the projector beams images of the night sky onto the interior of the planetarium's dome, and the virtual-reality presentations on cosmic phenomena at the **StarRider Theater**.

Behind the main building is **Doane Observatory**, which houses a telescope with a 20-inch (50cm) mirror. It's open for public viewing the

Below: a butterfly at the Peggy Notebert Nature Museum.

81

first Friday of every month and during special astronomical events, such as eclipses.

Chinese-American Museum of Chicago

238 West 23rd Street; tel: 312-949-1000; www.ccamuseum.org; Fri 9am–1.30pm, Sat–Sun 10am–5pm; charge; el: Red line to Chinatown; map p.136 C2

Located in a former warehouse of a wholesaler of Chinese groceries, the museum, staffed by volunteers, offers temporary and semi-permanent exhibits on such eclectic subjects as Chinese toys, from kites and puzzles to puppets, the lives of Chinese immigrants in the Midwest, and a detailed examination and celebration of that misunderstood foodstuff, tofu. Many of the objects and photographs here are gifts or on loan from neighborhood residents.

Clarke House

1827 South Indiana Avenue; tel: 312-745-0040; www.clarke housemuseum.org; tours Wed–Sun noon, 2pm; charge; bus: 1, 3, 4; map p.137 D1

This Greek Revival home, built in 1836, is probably the oldest house in the city. It looks pretty good for having been moved several times in its long life; the current one is near its original location. The interior provides a glimpse into domestic life in the 1840s and 1850s. Tours are offered through the nearby Glessner House Museum *(see right)*.

The Museum of Contemporary Photography sponsors the ongoing **Midwest Photographers Project**, which highlights work by up-and-coming and established photographers living and working in the Midwest. Visitors can make an appointment to see portfolios not currently on display.

Field Museum

1400 South Lake Shore Drive; tel: 312-922-9410; www.field museum.org; daily 9am–5pm; charge; el: Red line to Roosevelt; bus 6, 12, 146; map p.135 D4

The highlight of the Field, which focuses mainly on natural history, has to be 'Sue' (named for the paleontologist who found her – or him), at 42ft (13m) the largest fossil of a Tyrannosaurus rex ever found, as well as the most complete and best-preserved. Casts of some bones and teeth and CT scans are also on view. Other examples of impressive animal life throughout the ages include the stuffed remains of the 'Bushman', a lowland gorilla who made headlines from his home at the Lincoln Park Zoo.

Human history and culture is explored here as well. The exhibit 'Inside Ancient Egypt' depicts daily life in a variety of environments, from burial practices inside a tomb (the exhibit includes 23 mummies) to a recreation of a busy marketplace and a luxurious royal barge. Another devoted to Africa uses artifacts and multimedia to explore the untamed savanna and a virtual trip aboard a slave ship.

Glessner House Museum

1800 South Prairie Avenue; tel: 312-326-1480; www.glessner house.org; tours Wed–Sun 1pm, 3pm; charge; bus: 1, 3, 4; map p.137 D1

This massive granite home is one of the few remaining homes dating from when Prairie Avenue was the city's millionaire row. Inside the mood is quite different, with a warm English Arts and Crafts feel that will appeal to admirers of turn-of-the-century design movements. Most of the objects on view are from the Glessner estate, including wooden picture frames and

furniture carved by Isaac E. Scott, a Chicago artisan known for his Modern Gothic style, hand-painted ceramic tiles, and bronze casts of Abraham's face and hands, taken from life.

Museum of Contemporary Photography

600 South Michigan Avenue; tel: 312-663-5554; www.mocp.org; Mon–Sat 10am–5pm, Thur until 8pm, Sun noon–5pm; free; el: Red line to Harrison; map p.135 C3

The only Midwest museum devoted to photography, this little gem is a must for anyone interested not just in the beauty of photographs but the role and effects of such images on society and culture. The holdings range from Dorothea Lange's sepia-toned images of Americans suffering the poverty and hopelessness of the Depression to the often grotesque tableaux of Joel-Peter Witkin. Most big names are represented here, including Ansel Adams, Henri Cartier-Bresson, and Victor Skrebneski, with equal time given to commercial and purely artistic work.

National Vietnam Veterans Art Museum

1801 South Indiana Avenue; tel: 312-326-0270; www.nvvam.org; Tue–Fri 11am–6pm, Sat 10am–5pm; charge; bus: 1, 3, 4; map p.137 D1

Since its founding in 1981 this museum has promoted healing through art for Vietnam veterans suffering memories of war. It's now the only museum in Chicago whose permanent collection focuses on armed conflict. Temporary exhibits explore themes such as the effect of war on children and the stages of post-traumatic stress syndrome explored through art. The museum's centerpiece is a massive sculpture made up

Right: 'Sue' *(above)* and a Charles Darwin exhibit *(below)* at the Field Museum.

of more than 58,000 tinkling dog tags suspended from the two-story atrium, each one representing those who died during the Vietnam War.

Shedd Aquarium

1200 South Lake Shore Drive; tel: 312-939-2438; www.shedd aquarium.org; winter: Mon–Fri 9am–5pm, Sat–Sun 9am–6pm, summer: daily 9am–6pm; charge; el: Red line to Roosevelt; bus: 12, 146; map p.135 D4

For a long time after it opened in 1930, the Shedd was the largest indoor aquariumn in the world, with the greatest variety of sea life. Just inside the main rotunda is the 90,000-gallon (340,000l) Caribbean Coral Reef, where divers equipped with microphones feed and cavort with stingrays, sea turtles, and nurse sharks. Just behind and to the right of the reef are barrel-vaulted galleries housing the 90 habitats of freshwater and saltwater fish, reptiles, amphibians, and the occasional water-delling mammal. Here's where you'll find 'Granddad', an 80-year-old Australian lungfish that is the aquarium's oldest resident.

On the lower level, the Wild Reef is a series of connected habitats with floor-to-ceiling glass, home to sharks and other toothy predators. A glass floor allows visitors to see rays gliding by beneath their feet, while in other tanks colorful fish flit through coral.

But the pearl of the museum is surely the **Oceanarium**, opened in 1991 and usually overflowing with visitors. A wall of windows looks out on Lake Michigan, while inside the environment mimics the rocky coast of the Pacific Northwest. The ampitheatre features dolphin shows, while nearby a 'secluded' bay is home to the famous Beluga whales. Penguins and otters are displayed in naturalistic habitats. Note that the Oceanarium is set to reopen after maintenance in mid-2009. During this time the animals will be temporarily moved to facilities around the country.

Spertus Museum

610 South Michigan Avenue; tel: 312-322-1700; www. spertus.edu; daily 10am–6pm, Thur until 7pm, Fri until 3pm; charge; el: Red line to Harrison; map p.135 C3

In late 2007 the Spertus Institute – an institution devoted to Jewish studies and art, made up of the Spertus Museum, Spertus College, and the Asher Library – moved next door into its new home, a 10-story structure featuring a stunning glass facade and designed with ecologically responsible principles. The 10th floor houses temporary exhibits exploring issues of Jewish identity and culture, while directly below it you'll find a selection of some of the 15,000 objects in the museum's core collection: religious items, textiles, and art, along with a site-specific installation commemorating the Holocaust. The fourth floor

houses a new Children's Center, with climbing ropes, a toy theater, and mazes, all of which reflect the Jewish storytelling tradition.

South Side

DuSable Museum of African American History

740 East 56th Place; tel: 773-947-0600; www.dusable museum.org; Tue–Sat 10am–5pm, Sun noon–5pm; charge; bus: 3, 4; train: Metra to 57th Street; map p.138 B3

The museum, located in a former parks administration building on the edge of Washington Park, is fittingly named for Jean Baptiste Pointe DuSable, the Haitian fur trader who officially founded Chicago. Exhibitions chronicle the history

83

Internet by having visitors create a virtual avatar to accompany them throughout the exhibit, while another uses infrared cameras and databases to explain computer imaging. The Omnimax & 3D theater, with a five-story, wraparound screen, creates the experience of stumbling upon dinosaurs in the jungle or sea creatures in the ocean. Lines for the more popular attractions can be long, so it's wise to get here early or plan your visit accordingly.

Oriental Institute Museum
1155 East 58th Street; tel: 773-702-9514; www.oi.uchicago.edu; Tue–Sat 10am–6pm, Wed until 8.30pm, Sun noon–6pm; charge; bus: 55; train: Metra to 57th Street; map p.139 C3
Founded in 1919 by University of Chicago ancient Egyptian studies professor James Henry Breasted, the 'oriental' of the title refers to the ancient Near East. Galleries are arranged around a central courtyard and focus on various areas, among them Nubia, Assyria, and Persia. The Mesopotamian gallery features a massive 16ft (5m) -tall winged bull with a human head, unearthed in 1929 by the Institute's archeologists. Another highlight is found down the hall in the Egyptian gallery, a 170ft (50m) -tall statue of King Tut, the tallest ancient Egyptian statue in the Western Hemisphere. Special exhibits have focused on topics from daily life in Persia to the problem of looting in contemporary Iraq.

Robie House
5757 South Woodlawn Drive; tel: 773-834-1847; www.gowright.org; tours Mon–Fri 11am, 1pm, 3pm, Thur also 4pm, 5pm, also 6pm in summer, Sat–Sun every

and culture of Africans and African-Americans in Chicago and across the US.

The museum contains a replica of the office of Harold Washington, the first African-American mayor of Chicago, with many of his personal effects. Elsewhere there are displays of African art and objects, paintings by Harlem Renaissance artist Archibald Motley, and exhibits on the history of African-Americans in the military, with special attention to their achievements in aviation, such as the Tuskegee Airmen, who served in World War II. A 9-by-8ft (2.4-by-2.7m) carved wooden mural presents African-American history from the days of the slave trade to the 1960s.

Museum of Science and Industry (MSI)
57th Street and South Lake Shore Drive; tel: 773-684-1414; www.msichicago.org; Mon–Sun 9.30am–4pm, Sun 11am–4pm; charge; bus: 2, 6, 10, X28; train: Metra to 57th Street; map p.139 E3
Although the museum occasionally receives criticism for being a little too blindly pro-industry (that's where it gets some of its funding), that hasn't stopped it from becoming one of the city's most

popular tourist attractions over the years. Generations of Chicagoans have happy memories of touring the U-505, an actual German sub captured during WWII, and gazing at the Fairy Castle, an elaborate dollhouse featuring chandeliers studded with real gems and tiny printed books.

Other time-tested delights include a whispering gallery, which explains with physics why you can hear another person whispering on the other side of the room, a walk-in model of a human heart, and chicks in an incubator pecking their way out of their shells, part of an exhibit on genetics. Meanwhile, new exhibits conscientiously keep up with advances in science and technology. 'Networld' explains the

> The Museum of Science and Industry is housed in the only building left over from the 1893 World's Columbian Exposition. A complex of white plaster buildings housing exhibits covered more than 600 acres (240 hectares) in the area, and some 27 million people visited the grounds. The Beaux Arts structure, then known as the Palace of Fine Arts, was recast in limestone for its new life as the MSI.

30 minutes 11am–3.30pm; charge; bus: 6; train: Metra to 59th Street; map p.139 C3
Completed in 1909, Robie House is one of the finest examples of Frank Lloyd Wright's Prairie School homes, with its wide overhangs, art-glass windows, and overt horizontality. It was also one of his last; he left the Chicago area (and his family) shortly thereafter. The house has a similarly dramatic past; when his business failed, original owner Frederick C. Robie sold it to a seminary, which used it for dormitories and nearly tore it down. It was then donated to the University of Chicago and used for office space. Meanwhile, the house had deteriorated badly. Since 1997 it has been undergoing restoration overseen by the Frank Lloyd Preservation Trust, so some areas might be closed off.

Smart Museum of Art
5550 South Greenwood Avenue; tel: 773-702-0200; www.smart museum.uchicago.edu; Tue–Fri 10am–4pm, Thur until 8pm, Sat–Sun 11am–5pm; free; bus: 55; train: Metra to 57th Street; map p.138 C2
Located on the campus of the University of Chicago, the Smart Museum's 10,000

Below: the Frank Lloyd Wright Home and Studio.

objects tell the story of both Western and Eastern civilization over the last 5,000 years through the visual arts. Some of the most well-represented eras and areas include Old Master paintings, ancient Greek vases, sculpture by Matisse, Rodin, and Degas, and contemporary Chinese photography. Exhibitions curated by U of C staff provide new insights into those cultures as well as our own, and the museum occasionally teams up with other local art institutions for major events.

Oak Park

Frank Lloyd Wright Home and Studio
951 Chicago Avenue; tel: 708-848-1976; www.gowright.org; tours Mon–Fri 11am, 1pm, 3pm, Thur also 4pm, 5pm, 6pm in summer, Sat–Sun every 20 mins, 11am–3.30pm; charge; el: Green line to Oak Park
Wright built this home – then a relatively simple cottage – in 1889, using a front room on the second floor as his studio. Nine years later he moved it into the Studio Annex, an addition to house his growing practice. The entire building has been restored to its 1909 condition, the last year that Wright and his family lived here. Wright used the home as a laboratory for new ideas, and it offers a peerless insight into his mind.

Hemingway Birthplace Home
339 North Oak Park Avenue; tel: 708-848-2222; www.ehfop.org; Sun–Fri 1–5pm, Sat 10am–5pm; charge; el: Green line to Oak Park
Recently restored, the rooms in this Queen Anne-style home, where Ernest Hemingway was born and lived until the age of six, are decorated in the style of the turn of the 20th century, and include some original furnishings and

decorative touches. Charge includes entry to the Hemingway Museum *(see below)*.

Hemingway Museum
200 North Oak Park Avenue; tel: 708-848-2222; www.ehfop.org; Sun–Fri 1–5pm, Sat 10am–5pm; charge; el: Green line to Oak Park
The museum, a former church, features permanent and temporary exhibits of photos, manuscripts, videos, letters, and other material that documents the writer's life from his boyhood through much of the rest of his life, including his job as a reporter for the Kansas City Star and his experiences as an ambulance driver on the Italian front during WWI.

Around Chicago

Evanston Art Center
2603 Sheridan Road, Evanston; tel: 847-475-5300; www.evanstonartcenter.org; Mon–Thur 10am–10pm, Fri–Sat 10am–4pm, Sun 1–4pm; charge; el: Purple line to Central
The EAC enjoys a grand home in a mansion on Lake Michigan. It puts on six to eight exhibits a year, focusing mainly on Midwestern and Chicago artists; every year, it commissions an installation for the front lawn.

Mary and Leigh Block Museum of Art
40 Arts Circle Drive, Evanston; tel: 847-491-4000; www.block museum.northwestern.edu; Tue 10am–5pm, Wed–Fri 10am–8pm, Sat–Sun noon–5pm; free; el: Purple line to Davis Street; train: Metra to Davis Street
Part of Northwestern University, the museum was originally the repository for works of art the university received over the years. Artists represented include Albrecht Dürer, Rembrandt, and Jasper Johns. In the sculpture garden you'll find work by Joan Miró and Barbara Hepworth.

85

Music

Chicago is of course known for the blues, but there's a vast music scene that includes world-class classical orchestras and internationally known pop and rock performers. Venues range from gilded Beaux Arts music halls to dank holes-in-the-wall. Listed here are most major locations for concerts and shows, although there are always plenty of one-off musical events in parks, churches, and community centers. Note that some venues may not have regular hours of operation or that organizations may perform at various locales around town. See also *Festivals and Events, p.54–5*, and *Nightlife, p.92–3*.

Blues and Jazz

Besides the clubs listed below, you can catch many big names at the **Chicago Blues Festival** and **Chicago Jazz Festival** every summer *(see Festivals and Events, p.54)*. However, it can be even more fun to see them at local clubs. Popular musicians include Eddy 'the Chief' Clearwater, singer Koko Taylor, and legends Buddy Guy, David 'Honeyboy' Edwards, and Otis Rush. There's also a thriving contemporary jazz scene, of which big names

include Ken Vandermark, Kurt Elling, and Von Freeman.

VENUES
Andy's Jazz Club
11 East Hubbard Street, North Side; tel: 312-642-6805; www.andysjazzclub.com; Mon–Fri 11am–2am; Sat 5pm–2am, Sun 11am–1am; el: Purple, Brown line to Merchandise Mart; bus: 29; map p.132 C4
All types of jazz, from bebop to swing, offered nightly.
Blue Chicago
736 North Clark Street, North Side; tel: 312-642-6261;

www.bluechicago.com; daily 8pm–2am, Sat until 3am; el: Red, Purple, Brown line to Chicago; map p.132 B3
Dancing is encouraged at this venue, which features many big local names.
Blue Chicago on Clark
536 North Clark Street, North Side; tel: 312-661-0100; www.bluechicago.com; daily 8pm–2am, Sat until 3am; el: Purple, Brown line to Merchandise Mart; map p.132 B4
The sister club to Blue Chicago is smaller, and specializes in female performers.
b.l.u.e.s.
2519 North Halsted Street, Lincoln Park; tel: 773-528-1012; www.chicagobluesbar.com; daily 8pm–2am, Sat until 3am; el: Red, Purple, Brown line to Fullerton; bus: 8, 11; map p.133 D1
Long-time blues bar featuring mostly local acts. On Sundays the cover charge here includes admission to Kingston Mines *(see right)*.
Buddy Guy's Legends
754 South Wabash Avenue, South Side; tel: 312-427-1190; www.buddyguys.com; Mon–Fri

Left: Chicago Blues Festival.

Left: a performance at Andy's Jazz Club.

South Loop; tel: 312-360-0234; www.jazzshowcase.com; shows: Sun 4pm, 8pm, 10pm, Mon–Sat 8pm, 10pm; el: Blue line to LaSalle; bus: 29; map p.134 C3

Another long-time jazz club (the owner has been in the biz for over 50 years), which hosts Chicago greats along with up-and-comers.

Kingston Mines

2548 North Halsted Street, Lincoln Park; tel: 773-477-4646; www.kingstonmines.com; daily 8pm–4am, Sat until 5am; el: Red, Brown line to Fullerton; bus: 8, 74; map p.133 D1

A gritty bastion of the blues with a no-frills atmosphere – it's all about the music.

Lee's Unleaded Blues

7401 South Chicago Avenue, South Side; tel: 773-493-3477; Thur–Mon 8pm–2am, Sat until 3am; bus: 30

Down-home juke joint that attracts a neighborhood crowd that really gets into the performances.

New Apartment Lounge

504 East 75th Street, South Side; tel: 773-483-7728; daily 4pm–4am; el: Red line to 79th Street; bus: 4

Hardcore jazz fans head here for the Tuesday night jazz sessions with local performer Von Freeman and his quartet.

Pops for Champagne

601 North State Street, North Side; tel: 312-266-7677; www.popsforchampagne.com; Tue–Sat 8pm–2am; el: Red line to Grand; bus: 29, 65; map p.132 C4

Ritzy two-floor jazz venue with an intimate ambience in the performance area.

Rosa's Lounge

3420 West Armitage Avenue, West Side; tel: 773-342-0452; www.rosaslounge.com; Tue–Fri 8pm–2am, Sat 8pm–3am; el: Blue line to Belmont; bus: 73, 82

11am–2am, Sat 5pm–3am, Sun 6pm–2am; el: Brown, Orange, Pink, Purple line to Library; bus: 151; map p.137 C3

Owned by Chicago musician Buddy Guy, himself a blues legend, this large venue hosts mainly local performers during the week, larger touring acts on the weekends. Big names in pop and rock have been known to stop by to jam with Buddy throughout the years, such as Mick Jagger, Kid Rock, and John Mayer.

Checkerboard Lounge

5201 South Harper Avenue, South Side; tel: 773-684-1472; www.checkerjazz.org; daily 6pm–2am; train: Metra to 51st–53rd Street; map p.139 D1

Some say the old ambience was lost when the Checkerboard moved from its longtime Bronzeville home to Hyde Park, but the owner has been resolute about keeping the lounge a home for true blues and jazz lovers.

Green Dolphin Street

2200 North Ashland Avenue, Lincoln Park; tel: 773-395-0066; www.jazzitup.com; Tue–Thur 9pm–2am; Fri–Sat 8.30pm–3am, Sun 8pm–midnight; bus: 9

Blues gets a lot of attention, but the jazz scene in Chicago is thriving too. **The Jazz Institute of Chicago**, www.jazzin chicago.org, is a good online resource to get a handle on local happenings, including shows and special seminars.

Upscale, candlelit locale hosting a wide range of jazz styles, including Latin and big band.

Green Mill

4802 North Broadway Street, Uptown; tel: 773-878-5552; www.greenmilljazz.com; Sun 11am–4am, Mon–Fri noon–4am, Sat noon–5am; el: Red line to Lawrence; bus: 36, 81

The city's premier jazz club, a one-time speakeasy during Prohibition, is also reportedly the oldest in the country. Regular performers have weekly slots during the week. Arrive early to snag a seat in the velvet booths. Performers over the years have included Branford Marsalis and Patricia Barber, and you just might hear one of tomorrow's legends if you stop in.

Jazz Showcase

806 South Plymouth Court,

Basic but very friendly blues bar with a wide range of performers, from acoustic to avant-garde.

Underground Wonder Bar
10 East Walton Street, North Side; tel: 312-266-7459; www.undergroundwonder bar.com; daily noon–4am, Sat until 5am; el: Red line to Chicago; bus: 29; map p.132 C3
Live music every night of the year – mostly improvised blues and jazz, with some reggae, folk, and rock thrown in for good measure.

Velvet Lounge
67 East Cermak Road, South Loop; tel: 312-791-9050; www.velvetlounge.net; Mon 7.30pm–2am, Tue–Sun 8pm–2am; el: Red line to Cermak/Chinatown; bus: 3, 4, 21; map p.137 C2
Mostly experimental jazz is offered at this classic-style club, where there's a good view of the stage from almost every vantage point.

Classical

COMPANIES
Apollo Chorus
225 West Washington Street #2200, Loop; tel: 312-427-5620; www.apollochorus.org; el: Orange, Purple, Brown, Pink line to Library; train: Metra to Van Buren; bus: 3; map p.134 B2
Founded in 1872 to lift the

2120 South Michigan is the site of the office of **Chess Records**, the influential label known for recording blues artists including Howlin' Wolf, Aretha Franklin, and Chuck Berry. Later, blues-influenced bands the Rolling Stones and the Yardbirds made a point of recording here. It's now the offices of the Blues Heaven Foundation, which sponsors occasional free concerts and promotes the continuation of the blues in Chicago.

---

city's spirit after the Great Chicago Fire, the group is made up of 150 men and women, who sing classical choral masterpieces, including a very popular Handel's *Messiah* at Christmastime.

Ars Antigua
Various locations; tel: 510-495-6721; www.arsantigua presents.com
Chamber ensemble specializing in Baroque music.

Chicago Chamber Musicians
Various locations; tel: 312-819-5800; www.chicagochamber music.org
15-member group that also features a brass quintet and a string quartet.

Chicago Opera Theater
Harris Theater, 205 East Randolph, Loop; tel: 312-704-8420; www.chicagooperatheater.org; el: Brown, Purple, Green, Pink, Orange line to Randolph/Wabash; map p.135 D1
The group, which puts on operas from the 17th through the 20th centuries, offers performances in more intimate settings than is traditional.

Chicago Philharmonic
Northwestern University, Pick-Staiger Concert Hall: 50 Art Circle Drive, Evanston; tel: 847-866-6888; www.chicago philharmonic.homestead.com; el: Purple line to Foster
Features many members of the Chicago Symphony Orchestra moonlighting during its off-season.

Chicago Sinfonietta
Various locations; tel: 312-236-3681; www.chicago sinfonietta.org
The Sinfonietta performs music in the classical, contemporary, and Romantic genres, including new works by emerging composers.

Chicago Symphony Orchestra
Symphony Center, 220 South Michigan Avenue, Loop; tel: 312-

294-3000; www.cso.org; el: Orange, Purple, Brown, Pink, Green line to Adams/Wabash; bus: 3; map p.135 C2
One of the finest classical orchestras in the country. Past musical directors have included Sir Georg Solti and Daniel Barenboim, as well as distinguished guests such as Aaron Copland, John Williams, and André Previn.

Grant Park Orchestra and Chorus
Millennium Park, 55 North Michigan Avenue, Loop; tel: 312-742-7638; www.grantparkmusic festival.com; map p.135 C2
Performs as part of the Grant Park Music Festival, the only free outdoor classical music series in the US. Concerts take place in the landmark **Jay Pritzker Pavilion** in Millennium Park, except for the city's Independence Day celebration, when the group heads back to its original home in Grant Park.

Light Opera Works
Northwestern University, Cahn Auditorium, 600 Emerson Street, Evanston; tel: 847-869-6300; www.light-opera-works.org

Classic American musicals and European operettas in suburban Evanston.

Lyric Opera of Chicago
20 North Wacker Drive, Loop; tel: 312-332-2244; www.lyric opera.org; el: Brown, Orange, Pink, Purple line to Washington/Wells; train: Metra to Union Station; map p.134 B2
Internationally known opera company offering top-notch productions of classic operas with major names. Tickets can be tough to score and are pricey, but it's worth the effort. Performances take place in the splendid Civic Opera House (see Venues, right). English subtitles are provided.

Music in the Loft
1017 West Washington Boulevard, West Side; tel: 312-243-9233; www.musicintheloft.org; bus: 8; train: Metra to Ogilvie Transportation Center Station; map p.134 A2
Younger musicians feature as part of this chamber music series, including students and promising young stars.

Music of the Baroque
Harris Theater, 205 East Randolph, Loop; tel: 312-551-1414;

www.baroque.org; el: Brown, Purple, Green, Pink, Orange line to Randolph/Wabash; map p.135 D1
Chorus and orchestra specializing in 18th-century masterpieces by composers including Handel and Bach. Members hail from the Chicago Symphony Orchestra and the Lyric Opera.

Rembrandt Chamber Players
Merit School of Music, 38 South Peoria Street, West Side; tel: 773-929-7277; www.rembrandt chamberplayers.org; bus: 8; map p.134 A2
The name of this seven-member group (including players from the CSO and the Lyric) is a bit misleading, as performances include not just Baroque music but new compositions, including specially commissioned works.

VENUES
Civic Opera House
20 North Wacker Drive, Loop; tel: 312-419-0033; www.civicopera house.com; el: Brown, Orange, Pink, Purple line to Washington/Wells; train: Metra to Union Station; map p.134 B2
The 1929 building with a splendid Art Nouveau/Art Deco interior is the home of the Lyric Opera, but it also hosts other classical groups as well as the occasional pop performance.

Joan W. and Irving B. Harris Theater Music and Dance
Harris Theater, 205 East Randolph, Loop; tel: 312-551-1414; www.baroque.org; el: Brown, Purple, Green, Pink, Orange line to Randolph/Wabash; map p.135 D1
A diverse group of small and medium-sized musical and

Left: an orchestra plays at the Jay Pritzker Pavilion in Grant Park.

> If you've no time or inclination for a full-on classical concert, the **Grant Park Orchestra and Chorus** rehearses in Millennium Park during the day in summer. Seats and docent talks are offered, but it's also pleasant just to watch from the side. A schedule is offered at the orchestra's website *(see listing, left)*.

dance companies call this space home, and the theater also hosts traveling ensembles. Opened in 2003, it was the first new performance space built downtown since 1929. The stage, set in a cube, the stainless steel accents, and muted color palette offer a contemporary viewing experience to complement the city's many traditional concert halls.

Symphony Center
220 South Michigan Avenue, Loop; tel: 312-294-3000; www.cso.org; el: Orange, Purple, Brown, Pink, Green line to Adams/Wabash; bus: 3; map p.135 C2
Designed by Daniel Burnham in a pastiche of styles, including Beaux Arts and Georgian, this lovely concert hall is the jewel of the classical music community, even more so since a major overhaul in 1997 improved sightlines and acoustics. The soaring Orchestra Hall is an appropriately grand home for the CSO, while a new pedestrian arcade and a stunning atrium with a winding staircase combine opulence and warmth.

Contemporary

Chicago's rock and pop scene, which produced big acts like Liz Phair and the Smashing Pumpkins in the 1990s, is still going strong. There are also big audiences for alternative country, world music, hip-hop, and any number of ethnic genres.

VENUES

Abbey Pub

3420 West Grace Street, Avondale; tel: 773-478-4408; www.abbeypub.com; check website for shows; bus: 80, 82

It's a bit out of the way, but a lack of attitude and a roomy main room and balcony make this a comfortable venue for pop and Celtic-tinged gigs.

Aragon Ballroom

1106 West Lawrence Avenue, Uptown; tel: 773-561-9500; www.aragon.com; check website for shows; el: Red line to Lawrence; bus: 36

One of the lovelier concert halls, the Aragon was built in 1926 with an interior meant to resemble a Spanish courtyard. Appropriately, today it hosts many Spanish-language concerts as well as rock bands.

Beat Kitchen

2100 West Belmont Avenue, Lakeview; tel: 773-281-4444; www.beatkitchen.com; Sun 11.30am–2am, Mon–Fri 4pm–2am, Sat 11.30am–3am; bus: 50, 77

Acts here range from high-profile to no profile, but they've all got that underground feel.

Double Door

1572 North Milwaukee Avenue,

Below: Schubas Tavern is a good bet for rock gigs.

Wicker Park; tel: 773-489-3160; www.doubledoor.com; Tue–Fri 8pm–2am, Sat 8pm–3am; el: Blue line to Damen; bus: 50, 56, 72

Local and touring bands with a slightly mainstream vibe play here (the Rolling Stones once even stopped by for a surprise gig). A lounge area downstairs with videogames and a pool table provides respite from the often crowded main floor.

Elbo Room

2871 North Lincoln Avenue, Lincoln Park; tel: 773-549-5549; www.elboroomchicago.com; daily 7pm–2am, Sat until 3am; el: Purple, Brown line to Diversey; bus: 11, 76

The music action – soul, rock, reggae, punk, and more – happens downstairs, especially right in front of the band, where there's a lot of dancing. There's seating available around the room for more mellow patrons.

Empty Bottle

1035 North Western Avenue, West Side; tel: 773-276-3600; www.emptybottle.com; Mon–Wed 5pm–2am, Thur–Fri 3pm–2am, Sat noon–3am, Sun noon–2am; bus: 49, 70

Consistently reliable rock club known for booking underground bands with buzz. The scruffy surroundings only add to its indie credibility.

FitzGerald's

6615 Roosevelt Road, Berwyn; tel: 708-788-2118; www. fitzgeraldsnightclub.com; Sun 5pm–2am, Tue–Sat 7pm–2am; el: Blue line to Oak Park

City dwellers trek out to the suburbs for zydeco, folk, country, and other roots music at this old-style roadhouse. The polite audiences tend to be a bit older but are no less enthusiastic for that.

Hideout

1354 West Wabansia Avenue, Wicker Park; tel: 773-227-4433; www.hideoutchicago.com; Tue

7pm–2am, Wed–Fri 4pm–2am, Sat 7pm–3am, Sun–Mon check listings for shows; bus: 72; train: Metra to Clybourn

Located on a side street in an industrial area, the reason for this country-tinged rock club's name quickly becomes apparent. With its divey, recroom charm and cheap booze, it's a popular oasis for local musicians and fans alike.

House of Blues

329 North Dearborn Street, North Side; tel: 312-923-2000; www.hob.com; Mon–Fri 11am–2am, Sat 4pm–12.30am, Sun 4pm–midnight; el: Brown, Purple line to Merchandise Mart, Blue line to Clark/Lake; map p.134 C1

Admittedly the House of Blues is part of a chain, but it's still fun to take in a concert at this venue, which attracts national acts as well as Chicago bands of all genres, tucked between the towers of Marina City.

Martyrs'

3855 North Lincoln Avenue, Roscoe Village; tel: 773-404-9494; www.martyrslive.com; Mon–Fri 6pm–midnight, Sat 6pm–1am; el: Brown line to Irving Park; bus: 11

Located a bit outside the 'hip' neighborhoods, Martyrs', which feels more like a friendly watering hole than a club, tends to cater to more seasoned music fans.

Metro

3730 North Clark Street, Lakeview; tel: 773-549-0203; www.metrochicago.com; check website for shows; el: Red line to Addison; bus: 22

This mid-sized concert hall has roots in the local indie rock and pop music community dating to the early 1980s. It's still a popular venue at which to see emerging artists on their way to the big time.

Old Town School of Folk Music

4544 North Lincoln Avenue,

Ravenswood; tel: 773-728-6000; www.oldtownschool.org; check website for shows; el: Brown line to Western; bus: 11
It's not just folk songs and acoustic guitars here. The calendar might feature an evening of contemporary Filipino music, a Zimbabwean drummer, or Middle Eastern song and dance.

Riviera Theatre
4746 North Broadway Avenue, Uptown; tel: 773-275-6800; check local listings for shows; el: Red line to Lawrence; bus: 36
One of the nicest mid-sized venues in town, with a beautiful ceiling and cool round windows. But that doesn't deter mosh pits from forming in the audience.

Schubas Tavern
3159 North Southport Avenue, Lakeview; tel: 773-525-2508; www.schubas.com; Mon–Fri noon–2am, Sat 10am–3am, Sun 10am–2am; el: Red, Brown line to Southport; bus: 77
The smallish back room, with its wood paneling and stuffed deer head, could be a lodge, except when it's packed with sweaty people grooving to the tunes emanating from the stage. The standing and style of the acts here vary enormously, but it's always a good bet for pop and rock.

Subterranean
2011 West North Avenue, Wicker Park; tel: 773-278-6799;

Above: classic vinyl at Reckless Records.

www.subt.net; daily 7pm–midnight; el: Blue line to Damen; bus: 72, 50, 56
Hip-hop, indie rock, reggae, and more all find common ground here. Music happens on the second floor; if you can't see the band, head to the wraparound balcony.

Record Stores

Dave's Records
2604 North Clark Street; tel: 773-929-6325; www.daves recordschicago.com; Mon–Thur, Sat–Sun 11am–8pm, Fri noon–7pm; bus: 36, 22; map p.133 D1
Dave's stocks vinyl only – and lots of it.

Dr Wax
5225 South Harper Avenue #D; tel: 773-493-8696; www.drwax.com; Mon–Sat 11am–8pm, Sun noon–6pm; bus: 6; train: Metra to 53rd Street Hyde Park; map p.139 D2
Great selection of local records, geared specifically to the neighborhood in each location. Also at: 2523 North Clark Street; tel: 773-549-3377; Mon–Sat 11am–7pm, Sun 11am–6pm; bus: 22, 36; map p.133 D1

Dusty Groove
1120 North Ashland Avenue; tel: 773-342-5800; www.dusty

groove.com; daily 10am–8pm; el: Blue line to Division; bus: 9, 70
DJs love browsing here for hard-to-find funk, hip-hop, and jazz records.

Jazz Record Mart
27 East Illinois Street; tel: 312-222-1467; www.jazzmart.com; Mon–Sat 10am–8pm, Sun noon–7pm; el: Orange, Brown, Purple, Green, Pink line to State/Lake; map p.132 C4
Run by a founder of Delmark Records, one of the most respected names in blues and jazz, this cavernous store has everything: used, new, rare, obscure, mainstream, in forms from the 45 to CDs.

Reckless Records
3161 North Broadway; tel: 773-404-5080; www.reckless.com; daily 10am–10pm, Sun until 8pm; el: Red, Brown line to Belmont; bus: 36, 77
The place for indie music, although you can find any genre here. Listening stations offer employees' picks, and the vinyl offerings are in good shape at good prices. Also at: 1532 North Milwaukee Avenue; tel: 773-235-3727; daily 10am–10pm, Sun until 8pm; el: Blue line to Damen; bus: 56, 50

Every week two major music columnists – Greg Kot of the *Chicago Tribune* and Jim DeRogatis of the *Chicago Sun-Times* – offer amusing, informed, and occasionally infuriating thoughts on popular music and other related topics on their radio show, *Sound Opinions*. It airs locally on Chicago Public Radio, 91.5, and is also available via podcast on their website, http://soundopinions.org.

Nightlife

The club scene in Chicago is concentrated around the River North area, where on weekends the traffic is bumper-to-bumper and establishments writhe with crowds, while there is also a newer scene in the gritty Fulton Market neighborhood. For a slightly less frenetic environment, head out early in the week or try one of the city's many cool lounges, which offer a clubby atmosphere minus the aggressive meat market. For places just to grab a drink, see *Bars, p.34–7*, or for further dance- and music-oriented evening activities, see *Gay and Lesbian, p.60–61*, and *Music, p.86–91*.

Dance Clubs

Angels & Kings
710 North Clark Street, North Side; tel: 312-482-8600; www.angelsandkings chicago.com; Wed–Mon 8pm–2am, Sat until 3am; el: Red, Brown line to Chicago; bus: 66, 22; map p.132 B3

Angels & Kings brings a much-needed rock mentality to the glitzy River North club scene. The celebrity aura (it's co-owned by Pete Wentz of the band Fall Out Boy) is counterbalanced by the industrial-clubhouse look.

Crobar
1543 North Kingsbury Street, Old Town; tel: 312-266-1900; www.crobar.com; Wed, Fri 10pm–4am, Sat 10pm–5am; el: Red line to North/Clybourn

If you're looking for sweaty dance-floor hedonism, you'll find it at Crobar. The South

> House music is reported to have evolved in Chicago thanks largely to Frankie Knuckles, a DJ who worked at the now defunct club Warehouse in the late 70s and early 80s, mixing disco with other styles of music.

Above: ready to party at Crobar.

Beach-esque interior behooves patrons to dress their best, even though some people end up taking it off.

Funky Buddha Lounge
728 West Grand Avenue, West Side; tel: 312-666-1695; www.funkybuddha.com; Wed–Fri 9pm–2am, Sat 9pm–3am, Sun 9pm–midnight; el: Blue line to Grand; bus: 8, 65; map p.132 A4

Anything goes at this almost New Agey dance and DJ club, which draws a mixed clientele and offers a similarly varied range of music, from reggae to house. Cocktails are mixed with organic juices.

Le Passage and The Drawing Room
937 North Rush Street, Gold

Coast; tel: 312-266-2694; www.lepassage.com; Drawing Room: Wed–Sun 6pm–4am, Sat 6pm–5am; Le Passage: Thur–Sun 9pm–4am, Sat 6pm–5am; el: Red line to Chicago; bus: 22, 66; map p.132 C3

Down a cobblestone alley in the swanky Rush Street area, Le Passage offers lots of loungey seating on which to see and be seen. The small dance floor is usually swarming with beautiful people gyrating to hip-hop and R&B.

Liar's Club
1665 West Fullerton Avenue, Lincoln Park; tel: 773-665-1110; daily 8pm–2am, Sat until 3am; bus: 9, 74

This offbeat bar with a disco lounge (complete with mirror ball) is a dying breed in Chicago: a comfortable place to dance without getting gouged at the bar. Music is heavy on danceable tunes from the 70s through the 90s.

Neo
2350 North Clark Street, Lincoln Park; tel: 773-528-2622; www.neo-chicago.com; daily 10pm–4am, Sat until 5am; bus: 74, 22; map p.133 D1

Black-painted club brings out

Left: hitting the decks at SmartBar.

beats as well as deep house. The 10,000 sq ft (930 sq m) of space includes a warehouse-like upper level with fog machines and multimedia.

Lounges

Lumen
839 West Fulton Street Market, West Side; tel: 312-733-2222; www.lumen-chicago.com; Tue–Fri 8pm–2am, Sat 8pm–3am; bus: 8; map p.134 A1
Determinedly chic but surprisingly unpretentious lounge, with low seating, an open floor plan, and easy-to-mingle vibe.

Sonotheque
1444 West Chicago Avenue, West Side; tel: 312-226-7600; www.sonotheque.net; daily 7pm–2am, Sat until 3am; bus: 66
Glam space with a minimalist edge draws an alternative crowd and high-profile DJs, who spin inside a glass booth.

Stone Lotus
873 North Orleans Street, North Side; tel: 312-440-9680; www.stonelotuslounge.com; Tue–Fri 8pm–2am, Sat 8pm–3am; el: Red line to Grand; map p.132 B3
Clubbing is mixed with a Zen-like interior at this high-end 'liquor spa,' where only the best libations are consumed. The DJs are known for their creative mash-ups.

The el runs all night and many buses do too, although you may be waiting a while. Some clubs are located in desolate areas, so a cab may be your best bet if you plan to dance the night away. *See Transportation, p.125.*

---

the black-garbed Goth/industrial crowd. Thursday nights are devoted to 80s club classics, a great night for spotting Robert Smith lookalikes.

Rednofive
440 North Halsted Street, West Side; tel: 312-421-1239; www.rednofive.com; Thur–Sun 10pm–4am, Sat until 5am; el: Blue line to Grand; bus: 56; map p.132 A4
Set in the hipper-than-hip Fulton Market area, this opulent spot is where everyone ends up when they're not ready to go home. An optimum choice for the wee hours.

SmartBar
3730 North Clark Street, Lakeview; tel: 773-549-0203; www.smartbarchicago.com; Wed–Sun 10pm–4am, Sat until 5am; el: Red line to Addison; bus: 22
Located just below the Metro *(see p.90)*, this long-time club has a roster of house DJs, but

you might see musicians who just played upstairs manning the turntable for a set. Dancing is a must, and the flavor of the crowd varies according to the theme night (punk, funk, industrial) or who's headlining at the Metro. It's also one of the most accessible clubs in the city (no snobby doormen).

Sound-bar
226 West Ontario Street, North Side; tel: 312-787-4480; www.sound-bar.com; Fri 9pm–4am, Sat 9pm–5am; el: Brown line to Chicago; bus: 156; map p.132 B3
The massive (20,000-sq-ft/1,850-sq-m) club offers the seminal dance and DJ experience, with nine bars and two dance areas, each with its own look and feel. The main dance floor features multimedia effects such as lasers and holographic images, while the lounge areas are more relaxed.

Zentra
923 West Weed Street, Old Town; tel: 312-787-0400; www.zentranightclub.com; Fri–Sun 9pm–4am; el: Red line to North; bus: 72
Flashy club with a global edge: you can dance to Hindi

Weary club-goers like to stop at the Diner Grill (1635 West Irving Park; tel: 773-248-2030), an old-fashioned greasy spoon right out of an Edward Hopper painting that's surprisingly good. Another popular destination for late-night grub is casual Mexican at La Pasadita, consistently voted as offering some of the best, most authentic tacos in the city. (1132, 1140, and 1141 North Ashland; tel: 773-384-6537, 773-278-0384).

93

Pampering

There's a lot to see in Chicago, but at some point a bit of relaxation and cosseting is appreciated. Choose from haven-like spas with an Eastern twist, ladylike sanctuaries, and communal bathhouses. Keep in mind that tipping technicians and massage therapists 15–20 percent of the cost of the service is customary. Meanwhile, cosmetics and bodycare junkies should head to the shopping mecca around Armitage Avenue and Halsted Street in Lincoln Park, where major cosmetics, bath, and skincare brands Lush, Benefit, Fresh, and L'Occitane all have storefronts brimming with beauty treats.

Bathhouses

Division Street Russian and Turkish Baths
1916 West Division Street, West Side; tel: 773-384-9671; call for current hours; el: Blue line to Division; bus: 70

The only remaining Russian bathhouse in the city, it has been serving the neighborhood for over 100 years. The highlight for many is the banya, a room in which extremely dry steam is produced by throwing water on heated granite boulders. The women's side has been closed

Below: a haven for men's pampering at Halo.

for years, but usually one night a week is reserved for ladies.

Paradise Sauna
2912 West Montrose Avenue, Lakeview; tel: 773-588-3304; Mon–Sat 7am–10pm, Sun 7am–9pm; el: Brown line to Francisco

This no-frills communal bathhouse is low on glamour, but it's clean and spacious, and while the largely Korean staff may not speak English perfectly, they're very welcoming. There are separate men's and women's facilities with showers, hot and cold pools, whirlpools, a sauna, a steam room, and even a nap area. The clientele is made up of a great mix of ethnicities and backgrounds. Massages and scrubs tend to be very brisk and thorough.

Beauty Stores

Blue Mercury
2208 North Halsted Street, Lincoln Park; tel: 773-327-6900; www.bluemercury.com; Mon–Fri 10am–7pm, Sat–Sun 10am–6pm; el: Red, Purple, Brown line to Fullerton; bus: 8, 74; map p.133 D2

With plenty of hard-to-find skincare lines and high-end

cosmetics from Trish McAvoy, Laura Mercier and Nars, this place is as irresistible as a candy store. Experts are on hand to show you the best way to apply foundation and eyeliner, and facials and waxing are offered as well.

Colorlabs Custom Cosmetics
857 West Armitage Avenue, Lincoln Park; tel: 773-525-9086; www.colorlabcosmetics.com; Mon–Wed 10am–6pm, Thur–Sat 10am–7pm, Sun 11am–6pm; el: bus: 8; map p.133 D2

Customized makeup isn't just for celebrities. Staff here will blend colors to your specifications on the spot for the perfect foundation, blush, or lipstick, or you can bring a discontinued shade. Products can be formulated according to your skin type.

Day Spas

Channing's Day Spa
54 East Oak Street, Gold Coast; tel: 312-280-1994; www.channings.com; el: Red line to Chicago; bus: 29; map p.132 C2

This posh spa takes its cues from the designer boutiques

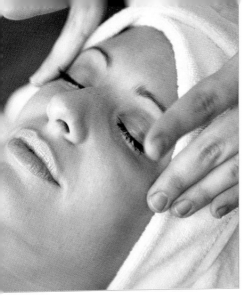

Left: after pounding the city streets, relax at a day spa.

Side; tel: 312-260-9000; www.tiffanikiminstitute.com; Mon–Tue 10am–7pm, Wed–Fri 9am–8pm, Sat 9am–7pm, Sun noon–5pm; el: Brown line to Chicago; bus: 66; map p.132 B3
Nearly all of your relaxation and skincare needs can be met at this three-story facility. Downstairs is the spa area, with burbling fountains and plush waiting rooms. Upstairs one area is devoted to wellness, with practitioners of Chinese medicine offering herbal and alternative remedies.

Urban Oasis
12 West Maple Street #3, Gold Coast; tel: 312-587-3500; www.urbanoasis.biz; Mon noon–8pm, Tue–Thur 10am–8pm, Fri 9am–7pm, Sat 9am–5pm, Sun 11am–5pm; el: Red line to Chicago; map p.132 C2
Soft music, lush greenery, and offers of tea help you forget the noisy, honking city outside. Everything is geared for total relaxation during massages, whether it's traditional Swedish or done with hot stones. Also at: 939 West North Avenue, Old Town; tel: 312-640-0001; el: Red line to North/Clybourn; bus: 72

Manicurists

Sole Nail Lounge and Beauty Emporium
1468 North Milwaukee Avenue, Wicker Park; tel: 773-486-7653; Tue–Fri 11am–8pm, Sat 10am–5pm; el: Blue line to Damen; bus: 50, 56
Mani-pedi joints are a dime a dozen, but not many places offer free cocktails while you have your tips buffed and your calluses smoothed – appropriate given the nightclub-rife neighborhood. Natural makeup, handbags, and cards are for sale upfront.

Several respected massage therapy schools in Chicago offer steeply discounted rates for massages with students. Teachers are on hand to keep an eye on things, but you're not allowed to request therapists with specific training or by gender. Options include the Chicago School of Massage Therapy (18 North Wabash; tel: 312-753-7990) and the New School for Massage, Bodywork, and Healing (800 North Wells; tel: 888-461-0114).

surrounding it. Ladies who lunch visit to be plucked, waxed, and buffed in an environment that's more Victorian home than high-tech facility.

Halo
3324 North Clark Street, Boys Town; tel: 773-348-6210; www.halochicago.com; Mon–Thur noon–9pm, Fri 10am–7pm, Sat 9am–6pm, Sun 11am–5pm; el: Red, Brown line to Belmont or Addison; bus: 22
Even men want to be pampered once in a while. This spa and salon offers treatments and grooming for men in a reassuringly masculine

environment. Along with the usual massage and skincare options are specials like 'the Crackberry,' a forearm massage for aches brought on by too much texting, and a five-minute back-scratching session for $10. Also at: 21 West Elm Street, Gold Coast; tel: 312-642-4256; el: Red line to Chicago or Clark/Division; map p.132 C2; and 1655 North Damen Avenue, Wicker Park; tel: 773-342-4256; el: Blue line to Damen; bus: 50

Thousand Waves Spa for Women
1212 West Belmont Avenue, Lakeview; tel: 773-549-0700; www.thousandwavesspa.com; Tue noon–5.30pm, Wed–Thur noon–9pm, Fri–Sun 10am–7pm; el: Red, Brown line to Belmont; bus: 77
Show up before your appointment for a massage or detoxifying herbal wrap and you can hang out in the Japanese-inspired redwood sauna, the eucalyptus steam bath, or the hot tub for an hour. Or you can skip the spa appointment altogether and just relax in the baths for a nominal fee.

Tiffani Kim Institute
310 West Superior Street, North

Parks and Beaches

Visitors to Chicago are often stunned by the miles of lakeshore and the ease of access to it. The city's 33 beaches range in character from busy centers for sport and socializing to quiet havens perfect for sun-worshipers craving solitude. The adjoining parks offer gorgeous landscaping and gardens, and public art, drawing picnickers as well as office workers taking a break for lunch. Unless otherwise noted, public parks are open from 6am to 11pm. For more information about things to do and see in the city's parks, see *Children, p.40–41, Festivals and Events, p.54–5, Music, p.86–91, Public Art, p.100–3,* and *Walks, Tours, and Views, p.126–9.*

The Loop

Grant Park

337 East Randolph Street; tel: 312-742-7648; free; el: Brown, Orange, Green, Pink line to Randolph, Madison, or Adams, Red, Blue lines to Washington, Monroe, Jackson, Harrison, or Roosevelt; map p.135 D2

This sprawling 310-acre (125-hectare) park, which stretches from Randolph Street all the way down to Roosevelt Road, is often referred to as the city's 'front yard.' Residents do use it as such, to the point of inviting the 'neighbors' over for major events such as **Taste of Chicago** and **Chicago Blues Festival**. However, it's a beautiful spot to visit on its own, with traditional landscaping as well as areas devoted to the native flora of the prairie. The glorious Buckingham Memorial Fountain, near Columbus Drive and Congress Parkway, was modeled after one at Versailles, and indeed the feel of this section of the park is very Parisian, with its pebbled allees and old-fashioned con-

cession stands. The fountain's design includes four sea horses that are symbolic of the four states around Lake Michigan: Wisconsin, Illinois, Indiana, and Michigan. There are several smaller parks-within-the-park, such as the charming **Spirit of Music Garden**, tucked into a niche next to Michigan Avenue, and the **Museum Campus**, a relatively new green space sprinkled with paths and public art that connects Grant Park with the **Shedd Aquarium**, the **Field Museum**, and the **Adler Planetarium**.

SEE ALSO FESTIVALS AND EVENTS, P.54, 55; MUSEUMS AND GALLERIES, P.81, 82, 83

Millennium Park

55 North Michigan Avenue; tel: 312-742-1168; free; el: Red, Blue line to Washington; bus: 3, 4, 6, 145, 147, 151; map p.135 C2

True to its name, Millennium Park, a former railyard that is the latest addition to the Chicago park system, has a very modern feel. Frank Gehry's undulating silver bandshell, the **Jay Pritzker Pavilion**, seems to shimmer in the sun, and the massive

Right: summer volleyball on Oak Street Beach.

Left: runners in the Chicago Marathon *(see p.55, 119)* make their way through Millennium Park.

The area around the south end was originally the city's public cemetery. The bodies were moved in the 19th century, but the Crouch family tomb remains, a lonely mausoleum near the **Chicago History Museum**.

Despite the park's gloomy beginnings, this is one of the most delightful open areas in Chicago, landscaped with lagoons and ponds that attract area wildlife. The **Alfred Caldwell Lily Pool**, directly in front of the zoo, features stones and paths designed to replicate the look of a river cutting through glacier-created ravines. On the park's north side is the **Montrose Point Bird Sanctuary**, a resting spot planted with bird-friendly greenery that brings over 300 species of migratory birds.

Nearly every kind of sports can be played here, making it

The city's largest and most popular 'park' may be the practically unbroken 18 miles (29km) of paved lakefront bike and walking paths. They can get quite clogged on summer weekends with fast-moving cyclists as well as meandering groups of walkers, so be sure to obey the rules to avoid collisions: cyclists, in-line skaters, and other fast-moving traffic stay in the inner lanes, walkers and slower traffic should stick to the outer lanes. Always look both ways before crossing the path. The path is always busiest from Lakeview to around Navy Pier; it clears up considerably as you go further north and south of downtown. See also Walks, Tours, and Views, p.126.

Great Lawn, over which crisscross a framework of stainless steel bars, provides plenty of space for visitors to plunk down a blanket or two to take in the many free concerts and events here. Aside from the lawn, though, this is definitely more of a walker's park, with its many promenades and a sinuous bridge of wood and brushed stainless steel that crosses Columbus Drive to deposit visitors in Grant Park. Bike rental is available at the **McDonald's Cycle Center**, which also offers free indoor parking for bikes. Maps and information about daily events and food options are available at the Welcome Center on the north end.

Gold Coast
Oak Street Beach
Oak Street at Lake Shore Drive; free, el: Red line to Chicago; bus: 145, 146, 147, 151; map p.133 C2
This is definitely the city's most glamorous beach, what with the proximity to posh Oak Street and the expensive highrises just abutting it. But

among the tanned and toned young bodies are plenty of families and regular folks making the most of the summer. On weekends it gets pretty crowded here with all of the traffic on the bike and walking path along the lakefront, but the beach itself is relatively calm, aside from the shrieks of small children at the water's edge. There are concession stands along the path, while the **Oak Street Beachstro** offers sit-down dining and the opportunity to drink alcohol legally on the beach.
SEE ALSO BARS, P.34

Lincoln Park and Old Town
Lincoln Park
Lake Shore Drive btwn Hollywood/North; tel: 312-742-7726; free; bus: 145, 146, 147, 148, 151, 156; map p.133 E2
By sharing its name with the neighborhood, the location of this 1,200-acre (490-hectare) green space causes some confusion: it actually goes as far north as Hollywood Avenue and ends at North Avenue to the south, making it the city's largest public park.

Above: lush flowers and plants at the Lincoln Park Conservatory.

a magnet for sports clubs and anyone with an active lifestyle. Facilities include fields for playing soccer, football, and baseball; tennis courts; a canal for rowing; and even a nine-hole public golf course that features the lake as a dramatic backdrop.

Of course, many will visit the park to take advantage of the much-loved, free **Lincoln Park Zoo**, which gets very busy in the summer.
SEE ALSO CHILDREN, P.41; MUSEUMS AND GALLERIES, P.80

Lincoln Park Conservatory
2391 North Stockton Drive; tel: 312-742-7736; www.chicago parkdistrict.com; daily 9am–5pm; free; bus: 145, 146, 147, 148, 151, 156; map p.133 E1
Inside the four Victorian-style green houses are blooms both exotic and familiar. It's always warm inside, even on the coldest days, making this a great place to warm up after a cold day at the zoo.

North Avenue Beach
North Avenue at Lake Shore Drive; tel: 312-742-7529; www.chicagoparkdistrict.com;

daily dawn–dusk; free; bus: 72, 22, 36, 151, 156; map p.133 E2
This is definitely the city's party beach, popular with single men and women for the festive atmosphere (enhanced by live music) and the ogling opportunities provided by some 50 volleyball courts. There's even an outdoor gym for the musclebound to lift weights in the fresh air (or enjoy even more ogling). Umbrella and bike rentals are available at the boat-shaped fieldhouse, which is also where restrooms and showers are located. The open rooftop houses a bar and grill with good views of the bikini-and-bicep scene.

West Side

Garfield Park Conservatory
300 North Central Park Avenue; tel: 312-746-5100; www.garfieldconservatory.org; daily 9am–5pm, Thur until 8pm; free; el: Green line to Central Park
Since a major restoration in the 1990s, the conservatory has been undergoing some-

thing of a renaissance, with residents and visitors alike rediscovering this forgotten jewel. The glass-and-steel structure, designed by renowned landscape artist Jens Jensen, is meant to resemble a simple haystack. In the interior, Jensen added signature touches like stonework and waterfalls to simulate a natural environment. Rooms are devoted to aroids, desert plants, and palms, while a children's garden lets kids touch and smell the plants. Small ones and

Drinking alcohol is illegal in Chicago's parks, which may put a dent in your plans for a romantic picnic. However, people do bring drinks to free outdoor concerts in Millennium Park and are generally not bothered as long as it's done discreetly (although you do so at your own risk). For events such as the **Chicago Blues Festival** and **Taste of Chicago**, alcohol can be purchased from official vendors.

anyone with a sweet tooth will want to check out the Sweet House, filled with sugar cane, fig and mango trees, and cocoa plants. Save time for the outdoor garden, which was inspired by that of Impressionist painter Claude Monet at his home in Giverny, France.

South Loop

Northerly Island
1400 South Lynn White Drive; tel: 312-745-2910; www.chicagoparkdistrict.com; free; bus: 12, 146; map p.135 E4
Formerly the site of Meigs Field, a small airport for light civilian aircraft, the reinvention of the area as Northerly Island was in line with the original plan of city planner Daniel Burnham, who envisioned a series of manmade islands along the lakeshore. Connected by a causeway to Burnham Park, the island is crisscrossed with paths and covered in wild prairie grasses and plants. The quiet and the spectacular, unimpeded views of lake and skyline make it a truly unique haven in the city.

South Side

Jackson Park
6401 South Stony Island Avenue; tel: 773-363-6971; www.chicagoparkdistrict.com; Mon–Fri 9am–10pm, Sat–Sun 9.30am–5.30pm; free; el: Green line to East 63rd Street; map p.139 E4
The highlight of the park is the Wooded Island, reached via footbridge over a lagoon. The island's Osaka Garden, a remnant of the 1893 World's Columbian Exposition, is regularly lauded as one of the city's most beautiful and little-known oases of beauty and solitude. Stone walkways, a wooden bridge, and Japanese lanterns make the

city – indeed the Western world – seem very far away.
On the park's southern end is the **South Shore Cultural Center**, designed in Mediterranean Revival style in 1916 by the architects of the Drake Hotel *(see Hotels, p.66)* for use as a country club. Peek inside to take a look at the ornate interior.

Promontory Point
5491 South Lake Shore Drive; tel: 312-742-4847; www.chicagoparkdistrict.com; daily 7am–9pm; free; el: Green line to Garfield; bus: 26; map p.139 E2
The Point, as it's often called, is a manmade peninsula with a striking limestone four-step revetment with great views of the downtown skyline and the nearby **Museum of Science and Industry**. Consequently you're more than likely to be the spectator to a wedding on any given spring or summer weekend. It's also a popular place for swimming, which is technically not allowed. The park itself features a number of lovely landscaping touches, including limestone 'council rings' for casual seating, as well as a water fountain topped with a bronze sculpture of a curled-up fawn with drinking fountains at different heights for humans, horses, and dogs.
SEE ALSO MUSEUMS AND GALLERIES, P.84

Around Chicago
Chicago Botanic Garden
1000 Lake Cook Road, Glencoe; tel: 847-835-5440; www.chicagobotanic.org; 8am–sunset; free; Metra: Union Pacific North Line to Glencoe free trolley from station to garden Apr 19–June 1 Sat–Sun 9.30am–5.30pm, June 1–Sept 1 Sat–Sun 9.30am–9.30pm, Mon, Tue, Thur 5–9pm) or Braeside

With 23 formal gardens and three native habitats spread over 385 acres (156 hectares), the Chicago Botanic Garden offers a comprehensive view of plants, flowers, and landscaping traditions. A sensory garden features raised beds to enhance the fragrace of the flowers and flora, while an English walled garden is made up of six secluded 'rooms.' The Evening Garden takes its cues from the sustainable, natural gardening style of today, with low-maintenance grasses and perennials. A 15-acre (6-hectare) prairie explores six different ecosystems typical of the landscape. A 1-mile (1.6km) section of the Skokie River winds though the garden, highlighting the natural beauty of the area, which is surrounded by forest preserves. Special activities such as musical performances, story-telling, and kite-making keep the little ones entertained. For anyone not up for trekking around or a quick overview, there's a 35-minute tram ride that hits the highlights.

Below: Lincoln Park is popular for dog-walking.

Public Art

First-time visitors to Chicago, rightfully expecting to see great architecture, may be surprised at the amount of mosaics, murals, and sculptures placed in public parks and plazas. They include not just the expected monuments to historical personages and events, but striking contemporary sculptures and politically charged murals. Major pieces are listed here, but for a comprehensive list of pieces with history and photos, the City of Chicago offers a free downloadable document on its website, www.cityof chicago.org, called 'Chicago Public Art Guide'; then just keep your eyes peeled as you stroll about.

The Loop

Cloud Gate, by Anish Kapoor (2004)

Millennium Park, SBC Plaza, Michigan Avenue btwn Madison/Monroe; el: Blue, Red line to Monroe, or Brown, Green, Orange, Pink line to Madison; map p.135 C2

Kapoor's curving, mirrorlike *Cloud Gate* sculpture (known colloquially as 'The Bean') has become the newest symbol of the city. Sun, sky, skyline, lake, and visitors are reflected in funhouse form on the shining surface, made from 168 plates of stainless steel. The 'gate' is formed by the arch beneath the 66ft (20m) -long piece, which measures 33ft (10m) high.

The bronze lions guarding the entrance of the Art Institute (see p.76) have done so for over 110 years. The playful regard with which they are held here is evident during the holiday season, when they wear wreaths, and during sports championships, when they've donned Bears helmets and White Sox caps.

Crown Fountain, by Jaume Plensa (2004)

Millennium Park, Michigan Avenue btwn Madison/Monroe; el: Blue, Red lines to Monroe, or Brown, Green, Orange, Pink line to Madison; map p.135 C2

Water cascades over two glass-block towers, which project a changing series of Chicagoans' faces. This irreverent, interactive fountain is a big hit with kids, especially when water spews from the faces' puckered lips onto the black granite reflecting pool below – a 21st-century twist on water-spouting gargoyles in more traditional fountains.

Defense, Regeneration, The Pioneers, and The Discoverers, by James Earle Fraser and Henry Hering (1928)

Michigan Avenue Bridge, Michigan Avenue and the Chicago River; bus: 2, 3, 143–8, 151, 157; map p.135 C1

Four relief panels on the bridge houses of the Michigan Avenue Bridge tell of incidents from the city's early days in classical style, from the earliest explorers and city fathers to the devastation and renewal caused by the Great Chicago Fire.

Flamingo, by Alexander Calder (1973)

Federal Plaza, Dearborn and Adams Streets; el: Red, Blue lines to Monroe or Jackson, Brown, Pink, Green, Orange line to Adams; map p.134 C2

You probably wouldn't know to look at it, but Calder's curving red abstract sculpture shares some design principles with the glass-and-steel Mies van der Rohe-designed buildings around it. If nothing else, the regularity of the backdrop provides a striking contrast.

The Four Seasons, by Marc Chagall (1974)

Bank One Plaza, Dearborn and Monroe Streets; el: Red, Blue line to Monroe; map p.134 C2

Chagall's 70ft (20m) -long, four-sided glass-and-stone mosaic is a whimsical, colorful piece showing people, fish, and birds frolicking above the city's skyline. After the piece was installed as a gift from the artist, he modified the design to reflect changes in the cityscape.

Left: *Cloud Gate*, or 'The Bean', in Millennium Park.

James R. Thompson Center Plaza, 100 West Randolph Street; el: Red, Blue line to Lake or Washington, Brown, Green, Orange line to Randolph/Wabash; map p.134 C1

The kinetic influences of graffiti and street culture are evident in this abstract fiberglass sculpture. The shapes here bring to mind giant pieces of a jigsaw puzzle leaning against each other.

Untitled, by Picasso (1967)

Daley Plaza, 50 West Washington; el: Red, Blue line to Lake or Washington, Brown, Green, Orange line to Randolph/Wabash; map p.134 C1

Picasso's Cubist contribution to Chicago caused comments and confusion when it was unveiled: was it a lion, a mythical creature, or the artist's Afghan hound? Everyone has their own answer to that question, and the piece has become one of the city's most recognizable and cherished icons.

***Miró's Chicago*, by Joan Miró (1981)**

Cook County Administration Building, 69 West Washington Street; el: Red, Blue line to Lake or Washington, Brown, Green, Orange line to Randolph/Wabash; map p.134 C1

The playful sculpture by the well-known Catalan artist, working in his signature Surrealist manner, resembling a woman with a fork rising from her head. It's meant to symbolize the earth and the heavens: the rounded base suggests the Earth-Mother, while the fork's tines stand in for rays of light. With stub-like 'arms' reaching from its middle, it seems to be ready for an embrace.

***Monument with Standing Beast*, by Jean Dubuffet (1984)**

Below: Marc Chagall's *The Four Seasons (left)* and Untitled, by Picasso *(right)*.

The elegant Art Nouveau entrance to the Metra South Shore train line, located at Michigan Avenue at Van Buren, brings a little bit of Parisian élan to Chicago. It was cast from the original molds designed by Hector Guimard, whose distinctive style based on organic forms can be seen at so many Metro stations in the City of Light, and assembled here by French workers in 2003.

North Side

Riverwalk Gateway, by Ellen Lanyon (2000)
South bank of the Chicago River, 400 East Wacker (at Lake Shore and Wacker Drive); bus: 6, 124; map p.133 D4
Finding this installation is half the fun: it's along a trellised passageway underneath Lake Shore Drive that connects the Riverwalk with the lakefront path. Sixteen panels of painted ceramic

tile murals tell the history of the river, starting with the arrival of the first European explorers in 1673. Twelve decorative panels portray iconic sights around town as well as natural phenomena.

Lincoln Park and Old Town

Abraham Lincoln, by Augustus Saint-Gaudens (1887)
Lincoln Park, Clark Street and North Avenue; bus: 11, 22, 36, 72, 73, 151, 156; map p.133 E3
Among the many statues of historic personages in Lincoln Park, Saint-Gaudens's rendering of a standing Abraham Lincoln, now an official Chicago landmark, is particularly arresting. Lincoln's introspective expression – he is apparently about to give a speech, having risen from a chair – was the result of the artist's glimpse of the president in 1860 and influ-

enced portraits of him for years to come.

West Side

Alto al Desplazamiento Urbano de Pilsen, by José Guerrero, Héctor Duarte, and others (from 1997)
18th Street and Bishop Street; el: Pink Line to 18th Street
This boldly drawn, politically charged painted mural decries the increasing gentrification of the Pilsen area, where rising housing prices may eventually force out the strong Latino community there. The mural shows workers and residents flanked by portraits of labor leader César Chávez and Mexican Revolution hero Emiliano Zapata under the eagle symbol of the United Farm Workers.

Batcolumn, by Claes Oldenburg (1977)
Harold Washington Social Security Administration Building Plaza, 600 West Madison Street; el: Brown, Orange, Pink line to Washington/Wells; map p.134 B2
Swedish artist Oldenburg indulged in his love for playing with scale with this 100ft (30m) -tall latticed steel baseball bat, which also references the city's fascination with skyscrapers and height.

Haymarket Memorial, by Mary Brogger (2004)
Desplaines Street between Randolph and Lake; el: Pink, Green line to Clinton; map p.134 A1
Placed on the site of the Haymarket Affair, an 1886 bombing at a labor rally that led not only to the deaths of several police officers and civilians but the executions of innocent men for the

Left: Joan Miró's Modernist sculpture in the Loop, *Miró's Chicago (see p.101).*

Right: the West Side is peppered with bright murals.

crime, the bronze sculpture is Chicago sculptor Mary Brogger's attempt to incorporate the many points of view of the incident – no easy feat given that feelings among the police and labor activists still run high over 100 years later. The wagon that the speakers stood on is shown in pieces, and the faceless figures around it could be putting it together or destroying it, touching on the conflicts between labor, business, and the police.

Untitled Mosaics
Orozco Academy/Cooper Academy; 1645 West 18th Place; el: Pink line to 18th Street; map p.136 A1
The outside of this elementary school is covered in mosaic portraits of notable Latinos throughout history such as artist Frida Kahlo and muralist Diego Rivera, as well as Aztec symbols and gods. Rendered in Venetian glass tiles, they're the work of an art teacher at the school and his students.

South Loop

Agora, **by Magdalena Abakanowicz (2006)**
Grant Park near Roosevelt Road; el: Red line to Roosevelt; bus: 3, 4, 146; map p.135 D3
On the southern end of Grant Park are 106 9ft (2.7m) -tall headless sculptures made of iron, spaced to encourage people to walk around in them, as in a crowd. Although apparently indistinguishable, Polish artist Abakanowicz created details like the figures' bark-like surface by hand. Viewed from a distance the effect is eerie; up close it feels rather like walking in a forest of strange, immobile creatures.

Man Enters the Cosmos, **by Sir Henry Moore (1980)**
Outside Adler Planetarium, 1300 South Lake Shore Drive; bus: 146, 12; map p.135 E4
The medieval-looking bronze sundial at once evokes the universe as well as the Earth in its spherical shape.

South Side

Fountain of Time, **by Lorado Taft (1922)**
Washington Park, 5531 South Martin Luther King Drive; el: Green line to 55th Street; map p.138 A2
Chicago sculptor Lorado Taft's representation of man's relationship to time shows a hooded Father Time standing across a reflecting pool from a mass of humans engaged in life: kissing, playing, fighting, despairing. There's even a self-portrait of the artist among the figures. Taft was inspired by the opening lines

from Henry Austin Dobson's poem *The Paradox of Time*: 'Time goes, you say? Ah, no. Alas, time stays; we go.' A restoration started in 2002 has greatly improved the appearance and details of the reinforced-concrete structure.

Below: the iconic statue of Abraham Lincoln.

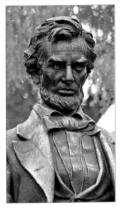

103

Restaurants

Chicago has climbed to the forefront of the international dining scene as one of the best destinations for experimental 'molecular gastronomy' cooking, as well as for its many fine-dining restaurants that offer fusion-oriented menus made from hand-picked local and organic ingredients. For ethnic dining it is a bonanza as well, with inexpensive eateries offering a peek into various regional cuisines. Of course, local specialties deep-dish pizza and hot dogs are still a must-do on most visitors' lists. For more information on the city's gustatory character, see *Food and Drink, p.56–9.*

The Loop

AMERICAN

Atwood Café
1 West Washington Street; tel: 312-368-1900; www.atwood cafe.com; Breakfast: Mon–Fri 7am–10am, Sat 8am–10am, Brunch: Sun 8am–3pm, Lunch: Mon–Sat 11.30am–3.45pm, Dinner: daily 5–10pm, Fri–Sat until 11pm; $$$; el: Red, Blue line to Washington; bus: 3, 145, 147, 151; map 134 C2
The sumptuous surroundings – velvet draperies and chandeliers – belie the relaxed atmosphere and straightfor-

Below: afternoon tea at the Atwood Café.

ward menu, mainly upscale comfort food: pot pie, organic pork chops, and even calamari fried with a graham cracker crust. In summer the sidewalk seating offers an excellent post for people-watching in one of the busiest areas of the Loop, while winter brings afternoon tea service.

Hannah's Bretzel
180 West Washington Street; tel: 312-621-1111; www. hannahsbretzel.com; Mon–Fri 7am–5pm; $; el: Red line to Washington; map p.134 B2
Fresh, organic, and natural ingredients are a mainstay of this casual eatery, of which the centerpiece are the bretzels (bready pretzels), which come in different flavors and can be dabbed with cheese or ham. There are also sandwiches served on whole-wheat baguettes. Also at: 233 North Michigan Avenue; tel: 312-856-1111; el: Brown, Pink, Green, Orange, Purple line to State/Lake; map p.135 C1

Heaven on 7
111 North Wabash Avenue, 7th floor; tel: 312-263-6443; www.heavenonseven.com; Mon–Fri 8.30am–5pm, Sat 10am–3pm; $$; el: Orange, Brown, Green, Purple line to Randolph/Wabash or State/Lake; bus: 20, 29; map p.135 C1
Tucked away on the seventh floor of an office building, this cozy New Orleans-themed restaurant does a busy lunchtime business in Cajun and Creole classics in a room studded with kitschy Mardi Gras souvenirs, including scores of hot sauce bottles. Chef-owner Jimmy Bannos prides himself on offering authentic gumbo, jambalaya, and etouffees. Also at 600 North Michigan Avenue; tel: 312-280-7774; Sun–Thur 11am–10pm, Fri–Sat 11am–11pm, Brunch: Sat–Sun 11am–2pm; el: Red line to Grand; bus: 3, 65, 145, 147, 151; map p.133 C3

EUROPEAN

Everest
440 South LaSalle Street; tel: 312-663-8920; www.everest restaurant.com; Tue–Thur 5.30–9pm, Fri 5.30–9.30pm, Sat 5–10pm; $$$$; el: Red line to Adams; map p.134 C2
Located on the 40th floor of the stock exchange, this fine-dining landmark offers an

Left: a seat with a view at the Signature Room.

Prices for an average three-course meal with a glass of wine, beer, or a cocktail:
$$$$ – over $60
$$$ – $45–$65
$$ – $20–$45
$ – under $20

unusual west-facing view and excellent Alsatian cuisine. Theatergoers can take advantage of a special early-bird dinner menu.

FUSION
Catch 35
35 West Wacker Drive; tel: 312-346-3500; www.catch35.com; Mon–Thur 11.30am–2pm, 5–9.30pm, Fri 11.30am–2pm, Fri–Sat 5–10.30pm, Sun 4–9pm; $$$$; el: Blue line to Clark/Lake; map p.134 C1
Watch business deals in the making at this upscale seafood restaurant, popular with expense-account holders. Freshness is of the utmost importance: there are dozens of specials on offer every day. Dishes are heavily influenced by Asian cuisine, but there are European and American touches on the menu as well.

Rhapsody
65 East Adams Street; tel: 312-786-9911; www.rhapsody chicago.com; Mon–Thur 11.30am–2pm, 5–9pm, Sat 5–10pm; $$$$; el: Blue, Red line to Monroe; map p.135 C2
Located behind Symphony Center (hence the name) and

popular for pre-concert dinners, Rhapsody specializes in innovative takes on classics, such as thyme-roasted Cornish game hen with grilled quince and scallops with leek confit. The pretty glass-walled dining room is rivaled only by the outdoor patio and garden.

North Side
AMERICAN
Billy Goat Tavern
430 North Michigan Avenue; tel: 312-222-1525; www.billygoat tavern.com; Mon–Fri 6am–2am, Sat 10am–3am, Sun 11am–2am; $; el: Red line to Grand; bus: 3, 29, 145, 151; map p.133 C4
This underground bar and

Leaving a tip of 15 to 20 percent (before tax) is not only customary, it's expected, as servers, who generally are paid below minimum wage, rely on them for their income. If service is unacceptable, you may decide to leave a lower amount or nothing at all, but you should let the restaurant's management (or the server directly, if you're brave enough) know the reason.

grill, made famous more than 25 years ago in a skit on the TV comedy show *Saturday Night Live*, is still offering up the cheeseburgers and chips (no fries here). Journalists, who make up a large percentage of the regulars, have been telling tales and drowning their sorrows here for years.

Giordano's Pizza
730 North Rush Street; tel: 312-951-0747; www.giordanos.com; Sun–Thur 11am–11pm, Fri–Sat 11am–midnight; $$; el: Red line to Chicago; map p.132 C3
One of the city's many classic pizzerias with several locations around town, Giordano's specializes in the stuffed version. There's usually a wait for the huge pies, with a long list of toppings, and there are even thin-crust versions available. Sandwiches, salads, and pasta round out the menu.

Pizzeria Uno
29 East Ohio Street; tel: 312-321-1000; www.unos.com; Sun 11am–11pm, Mon–Fri 11am–1am, Sat 11am–2am; $$; el: Red line to Grand; bus: 65; map p.132 C3
It's said that deep-dish pizza was invented here, and in fact this restaurant – along with its sister, Due, around the corner, both housed in old Victorian buildings – has become a cultural landmark. Consequently it's nearly always packed, although still worth the wait.

Signature Room
875 North Michigan Avenue; tel: 312-787-9596; www.signature room.com; Mon–Thur 11am–

105

Above: a mushroom ragout *(left)* at Charlie Trotter's *(see p.108)* and the legendary chef himself *(right)*.

2.30pm, 5–10pm, Fri–Sat 11am–2.30pm, 5–11pm, Sun 10am–2pm, 5–10pm; $$–$$$$; el: Red line to Chicago or Division; bus: 3,147, 151; map p.133 C3

Let's face it: here you're mostly paying for the view, a spectacular one from the 95th floor of the John Hancock Center. The lunchtime buffet is a bargain given the view and there's plenty of kid-friendly fare, while things get more elegant at dinner, with straightforward dishes like steak and lobster tail.

West Egg Café
620 North Fairbanks Court; tel: 312-280-8366; Mon–Fri 6.30am–10pm, Sat–Sun 7am–9pm; $; bus: 3, 157, 66; map p.133 C3

This bustling, casual café has something for everyone, from eggs and pancakes at breakfast to salads, burgers, and chicken for lunch and dinner. Fresh coffee in a carafe is provided at the table.

EUROPEAN
Café Iberico
739 North LaSalle Street; tel: 312-573-1510; www.cafe iberico.com; Mon–Thur 11am–11.30pm, Fri 11am–1.30am, Sat noon–1.30am, Sun noon–11pm; $$; el: Brown line to Chicago; bus: 65; map p.132 B4

The crowds of Spanish nationals are a clue that the tapas here – traditional offerings like *gambas a la plancha* and *tortilla española* – are delicious and authentic. The non-Spanish apparently agree: the aura goes from convivial to plain loud as the night goes on.

Cyrano's Bistrot and Wine Bar
546 North Wells Street; tel: 312-467-0546; www.cyranos bistrot.com; Mon–Thur 11.30am–2.30pm, 5.30–10.30pm, Fri–Sun 4.30–11pm; $$$; el: Brown, Purple line to Merchandise Mart; bus: 65; map p.132 B3

Framed mirrors, French-speaking staff and patrons, and escargots and frog legs on the menu provide the taste and feel of a traditional French bistro. Chef Didier Durand, who has plied his talents at several upscale French restaurants through the years, brings the same precision and skill to this charming and affordable establishment.

Quartino
626 North State Street; tel: 312-698-5000; www.quartinochicago. com; daily 11.30am–2am; $$; el:

Prices for an average three-course meal with a glass of wine, beer, or a cocktail:
$$$$ – over $60
$$$ – $45–$65
$$ – $20–$45
$ – under $20

Red line to Grand; bus: 3, 29, 145, 151; map p.132 C3

Modeled after an Italian wine bar, or *enoteca*, Quartino offers small plates of house-cured salami, Italian cheeses, and hot and cold specialties like veal meatballs and thinly sliced beef carpaccio. For those who don't want to share tapas-style, there are plenty of main dishes, including pasta and pizza. This is also one of the few restaurants that offer good wines by the carafe, half-carafe, and quarter-carafe (or *quartino*).

Spiaggia
980 North Michigan Avenue; tel: 312-280-2750; www.spiaggia restaurant.com; Mon–Thur 6–9.30pm, Fri–Sat 5.30–10.30pm, Sun 6–9pm; $$$$; el: Red line to Chicago or Division; bus: 3, 145, 147, 151; map p.133 C3

The dining room at this formal northern Italian palace in a high-rise offers terrific views of the lake and Oak Street Beach. The grand surroundings don't dwarf the food, which is top-notch. The café next door offers a more casual setting (no jackets required) and slightly lower prices.

FUSION
Tru
676 North Saint Clair Street; tel: 312-202-0001; www.tru restaurant.com; Mon–Thur 5.30–

10pm, Fri–Sat 5–11pm; $$$$; el: Red line to Chicago; bus: 3, 145, 147, 151; map p.133 C3

Tru, a temple of experimental haute cuisine overseen by well-known chef Rick Tramonto, is also famous for its whimsical touches, such as a small Lucite staircase holding tastes of caviar and upholstered 'poufs' that ladies can set their handbags on. Don't skip the desserts, which are just as innovative as the savory options.

Vermilion

10 West Hubbard Street; tel: 312-527-4060; www.the vermilionrestaurant.com; Mon–Fri 11.30am–2.30pm, daily 5–10pm, Fri–Sat until 11pm; $$$; el: Orange, Brown, Purple, Green, Pink line to State/Lake; bus: 29; map p.132 C4

Indian cuisine gets a dusting of Latin flair. Beverage offerings include *aguas frescas* – fruits blended with water – and mango-mint lassies. For lunch there's a three-course prix fixe offering for excellent value.

LATIN AMERICAN
DeLaCosta

465 East Illinois Street; tel: 312-464-1700; www.delacosta chicago.com; Mon–Fri 11.30am–2.30pm, daily 5–10pm, Fri–Sat until 11pm; $$$$; el: Red line to Grand; bus: 65; map p.133 D4

Located just east of Navy Pier, this giant Nuevo Latino restaurant, with a solarium and private 'cabanas', offers a similarly festive ambience, albeit for sophisticated grownups. Seafood, which can also show Caribbean and Asian influences, is a specialty.

Frontera Grill

445 North Clark Street; tel: 312-661-1434; www.frontera kitchens.com; Lunch: Tue–Fri

11.30am–2.30pm, Brunch: Sat 10.30am–2.30pm, Dinner: Tue 5.30–10pm, Wed–Thur 5–10pm, Fri–Sat 5–11pm; $$$; el: Pink, Brown, Green, Blue, Purple, Orange line to Clark/Lake; bus: 65; map p.132 B4

Celebrated chef Rick Bayless highlights the lesser-known specialties of regional Mexican cuisine: tacos filled with skate wing, complex mole sauces, and corn masa croquettes stuffed with goat meat.

Gold Coast

AMERICAN
Gibson's

1028 North Rush Street; tel: 312-266-8999; www.gibsons steakhouse.com; daily 11am–2am; $$$$; el: Red line to Chicago or Clark/Division; bus: 66, 70; map p.132 C2

Classic steakhouse offering old-school fare like filet mignon, lamb chops, and lobster in a glitzy atmosphere. The moneyed, powerful crowd includes local politicians and other city bigwigs.

The Pump Room

1301 North State Parkway; tel: 312-266-0360; www.pumproom. com; Mon–Fri 6.30am–11am, 11.30am–2pm, 5–10pm, Sat 7am–11am, 11.30am–2pm, 5–10pm, Sun 11.30am–2pm, 5–10pm; $$$$; el: Red line to Division; map p.132 C2

Once one of the city's poshest dining establishments, The

In 2006 the Chicago City Council voted to ban the sale of foie gras in restaurants due to concerns about the force-feeding of geese and ducks. Animal rights activists cheered and area foodies were horrified. The law made headlines worldwide and was considered embarrassing for a city that is in the spotlight for its acclaimed restaurants. The ban was overturned two years later.

Pump Room is no longer a must-try destination, except for its historical significance. Celebrities no longer stop by to eat in the famed Booth One, but plenty of tourists still want to feast on French-American dishes in the pretty wood-paneled room with leaded glass windows. Live jazz on the weekends gives the place a neighborhood feel.

Lincoln Park and Old Town

AMERICAN
Half Shell

676 West Diversey; tel: 773-549-1773; www.halfshell chicago.com; Mon–Sat 11.30am–11pm, Sun noon–11.30pm; $$; el: Brown, Purple line to Diversey; bus: 22, 36, 76; map p.133 D1

This long-time bar and grill is generally acknowledged to be a bit of a dive, but the seafood – raw oysters, crab

Right: Gibson's is the star of the Rush Street social scene.

legs, and fried fish – is fresh, and the prices are excellent.

The Wiener's Circle
2622 North Clark Street; tel: 773-477-7444; daily 11am–4am, Fri–Sat until 5am; $; el: Brown, Purple line to Diversey; bus: 22, 36, 76; map p.133 D1
There's no better place to try a traditional Chicago hot dog that this late-night stand. Half the fun is provided by the counter staff, who are famous for their gleeful insults to customers.

EUROPEAN
La Creperie
2845 North Clark Street; tel: 773-528-9050; www.lacreperie usa.com; Tue–Fri 11.30am–11pm, Sat 11am–11pm, Sun 11am–9.30pm; $$; el: Brown, Purple line to Diversey; bus: 22, 36, 76; map p.133 D1
Pleasingly quaint, wood-paneled hideaway with both savory and sweet crepes, filled with anything from chicken curry to Nutella and bananas. The budget-minded prices draw a largely younger crowd.

FUSION
Alinea
1723 North Halsted Street; tel:

312-867-0110; www.alinea-restaurant.com; Wed–Fri 5.30–9.30pm, Sat–Sun 5–9.30pm; $$$$; el: Red line to North/Clybourn; map p.133 D3
Chef and co-owner Grant Achatz is the toast of the town, having brought Chicago international attention for his avant-garde cuisine. Menus of 12 or 24 courses, many of them just one bite, are astonishing for their technical creativity, range of textures, and general tastiness.

Charlie Trotter's
816 West Armitage Avenue; tel: 773-248-6228; www.charlie trotters.com; Tue–Thur 6–9pm, Fri–Sat 5.30–9pm; $$$$; el: Brown line to Armitage; bus: 8; map p.133 D2
Since it opened in 1987, Charlie Trotter's has become a local institution and Chef Trotter a celebrity. The cuisine, based on fresh, healthy ingredients from hand-picked purveyors, draws from a variety of traditions, always with a light touch. The degustation menus include an all-vegetarian one.

North Pond Café
2610 North Cannon Drive; tel: 773-477-5845; www.northpond

restaurant.com; Brunch: Sun 10.30am, Lunch: Tue–Fri 11.30am–1.30pm, Dinner: Wed–Sun from 5.30pm; $$$$; bus: 76, 77; map p.133 E1
Beautifully situated in the heart of the park in a gorgeously restored Arts and Crafts building, North Pond complements its natural setting with seasonal menus focused on organic and sustainably produced foodstuffs, many from area farmers.

Lakeview to Andersonville

AMERICAN
Moody's Pub
5910 North Broadway; tel: 773-275-2696; www.moodys pub.com; daily 11.30am–1am, Sat until 2am; $; el: Red line to Thorndale; bus: 36
This casual eatery, known for its hamburgers, is best in warm weather, when the giant outdoor patio beckons and it becomes a delightful place to kick back for an hour or two with a beer.

Salt & Pepper
3537 North Clark Street; tel: 773-883-9800; Mon–Thur 7am–10pm, Fri–Sat 7am–midnight, Sun 7am–4pm; $; el: Red line to Addison; bus: 22, 36, 152
Retro-style cash-only diner that's great for a quick burger or sandwich and an old-fashioned milkshake, served by agreeably sassy waitresses. Also at: 2575 North Lincoln Avenue; tel: 773-525-8788; Mon–Sat 7am–10pm, Sun 7am–4pm; el: Red, Purple, Brown

Left: elegant, fine dining style at Charlie Trotter's.

Right: you can't miss it:
Mexican eatery Nuevo Leon.

line to Fullerton; bus: 74; map
p.133 D1

EUROPEAN
Hopleaf
5148 North Clark Street; tel:
773-334-9851; www.hop
leaf.com; Bar: daily 3pm–2am,
Sat until 3am, Kitchen: daily 5–
11pm, Fri–Sat until midnight;
$$; el: Red line to Berwyn; bus:
22, 92
The restaurant in the back of
this bar – which specializes in
Belgian-style ales – offers
casual European fare like
mussels cooked in ale and
accompanied by thin-cut
frites and aioli.

LATIN AMERICAN
Tango Sur
3763 North Southport Avenue;
tel: 773-477-5466;
www.tangosur.com;
Mon–Thur 5–10.30pm, Fri–Sat
5–11.30pm, Sun noon–11pm;
$$; el: Brown line to Southport;
bus: 9, 22, 80
Tango Sur does steak the
Argentinian way – big slabs
of beef accompanied by gar-
licky chimichurri sauce and
wedges of potatoes. The fact
that it's BYOB makes it one
of the most affordable steak
restaurants in town.

West Side
AMERICAN
Al's #1 Italian Beef
1079 West Taylor Street; tel: 312-
226-4017; www.alsbeef.com;
Mon–Thur 9am–11pm, Fri 9am–
1am, Sat 10am–1am; $; el: Blue
line to UIC-Halsted; map p.134 A3
Since 1938 Al's has been
serving up the quintessential
Chicago sandwich – beef
topped with peppers and
giardiniera – from this original
location. No tables here, only
counters, and make sure to
get lots of napkins.

Lou Mitchell's
565 West Jackson Boulevard; tel:
312-939-3111; www.loumitchells
restaurant.com; Mon–Sat
5.30am–3pm, Sun 7am–3pm; $;
el: Brown, Orange, Purple, Pink
line to Quincy; map p.134 B2
This is *the* breakfast spot in
Chicago, with lines to match,
especially on weekends. The
classic diner offerings, such
as French toast, omelets, and
club sandwiches, are complemented by baskets of doughnuts and Milk Duds to take
the edge off while you wait.

Nuevo Leon
1515 West 18th Street; tel: 312-
421-1517; www.nuevoleon
restaurant.com; daily 7am–
midnight; $$; el: Pink, Blue line
to 18th; bus: 9
Specialties are from the
northern Mexican state of
Nuevo Leon, known for its
meat-based cuisine. Basics
like *chiles rellenos* and skirt-
steak tacos are done well,
while the more adventurous
can opt for *lengua a la Mexi-
cana* (sautéed tongue) or
menudo (tripe soup). Note
that the restaurant is BYOB.

EAST ASIAN
Sushi Wabi
842 West Randolph Street; tel:
312-563-1224; www.sushi
wabi.com; Lunch: Mon–Fri
11.30am–2pm, Dinner: daily
5–11pm, Wed–Sat until midnight;
$$$; el: Pink, Green line to
Clinton; bus: 8; map p.134 A1
Sushi Wabi offers super-fresh
fish in a loungey atmosphere,
complete with DJ. The menu
includes a make-your-own-
maki section, and you don't

have to choose just one kind
of sake – order a sampler of
three instead.

EUROPEAN
Santorini
800 West Adams Street; tel:
312-829-8820; www.santorini
chicago.com; daily 11am–
midnight, Fri–Sat until 1am;
$$$; el: Blue line to UIC-Halsted;
bus: 8; map p.134 A2
Santorini distinguishes itself
from the many other Greek
restaurants in the area
thanks to its charcoal and
wood grill, which gives
added depth to even rela-
tively simple dishes like
whole fish and lamb chops.

Wicker Park
AMERICAN
Hot Chocolate
1747 North Damen Avenue; tel:
773-489-1747; www.hot
chocolatechicago.com; Brunch:
Sat–Sun 10am–2pm, Lunch:
11.30am–2pm, Dinner: Tue–Sun
5.30–10pm, Thur until 11pm,
Fri–Sat until midnight; $$$; el:
Blue line to Damen; bus: 50, 73
Pastry chef Mindy Segal
brings her expertise to her
restaurant's deliciously sinful
desserts (including several
variations of hot chocolate) as
well as the seasonal, contem-

BYOB stands for Bring Your
Own Bottle (or Beer). Many
restaurants without a liquor
license have permits that allow
diners to bring their own
alcohol (usually with no
corkage fee), although others
are strictly booze-free.

Left: a packed-out Dixie Kitchen and Bait Shop.

porary menu, which highlights American cooking at its best.

EAST ASIAN
Phoenix
2131 South Archer Avenue; tel: 312-328-0848; www.chinatown phoenix.com; Mon–Thur 8am–10pm, Fri–Sat 8am–11pm; $$; el: Red line to Cermak/Chinatown; bus: 21, 24, 62; map p.136 C2
Phoenix is open for dinner, but the big draw here is the dim sum, served daily. Language barriers can make it tough to find out exactly what you're getting at times, but no matter – it's all delicious.

EUROPEAN
Podhalanka Polksa Restauracja
1549 West Division Avenue; tel: 773-486-6655; Mon–Sat 9am–8pm, Sun 10am–10pm; $; el: Blue line to Division; bus: 9, 56, 70
It doesn't get much more authentic than Podhalanka, which looks like your grandma's finished basement but serves up some mighty fine Polish fare. Pierogis are a perennial favorite, as are the

filling soups. No alcohol is served – try the homemade fruit juice instead.

FUSION
Bongo Room
1470 North Milwaukee Avenue; tel: 773-489-0690; Mon–Fri 7.30am–2.30pm, Sat–Sun 9am–2.30pm; $$; el: Blue line to Damen; bus: 56
Diets go out the window once customers read the pancake options at this brunch and lunch place: it's hard to resist the siren call of lemon pineapple hotcakes. Sandwiches and salads round out the lunch offerings. Also at: 1152 South Wabash Avenue, South Loop; tel: 312-291-0100; Mon–Fri 8am–2.30pm, Sat–Sun 10am–2.30pm; el: Red, Orange, Green line to Roosevelt; bus: 12, 29; map p.135 C4

Prices for an average three-course meal with a glass of wine, beer, or a cocktail:
$$$$ – over $60
$$$ – $45–$65
$$ – $20–$45
$ – under $20

Green Zebra
1460 West Chicago Avenue; tel: 312-243-7100; www.green zebrachicago.com; Mon–Thur 5.30–10pm, Fri–Sat 5–11pm, Sun 10.30am–2pm, 5.30–9pm; $$$; el: Blue line to Chicago; bus: 66
Even hardcore carnivores won't miss the meat at Green Zebra, where the vegetarian cuisine is more haute than hippie. You can even wash it down with a choice of inventive non-alcoholic cocktails.

Rodan
1530 North Milwaukee Avenue; tel: 773-276-7036; www.rodan. ws; Mon–Thur 6pm–2am, Fri 5pm–2am, Sat–Sun 10am–3pm, 5pm–2am; $$; el: Blue line to Damen; bus: 56
This extremely cool lounge/restaurant hybrid offers funky decorative touches like a video screen and futuristic mirros in the bathrooms. The global menu veers heavily toward Asia with pit stops in Latin America.

Schwa
1466 North Ashland; tel: 773-252-1466; www.schwarestaurant.com; Tue–Sat 5.30–9.30pm; $$$$; el: Blue line to Division; bus: 9, 70
Another star on the local scene for its creative concoctions, Schwa differs from the others for its aggressively casual air – there are just 13 tables, and your server might just be chef Michael Carlson himself, ready to regale you with the history of the food on your plate.

LATIN
Irazu
1865 North Milwaukee Avenue; tel: 773-252-5687; www.irazu chicago.com; Mon–Sat 11.30am–9.30pm; $; el: Blue line to Western; bus: 49, 56
This family-owned Costa

Rican place has a utilitarian atmosphere, but the food – huge burritos, spicy steaks accompanied by fried plantains – is great and the portions are huge. Definitely leave room for one of the shakes, in flavors like blackberry, tamarind, and even oatmeal.

South Loop

EAST ASIAN

Oysy

888 South Michigan Avenue; tel: 312-922-1127; www.oysy sushi.com; Mon–Thur 11.30am–2.30pm, 5–10pm, Fri 11.30am–2.30pm, 5–11pm, Sat 5–11pm, Sun 5–9pm; $$; el: Red line to Roosevelt; bus: 29; map p.135 C3

Affordable, fresh sushi in an appealingly casual atmosphere draws both lovers of Japanese cuisine and local residents hanging out. Oysy, pronounced 'oh-see-she,' offers a wide range of nigiri and maki as well as innovative cooked dishes like lotus root tempura stuffed with chicken.

South Side

AMERICAN

Dixie Kitchen and Bait Shop

5225 South Harper Avenue; tel: 773-363-4943; www.dixie kitchenchicago.com; Sun–Thur 11am–10pm, Fri–Sat 11am–11pm; $$; bus: 28; train: Metra

Below: classic soul food can be found in the South Side.

to 53rd Street; map p.139 D2

All of the soul-food specialties of the south are available at this eatery, where the warm welcome is surpassed only by the portion sizes. Fried green tomatoes, oyster po-boys, and johnnycakes with peach butter are among the mouthwatering favorites.

Lem's

311 East 75th Street; tel: 773-994-2428; daily 2pm–2am, Fri–Sat until 4am; $; el: Red line to 79th Street; bus: 3, 4, 75

If you've got a car or a ride, it's worth the trek out to this carry-out-only rib shack, which is regularly listed among the best in the city for its big tubs of meaty ribs, which come covered in spicy sauce.

Soul Vegetarian East

205 East 75th Street; tel: 773-224-0104; www.soulvegetarian. com; Mon–Thur 7am–10pm, Fri–Sat 8am–11pm, Sun 8am–9pm; $; bus: 3, 75

The name isn't a misprint: here the soul food is stir-fried tofu, served with brown rice. Even non-vegetarians like the battered and fried vegetables and greens with cornbread.

Oak Park

EUROPEAN

Café le Coq

734 Lake Street; tel: 708-848-2233; Tue–Thur 5–9.30pm, Fri–Sat 5–10.30pm, Sun 11am–2.30pm, 4–9pm; $$$; el: Green line to Ridgeland

This delightful French restaurant is the pride of the dispiriting Oak Park restaurant scene, offering both classic dishes like steak frites as well as more imaginative fare. The decor is reminiscent of a Belle Epoque bistro.

Around Chicago

AMERICAN

Feed

2803 West Chicago; tel: 773-489-4600; Mon–Sat 11am–10pm; $$;

As in most major cities, often the food options nearest major sights are tourist joints offering mediocre food. For a quick, decent meal, chains like **Corner Bakery** and **Cosi**, which have locations all over the city, offer fresh, tasty sandwiches, soups, and the like – a healthier alternative to fast food.

bus: 65, 66

Chicken – cooked on a rotisserie and served up with salsa and tortillas on the side – is the specialty at this BYOB joint, in case you couldn't tell from the poultry pictures and paraphernalia about the room. The banana pudding, made with the traditional vanilla wafers, is excellent.

Hot Doug's

3324 North California Avenue; tel: 773-279-9550; www.hot dougs.com; Mon–Sat 10.30am–4pm; $; bus: 77

Hot-dog enthusiasts must find a way to get to this offbeat 'sausage emporium,' which is not easily accessible via public transportation. On Saturdays there's a line of customers down the block eager for classic dogs as well as gourmet offerings like pheasant sausage topped with foie gras mousse.

SOUTH ASIAN

Bhabi's Kitchen

6352 North Oakley; tel: 773-764-7007; daily noon–10pm; $$; bus: 49, 155

Just off Devon Avenue, the heart of the South Asian community here, dining at Bhabi's is like visiting the Indian uncle you never had. The gregarious owner is happy to advise guests on the best choices from the menu of Indian and Pakistani cuisine: spicy curries for the brave, biryanis for the fainter of heart.

Shopping

Americans love their malls, and Chicago is no exception – except that the city's malls are of the vertical kind, housed in high-rises. Packed with diverse shops, they're a great destination when an icy wind is blowing. While downtown, particularly Michigan Avenue, is the mainstream shopping drag, packed with all the well-known brands, be sure to head for other neighborhoods as well, where rents are much cheaper, for a fuller picture of the retail landscape. For more listings of specialised stores, see *Fashion, p.50–3*, *Food and Drink, p.56–9*, *Gay and Lesbian, p.60–61*, *Literature, p.72–3*, *Music, p.91*, and *Pampering, p.94*.

Shopping in Chicago

The main shopping areas are definitely downtown, along the **Magnificent Mile** and **State Street**. **River North** is a great destination for furniture and home decor – as is **Andersonville**, which is fast becoming known for several small independent shops with mid-century modern and antique finds. Lincoln Park is packed with small shops along stretches of **Clark and Lincoln Avenues** and around **Armitage Avenue and Hal-**

Below: shopping on the Magnificent Mile.

sted Street, while former industrial corridors along **Elston and Clybourn Avenues** offer plenty of big-box retailers. **Bucktown** and **Wicker Park**, known as a destination for cool clothes, also feature many eclectic outlets offering home accessories and gifts. There are plenty of little retail pockets scattered all over the city as well, and part of the fun is stumbling upon quirky shops off the beaten path.

Shopping Malls

If you spend any time on the Magnificent Mile, chances are you'll head into one of the city's vertical malls at some point or other. The malls generally house one or two major department stores, while the rest of the space is given to smaller shops.

The oldest and best-known is **Water Tower Place**, just across from the historical Water Tower on Michigan Avenue. Just north are **The 900 Shops** (named for its street number, not the number of stores), with **Bloomingdale's** as the largest

tenants. To the south, **Nordstrom** is the big draw at **The Shops** at North Bridge. **Chicago Place**, which **Saks Fifth Avenue** calls home, at press time had a lot of empty storefronts – plans for the building are unclear.

Antiques

Architectural Artifacts
4325 North Ravenswood Avenue, Ravenswood; tel: 773-348-0622; www.architecturalartifacts.com; daily 10am–5pm; el: Brown line to Montrose; train: Metra to Lawrence; bus: 9, 78
Chances are you're not in the market for a vintage marble mantelpiece, but there's a good chance you'll find something that fits in a suitcase in this 80,000-sq-ft (7,400-sq-m) space. Just bring money – it is quite expensive. Painted ceramic tiles and hand-painted store signs can be found among the more substantial pieces. If you've got enough cash, you can even take home pieces from significant buildings in the area, such as an Art Deco chandelier from the Civic Opera House.

Left: Macy's, formerly the beloved Marshall Field's.

Long-time shoppers swear it's not the same, although for basic department-store shopping it's a good bet, and the company has made a point of wooing locals, even selling the creations of local designers in the store. The seventh floor is the home of the Walnut Room restaurant, a popular stop for weary shoppers. Also at: Water Tower Place, 845 North Michigan Avenue, North Side; tel: 312-335-7700; Mon–Fri 10am–9pm, Sat 9am–10pm, Sun 11am–7pm; el: Red line to Chicago; bus: 151; map p.133 C3

Scout
5221 North Clark Street, Andersonville; tel: 773-275-5700; www.scoutchicago.com; Tue–Sat 11am–6pm, Thur–Fri until 7pm, Sun noon–5pm; bus: 9, 22, 64
This 'urban antique store' specializes in refinishing and rehabbing vintage pieces with simple, clean lines. On any given day you might find a clutch of stackable brushed-aluminum chairs, old croquet balls, a perfectly shaped black wooden dish, or new straw bags from Morocco. It's a great browsing destination after brunch or lunch.

Department Stores

Bloomingdale's
900 North Michigan, North Side; tel: 312-440-4460; www.bloomingdales.com; Mon–Tue, Thur–Sat 10am–8pm, Wed 10am–10pm, Sun 11am–7pm; el: Red line to Chicago; bus: 151; map p.133 C3
The name is commonly associated with New York, but Chicagoans have fallen in love with 'Bloomie's,' especially after the historic Marshall Field's was subsumed by Macy's *(see right)*. The

women's dress and trend-oriented departments are musts for fashionistas, as are the makeup counters on the first floor, where you'll have to run a gauntlet of black-clad staffers anxious to spray you with something. The men's department is a solid destination for everything from jeans to high-end suits. Note that the home store is at a different location, housed in the historic Medinah Temple (600 North Wabash Avenue; tel: 312-324-7500; Mon–Tue, Thur–Sat 10am–8pm, Wed 10am–10pm, Sun 11am–6pm; el: Red line to Grand; map p.132 C3).

Macy's
111 North State Street, Loop; tel: 312-781-1000; www.visitmacyschicago.com; Mon–Sat 10am–8pm, Sun 11am–6pm; el: Red, Blue line to Washington; map p.135 C1
In 2006 Marshall Field's, the venerable department store that was a Chicago institution for over 100 years, was bought by Macy's. The company decided to rename all the stores (even the historic State Street location, a local landmark) despite a public outcry and protestations.

Gifts

Andersonville Galleria
5247 North Clark Street, Andersonville; tel: 773-878-8570; www.andersonvillegalleria.com; Tue–Sat 11am–7pm, Fri until 8pm, Sun noon–5pm; bus: 9, 22
Artists, craftspeople, designers, and small businesses rent carrels from month to month in this spacious two-floor building, creating an indoor indie market. The merchandise runs the gamut: photography, mid-century modern light fixtures, and lots of accessories and jewelry.

For concentrated antiquing, head to Belmont Avenue between Damen and Western Avenues, where the shops range from storefronts with affordable secondhand treasures to galleries of expensive Louis XIV settees. In addition, every last weekend of the month from May to October brings the indoor-outdoor **Chicago Antique Market**, at 1350 West Randolph Street. More than 500 vendors bring in furniture, assorted bric-a-brac, and vintage clothing.

Art Effect
934 West Armitage Avenue, Lincoln Park; tel: 773-929-3600; www.arteffectchicago.com; Mon–Thur 11am–7pm, Fri 11am–6pm, Sat 10am–6pm, Sun noon–5pm; el: Brown, Purple line to Armitage; bus: 73; map p.133 D2
This airy, three-room store has a large selection of women's clothing and accessories, but the front room is a great destination for gifts – everything from birdhouses made from library books to ornate silver frames. It's hard to resist the urge to sniff-test every single candle and perfume in the shop.

Renegade Handmade
1924 West Division Street, Wicker Park; tel: 773-227-2707; www.renegadehandmade.com; daily 11am–7pm; el: Blue line to Damen or Division; bus: 50, 70
The founders of the fabulously successful Renegade Craft Fair opened this permanent location to provide crafted goods from independent designers and artists year-round. Check out the stuffed animals made from recycled sweaters, hand-painted posters, and notebooks featuring the covers of

secondhand textbooks and novels. Sewing and embroidery kits could set you on the path toward creating your own crafty wares.

RR#1
814 North Ashland Avenue, West Side; tel: 312-421-9079; www.rr1chicago.com; Mon–Sat 11am–7pm, Sun noon–5pm; el: Blue line to Division or Milwaukee; bus: 9, 66
The owners of RR#1, housed in an old 1930s apothecary complete with wooden glass-fronted cabinets and vintage vitrines, espouse the 'everything but the kitchen sink' philosophy. Every surface – and every taste – is covered, with gifts ranging from pretty floral paper lanterns and retro bicycle horns to porcelain teapots and vintagey cloth aprons.

Interiors and Housewares

CB2
3757 North Lincoln Avenue, Lincoln Park; tel: 773-755-3900; www.cb2.com; Mon–Fri 10am–8pm, Sat 10am–7pm, Sun 11am–6pm; el: Brown line to Addison; bus: 11, 50, 152
CB2 is the new contemporary arm of Crate & Barrel (see right), a well-known chain of

furniture and home stores founded in Chicago about 40 years ago. Here's where you'll find oddly shaped dishes, brightly colored wineglasses, and other fun items you never knew you needed, like chopsticks shaped like giant clothespins. Much of the sleek furniture is enticingly affordable. Also at: 800 West North Avenue; tel: 312-787-8329; el: Red line to North/Clybourn; bus: 8, 72; map p.132 A1

The Chopping Block
4747 North Lincoln Avenue, Lincoln Park; tel: 773-293-8490; www.thechoppingblock.net; Mon–Fri 10am–7pm, Sat 10am–6pm, Sun 10am–4pm; el: Brown line to Western; bus: 11, 49
Kitchenware store with everything for the home cook: high-end pots and pans, specialized cooking utensils and equipment, and must-have cookbooks. The cooking school offers a full roster of classes, including many one-offs. Also at: Merchandise Mart Plaza, Suite 107, North Side; tel: 312-644-6360; Mon–Fri 10am–9pm; el: Brown, Purple line to Merchandise Mart; map p.132 B4

Crate & Barrel
646 North Michigan, North Side; tel: 312-787-5900; www.crateandbarrel.com; Mon–Thur 10am–8pm, Fri 10am–9pm, Sat 10am–7pm, Sun 10am–6pm; el: Red line to Grand; bus: 147, 151; map p.133 C3
This beloved housewares and furniture retailer started out in Chicago in 1962, displaying—unsurprisingly—crates and barrels. In today's design-minded world it's hard to realise how groundbreaking this store was, with its contemporary yet functional and affordable merchandise. Today the look is a lot more

Left: Bloomingdale's home store, housed in the former Medinah Temple *(see p.113).*

sleek, but you'll still find everything from curvy glass carafes to leather sofas.

Grasshopper 510

1944 North Damen Avenue, Wicker Park; tel: 773-292-0510; www.grasshopper510.com; Mon–Sat 11am–7pm, Sun noon–5pm; el: Blue line to Damen; bus: 50, 73

All of the tableware, furniture, and gifts here are made according to eco-conscious and sustainable principles without sacrificing style. The owners truly believe in a green philosophy and incorporated many of the fixtures and built-in features left over from the previous tenant in the space to cut down on waste.

P.O.S.H.

613 North State Street, North Side; tel: 312-280-1602; www.poshchicago.com; Mon–Sat 10am–7pm, Sun 11am–5pm; el: Red line to Grand or Chicago; bus: 29; map p.132 C3

Those who like tableware and home accents with a history will love this Frenchified shop, which offers vintage hotel silver and restaurant china from defunct eateries. (A recent visit turned up china and silver service pieces from a private club in Chicago.) There are also drool-worthy pieces from Europe – cool flea-market treasures like vintage leather totes and perfectly distressed garden equipment, and new items like silver absinthe spoons and note cards featuring the Eiffel Tower. All in all it's akin to rummaging around in a shop on a Paris side street.

Sweden Shop

3304 West Foster Avenue, Albany Park; tel: 773-478-0327; www.theswedenshop.com; Mon–Sat 10am–6pm, Sun 10am–3pm; bus: 52, 64, 82

The new owners of this long-time business swept out all of the kitschy gnome dolls and Christmas ornaments in favor

Above: American Girl Place is hugely popular.

of housewares and gifts that show the best of cool Scandinavian design. Table linens and aprons printed with abstract patterns inspired by nature straddle classic and contemporary design. The store also carries popular Marimekko fabric from Finland, available by the yard.

Stationery and Cards

All She Wrote

825 West Armitage Avenue, Lincoln Park; tel: 773-529-0100; www.allshewrote.com; Mon–Thur 10am–7pm, Fri–Sat 10am–6pm, Sun 11am–5pm, el: Brown, Purple line to Armitage; bus: 8; map p.133 D2

The days of the handwritten note card never ended at this elegant little shop, where you can browse the selection of ready-made cards and stationery or order up a set with a monogram. There's a big gift section too, with pretty cloth tote bags, silver-tipped wine-bottle stoppers (which can also be monogrammed), and travel accessories.

Toys

American Girl Place

111 East Chicago Avenue, North Side; tel: 877-247-5223; www.americangirl.com; Mon–Thur 10am–7pm, Fri–Sat 9am–9pm, Sun 9am–7pm; el:

Red line to Chicago; bus: 3, 66, 145, 147, 151; map p.132 C3

This store/café/entertainment complex is heaven for little girls, who can browse dolls from the immensely popular American Girl series, each of which comes with a back story set in a different historical era, such as the days of slavery and the Great Depression. Here kids – or rather their parents – can buy matching clothes for doll and owner, stock up on books that detail the American Girls characters' adventures, and even get their dolls' hair styled.

Rotofugi

1953 West Chicago Avenue, Wicker Park; tel: 312-491-9501; www.rotofugi.com; Mon–Sat noon–8pm, Sun noon–5pm; bus: 9, 50, 66

Rotofugi is a toy store for adults. The merchandise actually falls under the heading of 'designer toys,' that is, limited-edition collectibles from a variety of pop-culture subgenres, especially anime and comics.

Museum gift shops can be a great place to find souvenirs. The **Museum Shop of the Art Institute** has posters, glass panels, and books related to permanent and temporary exhibits. The **Museum of Contemporary Art Store** is a great spot for those leaning more toward contemporary design, such as Alessi household utensils and silverware designed by the architect Zaha Hadid; it also has an excellent selection of jewelry by artists around the world. Over at the shop at the **Spertus Institute of Jewish Studies**, the collection of judaica, Jewish-oriented housewares, and books includes humorous touches like a Moses action figure.

Sport

Chicagoans take their sport seriously. The city's baseball, basketball, and football teams are a massive source of pride – even if some of their records are less than spectacular. They'll also take every opportunity to take part in activities, especially in summer, when the lakefront bustles with runners, cyclists, sailors, and kayakers. But even in winter there are options, from all-American bowling – admittedly usually less of a sport than a drinking opportunity – to ice-skating. These listings cover the major spectator sports in town, as well as options for participating in games and other activities around the city.

Baseball

Chicago Cubs
Wrigley Field, 1060 West Addison Street, Wrigleyville; tel: 774-404-CUBS; www.cubs.mlb.com; Feb–Sept; charge; el: Red line to Addison; bus: 22

The storied Cubs haven't won a championship pennant since 1908, but that hasn't stopped generations of fans from vowing 'wait 'til next year.' Watching games in historic and atmospheric Wrigley Field, with its ivy-covered walls and manual scoreboard, is often enough of a treat for baseball fans. Tickets are hard to come by due to the legions of devoted fans, so book far ahead or opt for standing-room tickets.

Chicago White Sox
US Cellular Field, 333 West 35th Street, South Side; tel: 312-674-1000; www.whitesox.mlb.com; Feb–Sept; charge; el: Red line to Sox/35th Street; bus: 24

In Chicago, there are Cubs fans and Sox fans, and never the twain shall meet. The rivalry derives chiefly from the different cultural and economic statuses of the affluent North Side (home of the Cubs) and the largely working-class South Side (where the Sox are headquartered). Although the Sox are considerably more successful than their counterparts to the north, (they won the World Series in 2005), it's considerably easier to obtain well-priced tickets to games.

Basketball

Chicago Bulls
United Center, 1901 West Madison Avenue, West Side; tel: 312-455-4000; www.nba.com/bulls; Oct–Apr; charge; el: Orange, Green, Purple line to Madison; bus: 19, 20

Chicagoans visiting other parts of the world are still greeted with accented cries of 'Michael Jordan!' The days when the legendary player helped lead the team to a half-dozen championships are over, but their games are still some of the most exciting in the city. Games take place at the impressive United Center, which the Bulls share with the Blackhawks hockey team (see p.118).

Bowling

A favorite Midwestern pastime for its associations with classic Americana. Lane reservations are a must, especially on weekends.

Diversey Rock N Bowl
2211 West Diversey Avenue, Lakeview; tel: 773-227-5800; www.drbowl.com; daily

Right: fans descend on Soldier Field for a Bears game.

Swimming in the lake is allowed only at beaches and other designated areas; if you are not sure, there are signs posted and sprayed on the rocks warning if it is prohibited. For serious swimmers, a pool may be a more attractive option. Check the **Chicago Park District**'s website, www.chicagoparkdistrict.org, for a list of public pools. Swimming in the Chicago River is not allowed and is a bad idea anyway – it's too polluted.

noon–2am, Sat until 3am; charge; bus: 49, 76

Typical bowling alley with a bar and greasy food, save for the flashy light show and loud rock music.

Timber Lanes
1851 West Irving Park Road, Lakeview; tel: 773-549-9770; Mon–Thur 11am–2am, Fri 6pm–2am, Sat–Sun noon–2am; charge; el: Brown line to Irving Park

One of the oldest alleys in the city, with a retro look and a good jukebox.

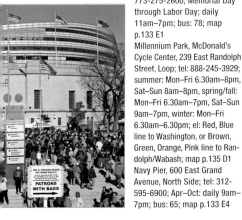

Cycling

Chicago's flat terrain and bike-friendly policies make two-wheeling it an excellent option for both exploring and general transportation. The **Chicagoland Bicycle Federation**'s website, www.biketraffic.org, offers plenty of resources and information on cycling events and rides.

Bike Chicago
www.bikechicago.com
Foster Beach, 5200 North Lake Shore Drive, Lincoln Park; tel: 773-275-2600; Memorial Day through Labor Day; daily 11am–7pm; bus: 78; map p.133 E1

Millennium Park, McDonald's Cycle Center, 239 East Randolph Street, Loop; tel: 888-245-3929; summer: Mon–Fri 6.30am–8pm, Sat–Sun 8am–8pm, spring/fall: Mon–Fri 6.30am–7pm, Sat–Sun 9am–7pm, winter: Mon–Fri 6.30am–6.30pm; el: Red, Blue line to Washington, or Brown, Green, Orange, Pink line to Randolph/Wabash; map p.135 D1

Navy Pier, 600 East Grand Avenue, North Side; tel: 312-595-6900; Apr–Oct: daily 9am–7pm; bus: 65; map p.133 E4

North Avenue Beach Boathouse,1600 North Lake Shore Drive, Old Town; tel: 773-327-2706; May–Oct: 9am–7pm, Nov–Apr: 8am–8pm; bus: 22, 72; map p.132 C1

Riverwalk, Wacker Drive and Columbus Avenue (stairs down to river), Loop; tel: 312-595-9600; Memorial Day–Labor Day: Sun–Sat 9am–5pm; el: Red line to Grand; bus: 3, 145, 147, 151; map p.135 D1

Hire bikes from the above locations.

SEE ALSO TRANSPORTATION, P.125

Football

Chicago Bears
Soldier Field, 1410 South Museum Campus Drive, South Side; tel: 847-615-BEAR (2327); www.chicagobears.com; Aug–Dec; charge; el: Red line to Roosevelt; bus: 12, 146; map p.135 D4

Known as the 'Monsters of the Midway,' the beloved Bears play 'rock 'em sock 'em' games in the new Solder Field Stadium, which blended the old Soldier Field with a contemporary structure (earning it the moniker 'the Mistake on the Lake' for its awkward look). The

Daley Bicentennial Plaza
337 East Randolph Street, Loop; tel: 312-742-7650; www.chicagoparkdistrict.com; Nov–Feb: Mon–Fri 8.30–10am (seniors only), 10am–3.30pm, Sat–Sun 8.30am–noon, 1–5pm; free (charge for skate rental); el: Green, Orange, Pink, Brown line to Randolph/Wabash, or Blue, Red line to Washington; map p.135 D1

Millennium Park
McCormick-Tribune Plaza, 55 North Michigan Avenue, Loop; tel: 312-742-5222; www.millenniumpark.org; Nov–Mar: daily 10am–10pm; free (charge for skate rental); el: Green, Orange, Pink, Brown line to Randolph/Wabash, or Blue, Red line to Washington; map p.135 C1

height of the fame came in the 1980s, when coach Mike Ditka led the team to a Super Bowl championship in 1984.

Hockey

Hockey doesn't enjoy the same broad fan base as other sports in Chicago, but the enthusiasm of dedicated fans helps make up for that. The two local teams are the Blackhawks and the Wolves. Tickets are fairly easy to come by, unless one of the team's big rivals is in town.

Chicago Blackhawks
United Center, 1901 West Madison, West Side; tel: 312-455-4000; www.blackhawks.nhl.com; Sept–Apr; charge; el: Orange, Green, Purple line to Madison; bus: 19, 20

Chicago Wolves
Allstate Arena, 6920 North Mannheim Road, Rosemont; tel: 847-724-GOAL; www.chicagowolves.com; Oct–June; charge; el: Blue line to Rosemont; bus: Pace 221

Ice-Skating

Winter brings the delightful experience of outdoor ice-skating downtown, surrounded by high-rises and the grandeur of some of the city's major parks. It's a good idea to call ahead as rinks are occasionally reserved for private parties.

Lake Michigan can't compete with the Bahamas or Australia for amazing diving – the water's murky in comparison to the tropics, and it's lean on brilliantly colored fish and aquatic plants – but people do it here anyway, usually checking out the remains of the many shipwrecks along the shore. **Dive Chicago** (www.divechicago.com) offers charter tours of sites for licensed scuba-divers from Burnham Harbor, as well as lessons. **Midwest Divers** (www.midwestdivers-il.com) wanders further afield but occasionally sponsors dives around the city.

Kayaking

Kayaking or canoeing along the Chicago River or the lake offers unusual views of great buildings as well as glimpses of wildlife in more residential areas. The companies below offer canoe or kayak hire.

Chicago River Canoe and Kayak
3400 North Rockwell Street, Lakeview; tel: 773-252-3307; www.chicagoriverpaddle.com; June–Aug: Mon–Fri 1–6.30pm, Sat–Sun 9am–7pm, Sept–Oct: Fri 1–5pm, Sat–Sun 9am–6pm; charge; el: Brown line to Rockwell

Kayak Chicago
tel: 630-336-7245; www.kayakchicago.com; May–Oct; charge Three locations: (river kayaking) 1501 North Magnolia, West Side; Wed–Sun 10am–7pm; el: Red line to North/Clybourn (lake kayaking) Montrose Beach, Montrose and Lake Shore Drive, Lincoln Park; Thur–Sun 10am–

7pm; bus: 145, 146, 147, 151; map p.133 C1
(lake kayaking) Leone Beach, 7032 North Sheridan Road, Rogers Park; Sat–Sun 10am–7pm; el: Red line to Jarvis; bus: 151

Running

The lakefront always beckons for practice, but for a list of upcoming races in the area, check the Chicago Area Runners Association website, www.cararuns.org.
Chicago Marathon
tel: 312-904-9800; www.chicagomarathon.com; Oct; charge
The annual race brings thousands of runners to Chicago, from beginners to professionals. The course begins and ends in Grant Park near Buckingham Fountain.
SEE ALSO FESTIVALS AND EVENTS, P.55

Sailing

Don't just look at the lake – get out on it. The view of the skyline from the water is truly stunning.
Chicago Sailing Club
Belmont Harbor, 3654 North

Above: participating in the Chicago Marathon.

Recreation Drive, Dock B, Lakeview; tel: 773-871-7245; www.chicagosailing.com; summer: daily 8am–9pm; charge; el: Red, Brown, Purple line to Belmont
Rentals, charters, and lessons are all offered here during the season.

Soccer

Soccer has never quite caught on as a major spectator sport in Chicago, like football or basketball, but the Chicago Fire games are affordable and family-friendly.
Chicago Fire
Toyota Park, 7000 South

Harlem, Bridgeview; tel: 888-MLS-FIRE; www.chicago.fire. mlsnet.com; Apr–Nov; charge; el: Orange line to Midway, then Toyota Park Express Pace bus

Skateboarding

Skate rats can perfect their ollies and half-pipes safely – at least for pedestrians – at skate parks around town.
Burnham Skate Park
3400 South Lake Shore Drive, South Side; tel: 312-747-2200; www.chicagoparkdistrict.com; daily 10am–10pm; free; bus: 2, 6, 10, 14, 26; map p.137 E3
Wilson Skate Park
4601 North Lake Shore Drive, Lakeview; tel: 312-742-PLAY; www.chicagoparkdistrict.com; daily 6am–11pm; free; bus: 145 146, 147, 151

Volleyball

Most of the volleyball action in Chicago happens around North Avenue Beach in summer *(see Parks and Beaches, p.98)*, where you might be able to engage in a pickup game. There are indoor games in winter as well. To take part or to find out where tournaments and games are happening, check with Spike Volleyball Chicago (http://spikevolleyballchicago.com).

Left: skating at the ice rink in Millennium Park.

119

Theater
and Dance

Chicago is a well-respected theater town, with everything from major musical productions to confessional solo performance. A diverse scene, many stages, and the presence of various playwriting incubators have made it a welcoming, affordable, and lively base for actors and writers to hone their craft. Theatergoers can catch premieres of works by new and established playwrights, big musicals, or off-Loop productions that embrace the unconventional. Show times and dates vary; check theater websites and local listings.

Theater

PLAYWRIGHTS IN CHICAGO

Probably the best-known playwright with strong ties to Chicago is **David Mamet**, who drew from certain residents' penchant for vulgarity to create stylized dialogue in such plays as *Sexual Perversity in Chicago* and *Glengarry Glen Ross*. **Lanford Wilson**, the author of such searing works as *Burn This* and *Balm in Gilead*, studied playwriting at the University of Chicago in the late 1950s. More recently a new generation of playwrights have been garnering acclaim, most notably **Tracy Letts**, a writer known for disturbing, occasionally violent plays who won a Pulitzer Prize for 2008's *August: Osage County*.

> The **Theater on the Lake**, a 400-seat theater on Fullerton Avenue at the lake, is a pretty setting for a series of plays in summer put on by small companies. Performances are listed in area magazines and newspapers, or call the box office (tel: 312-742-7994).

THE THEATER SCENE

In the early 1990s the city set about creating a downtown theater district, part of which involved regenerating some of the area's historic theaters. This is where you'll find big-budget Broadway plays and musicals, although some theaters (most notably the **Goodman**, *see p.121*) specialize in new dramatic works.

The off-Loop scene is known for edgier productions, many of which show the unmistakable influence of Chicago's comedy-improv scene. The long-running play *Late-Night Catechism*, based on the authors' experiences growing up Catholic in Chicago, and the monster late-night hit *Too Much Light Makes the Baby Go Blind* (see p.122), are prime examples of this phenomenon.

Other companies, most notably Lookingglass and Redmoon, incorporate elements of acrobatics and puppetry into their productions. There's also a small but strong experimental scene, much of it with roots in the Eastern European avant-garde tradition.

Above: advertising a production by the renowned Steppenwolf Theater Company *(see p.122)*.

THEATER DISTRICT

Bank of America Theatre
18 West Monroe Street, Loop; tel: 312-977-1700; www.broadwayin chicago.com; el: Orange, Brown, Purple, Green, Pink line to Madison/Wabash; map p.134 C2
Designed in 1906 as a venue for vaudeville, this theater has been hosting plays and musicals under various names since 1945. Many works have had their pre-Broadway premieres here, including the popular musical *Spamalot*.
Cadillac Palace Theatre
151 West Randolph Street,

aters. Every holiday season the company stages a popular production of Charles Dickens's *A Christmas Carol*.

OFF-LOOP

Chicago Dramatists

1105 West Chicago Avenue, West Side; tel: 773-583-4317; www.chicagodramatists.org; el: Blue line to Chicago; bus: 56, 66
The home of the nationally known playwriting development group shows new works here in an intimate 77-seat theater.

Chicago Shakespeare Theater

Navy Pier, 800 East Grand, North Side; tel: 312-595-5600; www.chicagoshakes.com; bus: 29, 65, 66, 120, 121, 124; map p.133 E4
The recipient of a 2008 Tony Award for best regional theater, the company stages imaginative yet accessible productions of the Bard's works – in fact, a large part of its mission is to engage students. The main stage, designed to resemble theaters common in the playwright's time, such as London's Globe Theatre, seats 500 around three sides, fostering an intimate experience.

Loop; tel: 312-977-1700; www.broadwayinchicago.com; el: Pink, Brown, Blue, Pink, Purple, Orange line to Clark/Lake; map p.134 C1
Built in 1926 by the well-known theater designers George L. and Cornelius W. Rapp, the interior of the Cadillac references the splendor of France's Fontainebleau and Versailles palaces. It reopened as a theater with the premiere of Elton John and Tim Rice's musical *Aida*.

Ford Center for the Performing Arts, Oriental Theatre

24 West Randolph Street, Loop; tel: 312-977-1700; www.broadwayinchicago.com; el: Brown, Green, Orange, Purple, Pink line to State/Lake; bus: 29; map p.134 C1
A former movie palace with an interior inspired by the Far East (and also designed by the Rapp brothers), the Ford is a venue for major musical productions including *Wicked*, which has been performed here on an open run since 2005.

Goodman Theatre

170 North Dearborn Street,

Loop; tel: 312-443-3811; www.goodmantheatre.org; el: Brown, Green, Orange, Purple, Pink line to State/Lake; bus: 29; map p.134 C1
Under the leadership of artistic director Robert Falls, a veteran of the 1970s off-Loop theater scene, the well-known company has built a distinguished reputation for diverse productions that range from classic plays to specially commissioned works, many by local playwrights. The theater itself, a new facility that opened in 2000, stretches for a city block and includes two the-

Below: Chicago is proud of it's theater scene.

Lookingglass Theatre Company

Water Tower Water Works, 821 North Michigan Avenue, North Side; tel: 312-337-0665; www.lookingglasstheatre.org; el: Red line to Chicago; bus: 3, 66, 145, 147, 151; map p.133 C3

Founded in 1988 by a group of students from Northwestern University, including former *Friends* star David Schwimmer, the company is known for staging fantastically creative, circus-like performances. Its home, with its 221-seat theater, is across the street from the historic Water Tower and is also one of the few structures in Chicago that survived the great 1871 fire.

Steppenwolf Theatre Company

1650 North Halsted Street, Old Town; tel: 312-335-1650; www.steppenwolftheatre.org; el: Red line to North/Clybourn; bus: 8, 72; map p.132 A1

One of the best-known theater companies in the country, Steppenwolf has garnered praise for its commitment to challenging works and the highest caliber of performance. Although many ensemble members (such as John Malkovich and Joan Allen) have gone on to fame in TV and movies, productions emphasize a collective vision rather than star power.

Victory Gardens Theater

2433 North Lincoln Avenue, Lincoln Park; tel: 773-871-3000; www.victorygardens.org; el: Red, Brown line to Fullerton; bus: 8, 74; map p.133 D1

This Tony Award-winning company has a long history of nurturing playwrights and producing world-premiere works in a mid-size format. Half of the plays are commissioned from the in-house ensemble of eight playwrights.

FRINGE AND EXPERIMENTAL

Chopin Theatre

1543 West Division Street, Wicker Park; tel: 773-598-8240; www.chopintheatre.com; el: Blue line to Division; bus: 9, 70

The theater, housed in a storefront building with a pretty terracotta facade, is the spot for avant-garde plays and performances, especially experimental Eastern European theater. Performances here regularly range outside the usual theater format, so be prepared for the breakdown of the fourth wall and other unusual formats. The space also hosts literary events, films, and the occasional musical performance, for a total of some 500 events annually, on average.

Live Bait Theater

3914 North Clark Street, Lakeview; tel: 773-871-1212; www.livebaittheater.org; el: Red line to Addison; bus: 22, 80

The small theater focuses on innovative works by up-and-coming playwrights, many with comic overtones. A highlight is the annual series of solo performances every summer.

Neo-Futurarium

5153 North Ashland Avenue (second floor), Andersonville; tel: 773-275-5255; www.neofuturists.org; bus: 9, 22

This is the home of the Neo-Futurists' long-running, late-night play *Too Much Light Makes the Baby Go Blind*, which is actually 30 plays in 60 minutes, which change every week. The free-wheeling atmosphere is obvious during the admission process: the cost is $7 plus whatever you roll on a six-sided die. Other works are just as offbeat – you might catch staged readings of notoriously bad movies or comedic monologues.

Redmoon Theater

1638 West Hubbard, West Side; tel: 312-850-8440; www.redmoon.org; el: Green, Pink line to Ashland/Lake; bus: 9, 65

Redmoon's spectacles – it would be inaccurate simply to call them plays – blend elements of puppetry, parades, and circuses to create a totally new type of performance that's accessible across ages, races, and cultures.

Trap Door Theatre

655 West Cortland, West Side;

Right: theaters are peppered all over the city.

Left: *Die! Mommie, Die!* by Chicago-based company, Hell in a Handbag Productions, who explore popular culture.

Hubbard Street Dance

Harris Theater, 205 East Randolph Street, Loop; tel: 312-850-9744; www.hubbardstreet dance.com; el: Brown, Green, Orange, Pink line to Randolph/Wabash; map p.135 D1

Company founder Lou Conte helped forge the company's signature innovative style starting in the 70s thanks to collaborations with such influential choreographers as Twyla Tharp and Jiri Kylian.

Muntu Dance Theatre

Various spaces and theatres; tel: 773-241-6080; www.muntu.com

Traditional African and African-American dance, music, and stories are the foundation for Muntu's original works.

River North Dance Company

The Ruth Page Center, 1016 North Dearborn Street, Gold Coast; tel: 312-944-2888; www.rivernorthchicago.com; el: Red line to Clark/Division; bus: 29, 70; map p.132 C2

The company's signature jazz-based style results in sleek, sophisticated works that are great fun to watch.

tel: 773-384-0494; www.trap doortheatre.com; bus: 9, 73; train: Metra to Clybourn

Originally a nomadic troupe wandering theaters in Europe, Trap Door still features Eastern European-style undertones of social and political commentary in its risk-taking productions.

Dance

Dance has a small but strong core fan base. Performances of smaller companies are sporadic; check local listings or websites for upcoming events.

BALLET

Joffrey Ballet

10 East Randolph Street, Loop; tel: 312-739-0120; www.joffrey.com; el: Red, Blue line to Lake or Washington, or Brown, Orange, Green, Purple, Pink line to Randolph/Wabash; map p.135 C1

One of the oldest and most prestigious ballet companies in the US, the Joffrey stages traditional classical ballets as well as more contemporary works. Its annual production of *The Nutcracker* is a local holiday tradition. It has recently moved to a new home in what has been named the Joffrey Tower, which also houses commercial premises, and boasts twice as much space as its previous location.

CONTEMPORARY

Breakbone Dance Company

Various spaces and theatres; tel: 773-841-BONE; www.breakbone.com

The company's fiery, emotional works are built around a kinetic technique called the Bodyslam, which seeks to use gravity rather than work against it.

The long-running show *Tony and Tina's Wedding* makes theater into an interactive experience, complete with dinner and drinks. Actors mingle and dance with 'guests' in the hit play, a satirical look at an extremely stereotypical Italian-American wedding, complete with big hair and goofy tuxedos. Performances are in the Pipers Alley complex in Old Town; check http://tonyntina.com or local listings for showtimes.

Transportation

The most visible public transportation system in the city, the 'el,' or elevated train (which, confusingly, includes sections of subway), doesn't offer blanket coverage of the city, but bus routes do tend to fill in the blank spots. For visitors sticking to the main areas, transportation won't be a problem – and if you do want to get further out, Metra trains, taxis, or even rental cars are readily available options. The flat terrain, plentiful bike lanes, and the gridlike city layout encourages cycling and walking. These listings provide an overview of the various choices for getting to and around the city.

Getting There

BY AIR
Chicago is serviced by two major airports. **O'Hare International**, 17 miles (27km) northwest of downtown, is a major flight hub and one of the busiest airports in the world. The cheapest and often most efficient method of getting to and from there is the el; the Blue line runs 24 hours a day, with trains every eight to 10 minutes, and the trip downtown takes about 50 minutes. The station is near the elevators to the main parking

Travelers are becoming more aware of the greenhouse gases produced by their journeys. It's possible to 'offset' the carbon dioxide created by your flight by purchasing credits that go towards projects that help reduce global warming. Sites such as **www.carbonfund.org** offer calculators to help you figure out your 'carbon footprint,' or how much carbon dioxide your activities produce. For a list of organizations offering carbon offsets, check out **www.carboncatalog.org**.

garage. A taxi ride to downtown will cost around $35–40.
Midway International Airport, 12 miles (19km) southwest of downtown, is much smaller and serves mainly budget airlines. It is accessible via the el's Orange line and takes about 45 minutes.
Airport Express (tel: 312-454-7800; toll-free: 800-654-7871; www.airportexpress.com) offers shuttle services between both airports and major downtown hotels; the cost of a one-way ticket for a single customer is $27 to O'Hare, $22 to Midway.

BY TRAIN
Amtrak trains depart and arrive at downtown's **Union Station** (225 South Canal Street; tel: 800-USA-RAIL; www.amtrak.com), which serves regional and national destinations. The Clinton stop on the Blue line is the closest el station.

BY BUS
Greyhound buses are a cheaper – but longer and less comfortable – option than train or air. The main station is at 630 West Harrison Street (tel: 312-408-5800;

www.greyhound.com), and the closest el stop is the Blue Line's Clinton station.

Getting Around
The main forms of public transportation in the area – the **Chicago Transit Authority** (**CTA**), **PACE** buses, and **Metra** trains – are overseen by the **Regional Transportation Authority** (**RTA**), which offers maps and trip planners using the entire system on its website, www.rtachicago.com.

THE EL
The el (elevated trains) rapid-transit system, run by the CTA (tel: 888-YOUR-CTA; www.transitchicago.com), consists of eight lines that serve downtown and outlying neighborhoods as well as a few suburbs. Service is generally efficient, although ongoing maintenance work on the tracks and structures can cause slowdowns during off-peak hours. The cost of a single ride is $2, and transfers to buses are 25 cents. You'll need to put the cash on a fare card, available from machines at all stations. If you are planning on using

Left: the distinctive el trains.

parking is expensive, and street parking often confusing. However, if you decide you must have a car, rental agencies have counters at both airports, as well as offices in the city. The best deals on parking downtown are probably at the Millennium Park, Grant Park, and East Monroe garages (www.grantparkparking.com).

TAXIS

Taxis can be hailed on the street or found at cab stands. The meter starts at $2.25 and goes up 20 cents every one ninth of a mile. There may be additional charges for extra passengers.

Yellow Cabs
Tel: 312-TAXICAB
Flash Cabs
Tel: 773-561-4444

WALKING

Walking is always an option in the city, although drivers don't always give pedestrians the proper right of way, so it's always a good idea to look both ways before setting off the curb, and only cross when signals say you may. As in all major urban areas, use caution at night and in isolated or high-crime areas.

SEE ALSO WALKS, TOURS, AND VIEWS, P.126–9

Below: yellow taxicabs can be hailed on the street.

From late May to early September, the city offers free trolley service to major tourist areas downtown, such as Navy Pier, daily from 10am to 6pm every 20 to 30 minutes. Trolleys also run around Lincoln Park, but only on weekends and holidays. For maps with routes and stops, tel: 877-CHI-CAGO; www.cityofchicago.org/Transportation/trolleys.

the el and buses extensively, consider a one-, seven-, or 30-day pass; special visitor passes offer unlimited use for up to five days.

BUSES

The el doesn't go everywhere, which is where buses come in handy. The network is extensive and confusing – your best bet is to pick up a system map or check out the CTA website, which features an online trip planner. Get passes and fare cards at el stations, Jewel and Dominick's grocery stores, and currency exchanges.

For travel beyond the reach of the CTA, you may end up transferring to a bus run by PACE, which services the suburbs (tel: 847-364-PACE; www.pacebus.com).

METRA TRAIN

Metra trains are used mainly by commuters to and from the suburbs, but they're another option when the el doesn't serve your destination and a bus would take too long. Most of the lines arrive at and depart from Union Station and the neighboring Ogilvy Transportation Center (tel: 312-322-6777; www.metrarail.com).

CYCLING

Chicago is officially a bicycle-friendly city *(see Sport, p.117)*. Some drivers haven't got the memo on this, however, so a helmet, lights, and reflectors are a good idea. Cyclists are expected to obey the rules of the road. Riding on the sidewalk is prohibited for anyone older than 12, unless it's a designated bike route.

DRIVING

Traffic, especially downtown, can be difficult, and Chicago drivers are not known for their patience. Furthermore, private

Walks, Tours, and Views

Prairie-sprung Chicago may not have any mountain vistas, but it does have a couple of record-breaking skyscrapers with 360 degree views, a long swathe of lakefront beaches and parks, and a growing riverfront promenade. These suggested walks stick mainly to downtown areas, but rambles through the city's other neighborhoods can be equally as scenic and rewarding. Devise your own, or take advantage of one of the companies offering themed tours. For more information on city tours, see *Architecture, p.31*.

Walks

Chicago River Walk

1½ hours
Start: LaSalle Street/West Wacker Drive, Loop; el: Brown, Purple, Orange, Pink, Green, Blue line to Clark and Lake; map p.134 C1
End: North Lake Shore Drive/ East Wacker Drive, Loop; bus: 6, 124; map p.135 D1

Start at the southeast corner of LaSalle Street and Wacker Drive, where there's a plaque commemorating the Eastland Disaster. On a July day in 1915, the steamer SS *Eastland*, hired to ferry Western Electric employees for a jaunt to Indiana, overturned on its side while still tied to the dock. Although it was

> Carriage rides around the city can be a romantic, albeit expensive, way to see the city, although the drivers don't always give much information about what you're seeing. Several companies keep carriages waiting around the Historic Water Tower off Michigan Avenue between Chicago Avenue and Pearson Street.

just feet from shore, 844 people drowned, mainly people caught below deck. It is still one of the greatest disasters to occur in the history of Chicago.

Head east along the riverside promenade for a happier sight, the twin towers of **Marina City**, known as 'the corncobs' for their resemblance to the vegetable *(see Architecture, p.32)*. The structures, planned to stem a tide of migration to the suburbs, were built to be a 'city within a city,' with a movie theater, a bowling alley, stores, and, naturally, a marina. Today the apartments inside are sought after for their retro styling and layout.

Continuing east on the promenade next to Wacker Drive, head down the stairs between Wabash and State to get to **Wabash Plaza**, a nice place to watch the river traffic go by, with its terraced lawn, benches, and a small fountain. It's also the site of the city's **Vietnam Memorial**, a slab of black granite engraved with the names of some 2,900 servicemen from

Illinois who gave their lives in the conflict.

Although there are plans under way to construct an unbroken riverfront promenade from Wells Street to the lakefront, for now you'll have to head back up to Wacker Drive. In the southwest tower of the Michigan Avenue bridge is the **McCormick Tribune Bridgehouse and Chicago River Museum** (tel: 312-977-0227; www.bridgehouse museum.org), where you can get a closer look at the gears and mechanisms that lift the bridge for large watercraft and explore exhibits about the bridge and the history of the river.

Step down to Lower Wacker Drive, where the Riverwalk, a paved path and promenade lined with flowerboxes and planters, really begins. There are a number of cafés and restaurants where you can sip a drink and relax in the sun, as well as a few souvenir shops and facilities for bike rental. Choose a spot east of Columbus Avenue to catch the spray of the **Nicholas J. Melas**

Left: a river tour boat passes by Marina City.

The underground pedway in the Loop is a little-known option for visitors and a godsend in winter, when strong, bitter winds make walking an unattractive proposition. The main route can be used to get all the way from Daley Plaza to Millennium Park. Signage is, unfortunately, spotty, so it's a good idea to download the system map, available on **www.chicagowalks.org**.

Centennial Fountain, located across the water at McClurg Court. From May to October, the fountain sends an arc of water across the river for 10 minutes every hour on the hour from 10am to 2pm and from 5pm to midnight.

Continue east to the underpass beneath Lake Shore Drive, where there's a trellised passageway, the **Riverwalk Gateway**, connecting the Riverwalk to the lakefront path. Along the sides are painted ceramic tile murals detailing important events in the history of the river. From here you can travel north or south along the lakefront path, or head across the river to **Navy Pier** (see Children, p.40).

Millennium Park to Northerly Island

2 hours

Start: *Cloud Gate*, Millennium Park, Loop; el: Brown, Orange, Green, Pink line to Randolph/Wabash or Madison/Wabash; map p.135 C2

End: Northerly Island, South Side; bus: 12, 146; map p.135 E4

This walk takes you through some of the city's newest and oldest park and offers great views of the skyline, lake, and the Michigan Avenue 'cliff.' You can end the walk early with a drink at **Kitty O'Shea's** (see Bars, p.37) or go on to finish at Northerly Island.

Start by checking out your reflection in *Cloud Gate* (see Public Art, p.100), the bean-shaped, silvery sculpture that is one of the city's newest symbols. When you're done admiring yourself – and the clouds, sky, and buildings – on its curved surface, walk east to the Great Lawn, where Frank Gehry's band-shell, the **Jay Pritzker Pavilion** (see Parks and Beaches, p.96), stands before you. If you're lucky you might be able to catch the **Grant Park Orchestra** (see Music, p.88) practicing for one of their concerts.

Continue east and cross over Gehry's undulating **BP Bridge**, which snakes across Columbus Drive to deposit you in **Grant Park** (see Parks and Beaches, p.96). As you head south, you'll pass gardens landscaped to highlight native prairie plants as well as more traditional designs. In spring and early summer, the scent of thousands of

Below: the Buckingham Memorial Fountain *(see p.128).*

The Chicago Loop Alliance offers free downloadable audio 'Loop the Loop' tours and maps of architectural landmarks, theaters, and public art in the downtown neighborhood, each lasting about an hour. You can even listen to them on their website, www.chicagoloop alliance.com, to figure out which one to take or to get a preview.

blooms from plants and trees wafts in the air.

Continue through the park, crossing East Monroe and Jackson Drives, and the trees open up to reveal **Buckingham Memorial Fountain** in all its glory. It was commissioned in 1927 by philanthropist Kate Buckingham and dedicated to the memory of her brother, a benefactor of the **Art Institute** (see Museums and Galleries, p.76). From April to October, the fountain's hourly water display is accompanied by lights and music after dusk.

Head east through the park to **Congress Plaza**, an arc-shaped area designed by city planner Daniel Burnham as a grand pedestrian entrance to Grant Park. The two monuments here, The Bowman and The Spearman, date from 1928 and were intended by sculptor Ivan Mestrovic to honor Native Americans in the area. From the top of the plaza you'll also have a nice view of the Michigan Avenue streetwall, or 'cliff,' a distinctive 12-block stretch of historic structures, including Louis Sullivan's **Auditorium Building** (see Architecture, p.31), on the northwest corner of Congress and Michigan. If you need rest and refreshment at this point, head across Michi-

gan to the **Hilton Chicago** (see Hotels, p.71), home of Kitty O'Shea's, the quintessential Irish bar, which has sidewalk seating in summer.

To continue, go south along the walkways that crisscross this section of the park. Between 11th Street and Roosevelt Road is Magdalena Abakanowicz's haunting sculptural installation *Agora* (see Public Art, p.103). From here, head east across the park, with its winding pathways and an underpass beneath Lake Shore Drive to the **Museum Campus**, usually lined with installations of often whimsical public art. Stroll between the neoclassical **Field Museum** and the **Shedd Aquarium** to head east toward the dome of the **Adler Planetarium** (see Museums and Galleries, p.81). Hang a right at the planetarium and you'll be on **Northerly Island**, formerly the site of a small air-

port and now a park with trees and native prairie grasses. You'll also see boats floating past on their way to and from **Burnham Harbor**, tucked in between the 'island' and the lakefront. Stroll past the **Charter One Pavilion**, a concert venue, to walk along the surprisingly quiet paths and to check out the panoramic views of the skyline.

Tour Companies

Bike Chicago
Tel: 888-BIKE-WAY;
www.bikechicago.com
The bike-rental company also offers guided bicycle and Segway tours.

Chicago Hauntings Ghost Tours
Tel: 888-446-7891;
www.chicagohauntings.com
The 'ghost bus' takes visitors to various creepy locations and sites rumored to be rife with supernatural happenings.

Right: the view from the John Hancock Center at sunset.

Chicago Neighborhood Tours

Tel: 312-742-1190; www.chicagoneighborhoodtours.com

Offers tours of neighborhoods, area churches and cemeteries, public art, and more.

Chicago Trolley and Double Decker Company

Tel: 773-648-5000; www.chicagotrolley.com

Chauffeured tours in old-fashioned trolleys and double-decker buses.

Untouchable Gangster Tours

Tel: 773-881-1195; www.gangstertour.com

Tours hit some of the most notorious locations from the gangster era, a bloody chapter in the city's history.

Views

John Hancock Observatory

875 North Michigan Avenue, North Side; tel: 312-751-3681,

Above: take a tour around Chicago's more residential neighborhoods, such as Lincoln Park.

www.johnhancockcenter.com; daily 9am–11pm; admission charge; el: Red line to Chicago; bus: 144, 145, 146, 147, 148, 151; map p.133 C3

The observatory's unparalleled views of the shoreline make it a coveted post during fireworks shows off Navy Pier (annually July 3, every Wednesday and Friday night from May to September), as well as festivals like the **Air and Water Show**, with its 94-floor-high view of the aircraft zipping around the lake. A screened-in Skywalk offers the unforgettable, occasionally nerve-wracking experience of the winds at this height. Crowds are lighter before 11am and after 5pm, although even at night the twinkling views of the city are impressive.
SEE ALSO ARCHITECTURE, P.32; FESTIVALS AND EVENTS, P.55

Sears Tower Skydeck

233 South Wacker Drive, Loop; tel: 312-875-96960; www.theskydeck.com; May–Sept: daily 10am–10pm, Oct–Apr: daily 10am–8pm; admission charge; el: Brown, Orange, Pink, Purple line to Quincy; map p.134 B2

At 1,450ft (440m), the Sears Tower offers an unusual vantage point for surrounding

architecture, the shoreline from Wisconsin to Michigan, and the lake. On cloudy and foggy days visibility can be severely limited, so choose a day that's relatively clear. To avoid the crowds, get there around opening time or wait until after 5pm, when you can also arrange your visit to coincide with the sunset. Exhibits and information placards provide historical and cultural context to the views, and there are plenty of high-powered telescopes to zoom in on interesting sights.
SEE ALSO ARCHITECTURE, P.33

The **Green Bay Trail**, open to bikes and walkers, heads north from suburban Wilmette all the way up to Lake Bluff – where it continues under a different name all the way to Wisconsin. Along the way it's lined with native plants such as Queen Anne's Lace and cattails, and there are plenty of opportunities to veer off and check out the gracious downtowns and stately homes of the North Shore area. For maps and information check the Forest Preserve of Cook County website, **www.fpdcc.com**.

Atlas

The following streetplan of Chicago makes it easy to find the attractions listed in our A–Z section. A selective index to streets and sights will help you find other locations throughout the city.

Map Legend

	Pedestrian area	**M**	Subway
	Notable building		Cathedral / church
	Park		Hospital
	Hotel		Bus station
	Urban area	✈	Airport
	Non urban area	**ℹ**	Tourist information
† †	Cemetery	★	Sight of interest
	Beach	**1**	Statue / monument

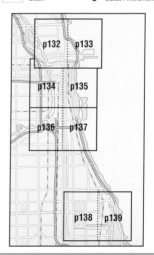

p132 p133

p134 p135

p136 p137

p138 p139

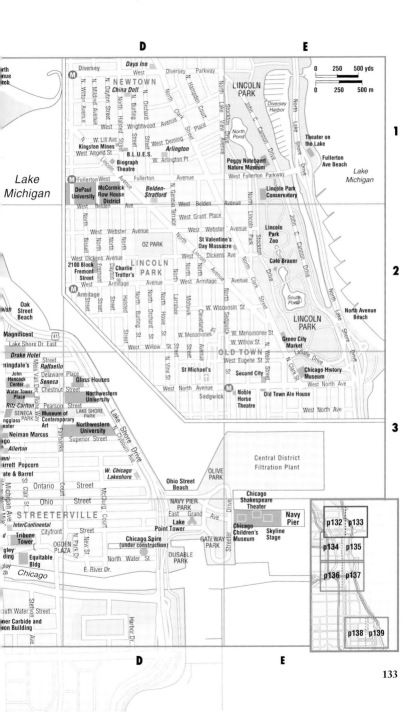

D **E**

0 250 500 yds
0 250 500 m

Diversey West
Days Inn West
Diversey Parkway

NEWTOWN
China Doll

LINCOLN PARK

Diversey Harbor

Theater on the Lake

Fullerton Ave Beach

Lake Michigan

Wrightwood Avenue

West Deming

Arlington
W. Arlington Pl

Kingston Mines
B.L.U.E.S.

Biograph Theatre

Fullerton West Fullerton Avenue

DePaul University

McCormick Row House District
Belden-Stratford

West Belden Ave

Peggy Notebaert Nature Museum

West Fullerton Parkway

Lincoln Park Conservatory

West Belden Avenue

West Grant Place

West Webster Avenue West Webster Avenue

Lincoln Park Zoo

OZ PARK

St Valentine's Day Massacre

Café Brauer

West Dickens Avenue

West Lincoln Dickens Ave

2100 Block Fremont Street
Charlie Trotter's

LINCOLN PARK

West Armitage Avenue West Armitage Avenue

South Pond

Armitage

LINCOLN PARK

Lake Michigan

Oak Street Beach

W. Wisconsin St

North Avenue Beach

W. Menomonee St. W. Menomonee St.

Magnificent
Lake Shore Dr. East

W. Willow St.

OLD TOWN

Green City Market

Drake Hotel
mingdale's Street

West Eugene St

Raffaello
John Hancock Center
Seneca
Glass Houses

St Michael's

Second City

Chicago History Museum

West North Ave

Water Tower Place
Chestnut Street

Ritz-Carlton Pearson Street

Northwestern University

West North Avenue

Noble Horse Theatre

Old Town Ale House

West North Ave

SENECA PARK
Museum of Contemporary Art
nglass
eater

Northwestern University

Superior Street

Neiman Marcus

Allerton
nni
arrett Popcorn
ate & Barrel

Central District Filtration Plant

Michigan Ave
ding

W. Chicago Lakeshore

OLIVE PARK

STREETERVILLE

Ontario Street

Ohio Street Beach

Chicago Shakespeare Theater

InterContinental
d
Tribune Tower

Ohio Street

NAVY PIER PARK
East Grand

Navy Pier

Cityfront

Lake Point Tower

Chicago Children's Museum
Skyline Stage

OGDEN PLAZA

Chicago Spire (under construction)

GATEWAY PARK

gley
ding
Chicago

North Water St

DUSABLE PARK

E. River Dr.

outh Water Street
er Carbide and
on Building

Harbor Dr.

p132 | p133
p134 | p135
p136 | p137
p138 | p139

1

2

3

D **E**

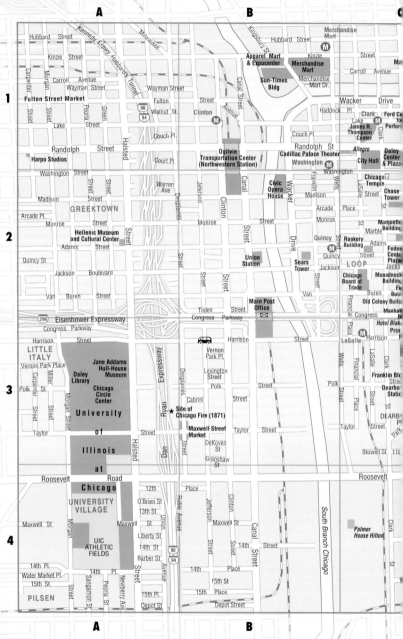

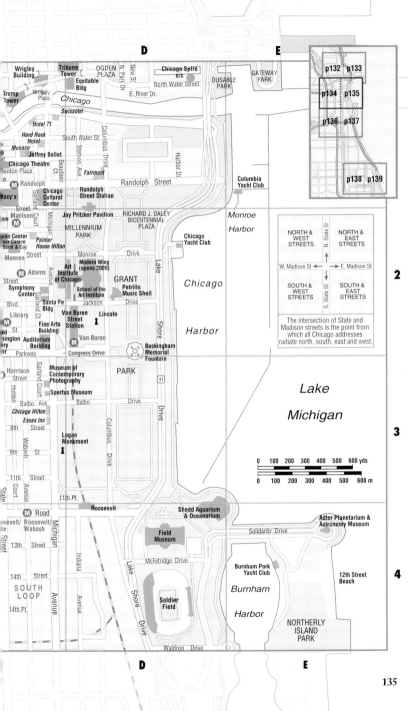

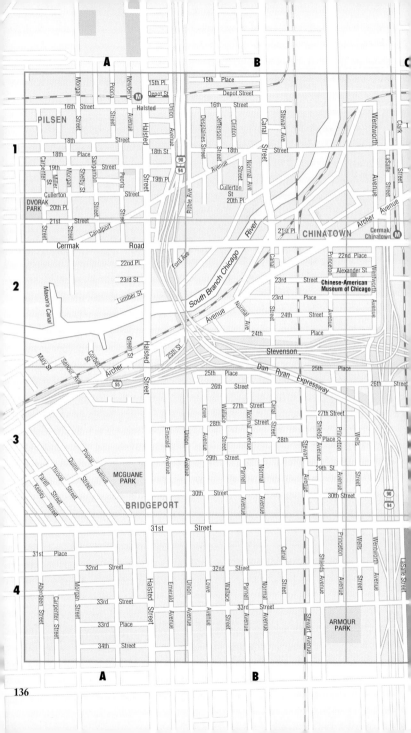

SOUTH LOOP

D

E

Waldron Drive

Street

Michigan

National
Vietnam
Veterans
Art Museum

18th Street

18th St

Wabash

18th

Street

Glessner House
Museum

Street

State

Second
Presbyterian
Church

St

Clarke
House

Street

Avenue

Cullerton

Prairie Avenue
Historic Distric

Lake

Burnham

St

Shore

Harbor

Dr. M.L. King Drive

Drive

21st

St

McCormick
Place
North

41

Blues Heaven
Foundation

Cermak   Road

Prairie

McCormick
Place
Lakeside
Center

Cottage Grove

Indiana

23rd

Street

Avenue

Street

Avenue

Calumet Ave.

McCormick
Place

Lake

24th

Street

Avenue

24th

Place

McCormick
Place
South

BURNHAM
PARK

Michigan

Expressway

25th   Street

55

26th   Street

26th

St

27th Street

Indiana Avenue

State

Wabash

Prairie Avenue

Calumet Avenue

Dr. M.L. King Drive

Ellis Avenue

Fort Dearborn Drive

Moe Drive

28th

Street

Avenue

28th Pl.

Vernon

29th   Street

Michigan

29th
Pl.

Avenue

Lake Park Avenue

h St

DUNBAR
PARK

Indiana Avenue

PRAIRIE
SHORES

30th   St

31st   Street

LAKE
MEADOWS
PARK

Lake Shore Drive

Illinois Institute
of Technology

32nd   Street

Street

Avenue

Giles

Calumet

Dr. M.L. King Drive

Rhodes Avenue

McCormick
Tribune
Campus Center

Wabash

Indiana

33rd   Street

Avenue

33rd St

41

State
Street
Village

Avenue

Avenue

Avenue

33rd   Place

S.R. Crown
Hall

34th

Street

0   100 200 300 400 500 600 yds

0   100 200 300 400 500 600 m

D

E

2

3

4

137

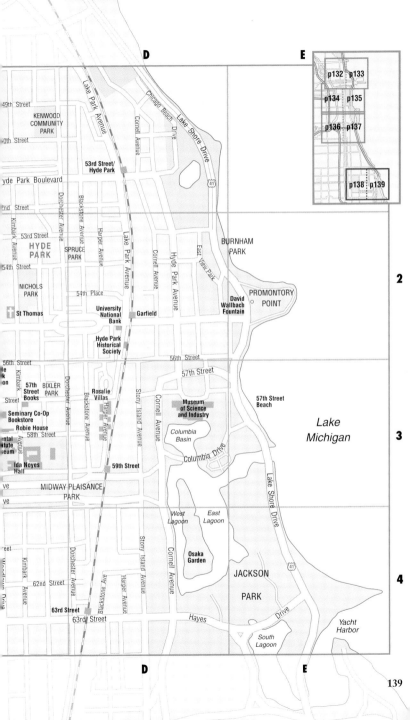

49th Street

KENWOOD
COMMUNITY
PARK

50th Street

Lake Park Avenue

Cornell Avenue

Chicago Beach Drive

Lake Shore Drive

53rd Street/
Hyde Park

Hyde Park Boulevard

52nd Street

Kimbark Avenue

Dorchester Avenue

Blackstone Avenue

Harper Avenue

Lake Park Avenue

Cornell Avenue

Hyde Park Avenue

East View Park

BURNHAM
PARK

2

53rd Street

HYDE
PARK

SPRUCE
PARK

54th Street

NICHOLS
PARK

54th Place

St Thomas

University
National
Bank

Garfield

David
Wallbach
Fountain

PROMONTORY
POINT

Hyde Park
Historical
Society

56th Street

56th Street

le
k
on

57th
Street
Books

BIXLER
PARK

Street

Seminary Co-Op
Bookstore

Robie House

ntal
tute
eum

Kimbark

Dorchester Avenue

Blackstone Avenue

Rosalie
Villas

Harper Avenue

Stony Island Avenue

Cornell Avenue

57th Street

Museum
of Science
and Industry

Columbia
Basin

57th Street
Beach

*Lake
Michigan*

3

58th Street

Ida Noyes
Hall

59th Street

Columbia Drive

ve

MIDWAY PLAISANCE
PARK

ve

Dorchester Avenue

Stony Island Avenue

Harper Avenue

West
Lagoon

East
Lagoon

Lake Shore Drive

reet

Kimbark
Avenue

62nd Street

Osaka
Garden

JACKSON

4

63rd Street

63rd Street

Hayes

PARK

Drive

South
Lagoon

Yacht
Harbor

p132 p133

p134 p135

p136 p137

p138 p139

D

E

D

E

Street Atlas Index

140

141

Index

Insight Smart Guide: Chicago
Compiled by: **Heather Kenny**
Edited by: **Sarah Sweeney**
Proofread and indexed by: **Neil Titman**

All Photography by: **APA/David Dunai**
except: **Alamy** 50, 52-53, 107, 109,
121B; **Rick Aguilar** 123; **Axiom** 120-
121; **Sandeep Babu** 130/131; **John
Berg** 92-93; **Chicago Institute of Art**
76/77, 77B; **Austin Clark** 2/3, 7t, 13t,
100-101, 104/105, 118, 128-129;
Corbis 63BL, 63T; **Eyevine** 53; **Getty**
44-45; **Greg Haus** 60-61; **Kobal** 74/75,
75B; **Leonardo** 11B, 65B, 65T, 66B,
66TL, 66TR, 69, 70B; **Library of
Congress** 62L, 62R

Picture Manager: **Steven Lawrence**
Maps: **James Macdonald**
Series Editor: **Jason Mitchell**

First Edition 2009
© 2009 Apa Publications GmbH & Co. Verlag KG Singapore Branch, Singapore.
Printed in Singapore by Insight Print
Services (Pte) Ltd

Worldwide distribution enquiries:
**Apa Publications GmbH & Co. Verlag KG
(Singapore Branch)** 38 Joo Koon Road,
Singapore 628990; tel: (65) 6865 1600;
fax: (65) 6861 6438

Distributed in the UK and Ireland by:
GeoCenter International Ltd
Meridian House, Churchill Way West,
Basingstoke, Hampshire RG21 6YR; tel: (44
1256) 817 987; fax: (44 1256) 817 988

Distributed in the United States by:
Langenscheidt Publishers, Inc.
36–36 33rd Street 4th Floor, Long Island
City, New York 11106; tel: (1 718) 784
0055; fax: (1 718) 784 0640

Contacting the Editors
We would appreciate it if readers would alert
us to errors or outdated information by
writing to:
Apa Publications, PO Box 7910, London SE1
1WE, UK; fax: (44 20) 7403 0290;
e-mail: insight@apaguide.co.uk
No part of this book may be reproduced,
stored in a retrieval system or transmitted in
any form or by any means (electronic,
mechanical, photocopying, recording or otherwise), without prior written permission of Apa
Publications. Brief text quotations with use of
photographs are exempted for book review
purposes only. Information has been obtained
from sources believed to be reliable, but its
accuracy and completeness, and the opinions
based thereon, are not guaranteed.

Chicago Transit Authority

Downtown (Loop) Map

Michigan Avenue
Wabash Avenue
State
Lake
Randolph
Madison
Monroe
Adams
Library
State Street
Harrison
Dearborn
Wacker St
LaSalle
Clark
Clark St
Washington
Street
Washington
Street
Jackson
Blvd
LaSalle
St
LaSalle Street
Station
Merchandise Mart
Orleans St
Randolph
Washington
Madison
Monroe
Adams
Jackson
Franklin
Wacker
Quincy
Street
Van Buren
St
Congress
Harrison
Drive

••• Subway train lines and station

▬ Elevated train lines, direction and station

System Map

EVANSTON
Linden
Central
Noyes
Foster
Davis
Dempster
Main
South Blvd
Howard

SKOKIE SWIFT
Skokie
Weekdays only
HOWARD

Jarvis
Morse
Loyola
Granville
Thorndale
Bryn Mawr
Argyle
Berwyn
Lawrence
Wilson
Sheridan
Addison
Belmont
Fullerton
Sedgwick
Clark/Division

Southport
Wellington
Diversey
Armitage
North/Clybourn

Paulina
Wellington

RAVENSWOOD
Kimball
Kedzie
Francisco
Rockwell
Western
Damen
Montrose
Irving Park
Addison
Belmont

Division
Chicago

Logan Square
California
Western
Damen

Belmont
Addison
Irving Park
Montrose
Jefferson Park
Harlem
Cumberland
Rosemont
O'Hare

O'HARE

Lake